International Marketing Blunders

Mistakes Made by Companies that Should Have Known Better

Michael White

World Trade Press
1450 Grant Avenue, Suite 204
Novato, California 94945 USA
Tel: (415) 898-1124
Fax: (415) 898-1080
USA Order Line: 800-833-8586
Email: sales@worldtradepress.com
http://www.worldtradepress.com

A Short Course in International Marketing Blunders
Michael White
Short Course Series Concept: Edward G. Hinkelman
Cover Design: Ronald A. Blodgett
Text Design: Seventeenth Street Studios, Oakland, California USA
Desktop Publishing: Valentina Pfeil

Disclaimer
This publication is designed to provide general information concerning aspects of international
trade. It is sold with the understanding that the publisher is not engaged in rendering legal or
any other professional services. If legal advice or other expert assistance is required, the services
of a competent professional person or organization should be sought.

Library of Congress Cataloging-in-Publication Data
White, Michael, 1951-
A short course in international marketing blunders : mistakes made
by companies that should have known better / Michael White.
p. cm. -- (The short course in international trade series)
Includes bibliographic references.
1. Export marketing. 2. International business enterprises--
Management. 3. Business failures.
ISBN 1-885073-60-7
I. Title: International Marketing Blunders. II. Title. III. Series.
HF1416 .W48 2001
658.8'48--dc21
       2001040146
        CIP

Printed in the United States of America

For my Dad, who told me a long time ago that everyone has a story.

PREFACE

The research for this book was no easy chore given the fact that companies are not as willing to talk about their failures as they are about their successes. Many hours were spent poring over primary source materials such as books, magazines, newspapers, and business journals, while an equal amount of time was spent referencing, cross-referencing and verifying information gleaned from dozens of Internet web sites.

My reliance on a large number of independent, and sometimes contradictory and conflicting, sources was eased considerably by the help and encouragement rendered by a solid company of fellow "ink-stained wretches" who have, themselves, burned the midnight oil on countless occasions to meet deadlines over the years. I refer to Martha Celestino, Sherrie Zhan, and Steve Barth, all former fellow staffers at *World Trade* magazine and outstanding friends and writers, in their own right.

A very great debt of gratitude also goes to international business consultants Patty Hirahara and Michael Moretti, who helped me greatly with my research into the Japanese way of doing business; Kristin Murphy, deputy trade commissioner of Mexico in Los Angeles; Anja Halle, editor at the International Centre for Trade and Sustainable Development in Geneva, Switzerland; and George Marshall, now retired senior vice president of marketing for Mitsui O.S.K. Lines (America), my former boss during my tenure with the company, and a good friend.

Many thanks also to the library staffs in the business departments of the central libraries of Long Beach, Burbank, Glendale, and Pasadena, California, as well as the very helpful staff at the Los Angeles Library's central branch. Also of great help were the staffs of the University of California campuses in Los Angeles, Irvine, and San Diego, as well as the California State University campus libraries in Northridge and Long Beach, who answered many telephone inquiries.

I also want to acknowledge those who spoke with me on the condition of anonymity, sharing their "blunders from hell" stories that their employers, or former employers, would have rather swept under the carpet. My interviews with them were always tinged with their profound sense of sadness at stupid mistakes —sometimes repeated over and over—that squandered opportunities, alienated employees and customers alike, and, in several cases, resulted in basically good companies being irreparably trashed. I hope they can read this book and derive some comfort in the hope that someone, somewhere, might learn from their own companies' blunders.

Also much gratitude to my wife Pam, and my sons Matthew and Nathaniel, for their help and support during another project "with a really tight deadline." It wasn't the first, and it probably won't be the last.

Michael White
Los Angeles California 2001

INTRODUCTION

THE ORIGINAL COLD CALL

In the mid-1990s, the petrified remains of a man were found in a frozen Alpine pass on the border between Italy and Switzerland. Scientists speculated that the man, who died some 2,000 years ago, was walking from his home village in what we now know as Italy to trade with or buy goods from the inhabitants of a village situated on the shore of Lake Geneva—most likely wheat or corn, as one of the artifacts found on his body was a bag of seeds slung over his shoulder.

The man, whoever he may have been, was obviously the kind of international business manager that many modern-day companies would kill for—willing even to freeze to death to make sure the goods got into the right hands.

No masters degree, no cell phone, no laptop computer. Pure business, no more, no less.

But if the eons that have passed since the "Iceman" set off on what was to be his final sales call have taught us anything, it's that everything old is, at some juncture, new again.

OLD OPPORTUNITIES IN NEW TIMES

Over the last decade, the world has seen what could, arguably, be called the most dramatic series of events in the history of global economics.

The political tensions that gripped the world since the end of World War II were, to a great extent, diffused with the rise of global capitalism and the demise of Communism. These evolutionary events have fused over the last decade with the growth of free-market economies, the tectonic shift of market forces in Asia and Latin America, and the increasing dependence of the world's lesser-developed nations on trade.

At the same time, new transportation systems and the surge of telecommunications technology have radically impacted how people and products move from place to place, while the Internet, satellite communications, and the ubiquitous personal computer have created a web of global connectivity unparalleled in history.

I can remember the heady days of the early 1990s when the Soviet Union was coming apart like a cheap cardboard suitcase in a heavy rain. It seemed that suddenly, almost ethereally, former vassal states—from Moldova and Latvia to Turkmenistan and Azerbaijan—found themselves thrust upon the world stage, almost blinded by the light of freedom, vulnerable, and almost totally bereft of any global identity apart from that crafted over the preceding three-plus generations in Moscow. In a flash, 15 new countries were created.

Further to the west, as students and border guards danced atop the Berlin Wall, East Germany ceased to exist. Close-by, Yugoslavia splintered into four autonomous states, while, elsewhere, two former enemies—the US and Vietnam—found themselves, after years of bitter animosity, laying a foundation that would eventually lead to the establishment of both diplomatic and trade ties. Free trade agreements and trade blocs such as the European Union (EU) and the Association of South East Asian Nations (ASEAN) have focused trade to directly impact both national and local economies, while, most recently, talk is rife of the

US ending its four-decades old trade embargo on Cuba; while at least one press report, commenting on the growing possibility of détente between North and South Korea, stated that "Coca-Cola has trucks already lined up at the border."

Simply put, there's a bigger world out there today than there was just ten years ago.

At last count, some 6 billion people populate 191 countries. Each of these countries has its own distinct culture, language, politics, and circumstances that have a direct impact on how, what, and why people buy certain products and reject others.

This makes marketing in an ever expanding and diverse world a critical issue to any company wanting to remain competitive in an increasingly globalized economy.

More opportunity to succeed, but more opportunities to fail, as more and more companies shift gears and move into the global trade fast lane—a fact underscored by a report in *Industry Week* magazine, showing that multi-nationals based in the US are likely to do business in 50 or more foreign countries, while American small and medium-sized firms—which number about 202,000 and account for 97% of the country's exporters—are pursuing business in as few as two and as many as 40.

The potential, they say, is limitless.

There's an old saying that "Success has many fathers, but failure is an orphan." While one might expect that established multi-national companies with huge marketing budgets would be immune from failure, the sad, but sometimes humorous, truth is that they're not.

In fact, many companies spend millions on product design, development, sales, and marketing only to fail miserably. Generally because they didn't do basic homework on the target market they were trying to penetrate. For others, the reasons for failure went much deeper.

This is a book about those failures.

TABLE OF CONTENTS

CHAPTER 1

The Why of
International Marketing Blunders

Why Sink When You Could Float?

IN MANY WAYS, A COMPANY IS LIKE A SHIP. No matter what specific purpose a ship was designed for—whether to carry cargo, passengers, or weapons of war—the vessel is compartmentalized, completely reliant on a efficient chain of command and responsibility, the smooth functionality of its machinery, and the competence of its crew. Every business enterprise, like each ship, has its own personality. The famous Liberty ships of World War II were, as one writer said, "built by the mile, and cut off as needed." They were all made to the same specifications and dimensions; in other words, basically, identical. But if you ask anyone who sailed on more than one of them, they'll say that each had its own personality and way of handling in similar sea and weather conditions.

The same is true for a company or business enterprise of any size. It is designed for a purpose, as well—to produce a product or provide a service and to generate a profit for its owner and shareholders. Like a ship, its success—and survival—depends on its ability to adapt, adjust to changing conditions, weather the rough spots, and optimize opportunities. The commanding management structure must constantly communicate, and, above all, always be aware of where the company has been, where it is, and where it's headed.

The Siren Call of Disaster

Just before midnight on July 25, 1956, two stately passenger ships were sailing through the fog near Nantucket Island, Massachusetts, the North Atlantic front gate to New York, at that time the busiest port in the world. The 697-foot-long *Andrea Doria*, pride of the Italian merchant marine, was on the last leg of a 4,000-mile transatlantic crossing to New York from her home port of Genoa. The sleek, white-hulled *Stockholm*, flagship of the venerable Swedish-American Line, was outbound from New York with a full manifest of 534 passengers headed for business or pleasure in the Scandinavian ports of Gothenburg and Copenhagen.

Nothing was amiss and the same scenario had been played out countless times before: ships inbound and outbound from a port pass each other every hour, following navigational "rules of the road" that govern their operation whenever another vessel comes into view, whether visually or on radar. Nothing indicated that the passing of these two ships would be any different from the passings of dozens of other ships that had sailed either in or out of the Port of New York that day.

Both ships were captained and officered by professionals with more than a century of combined experience on the high seas. Both ships were new, boasting the latest in radar and navigational equipment. Neither were hindered by any equipment breakdowns or malfunctions.

But what happened sent the elegant *Andrea Doria* to the bottom of Nantucket Sound and 57 people to their deaths; the *Stockholm* suffered severe damage that took six months to repair. Neither shipping company ever recovered its good reputation. More than 1,200 damage claims were registered for deaths, personal injuries, lost cargo and personal baggage—totaling a then-record $6 million. The controversy about the "whys" and "hows" continues to this day, still shrouded, like the disaster itself, in a blanket of fog.

Sailing through dense fog, each ship had the other clearly on its radar screen. Officers on both bridges knew of the other ship's presence, speed, and course. Each expected the other to reduce speed and apply the "rules of the road," which would have required the two ships to maintain a wide berth and pass each other showing the correct navigational lights. That awareness continued right up to the moment the *Stockholm* stabbed into the starboard side of the *Andrea Doria*—causing immediate flooding and a severe list. She sank the following morning and still rests today on her side, 235 feet beneath the surface of the North Atlantic.

"It was as if they [the ships' officers] were mesmerized," according to a marine underwriter involved in the disposition of the affair. "The people who should have known better and could have acted to remedy the situation as it was developing allowed themselves to become transfixed by the circumstances of the moment." As he described it, "the siren call of arrogance" combined with circumstance to create a situation that paralyzed their better judgment.

True, the tragedy of the *Andrea Doria* and the *Stockholm* literally was one of life and death, but the sum total of what happened on that cold, foggy night decades ago holds valuable lessons for international businesspeople who want to expand their companies in this culturally diverse and complicated world. Quite simply, incorrect assumptions and a failure to rely on accumulated experience combined with muddleheadedness to create a lamentable disaster. Their experience and their professionalism should have led to another outcome.

And no one is immune.

McDonald's and Coca-Cola: the Statement of Faith

McDonald's Corporation and The Coca-Cola Company certainly don't rank as amateurs in international marketing: a majority of each company's total annual revenue is derived from international sales. In fact, both firms—with a four-decades old supplier-buyer relationship—have become cultural archetypes for generations of consumers around the world. Both have spent hundreds of millions of dollars penetrating new markets, even modifying their core products to fit the widely divergent culinary tastes of consumers around the globe.

THE GREAT GLOBALIZATION

McDonald's Corporation—headquartered in the Chicago, Illinois, suburb of Oak Brook—operates 14,400 of its 27,000 total fast-food outlets in more than 120 countries outside the US. Those 14,400 outlets do more than 60 percent of the company's total business, which was $13.3 billion in sales in 1999. The company went global in the early 1970s, and found itself facing a dual challenge: To adapt the American hamburger and concept of fast food to a dazzling variety of international tastes, and to introduce beef as an everyday, common food.

For a company that concentrates on the basics, McDonald's is known as an innovator for tailoring its menu to suit the unique characteristics of virtually every foreign market it serves. It sells beer at its outlets in Germany, *McSpaghetti* pasta in the Philippines, mutton pies in Australia, and wine at its 760 beleaguered restaurants throughout France. Interestingly, the company's busiest franchise is in Moscow's Pushkin Square. The 28,000-square-foot outlet has served a steady stream of cheeseburgers, french fries, and *Chicken McNugget* meals to more than 250 million hungry Russians since opening for business in January 1990.

The Coca-Cola Company saw its future in the global market just after the turn of the last century. Founded in 1886 in Atlanta, Georgia, the company launched its international operations in 1906 with bottling operations in Cuba and Panama. In 1920, it built a production plant in France to supply the thirsty, war-weary European market. By 1929, the company boasted 64 bottling operations in 28 countries as far afield as Belgium and Japan.

Even a world war couldn't keep Coca-Cola from going global. In early 1942, braving attacks by German U-boats, merchantmen sailed the route from ports in the southeastern US with the company's secret syrup bound for Argentina. On the first day, street sales in Buenos Aires amounted to a little more than seven 24-bottle cases, but by the end of the following year sales had increased to more than 300,000 cases delivered by a fleet of 20 trucks.

In short, to say Coca-Cola commands the world's soft-drink market would be a serious understatement. In 1999, the company sold more than 230 brands of beverages in more than 200 countries with a full two-thirds of its $19.8 billion in sales generated by overseas operations. Amazingly, according to *Hoover's Online*, the company holds more than 50 percent of the international soft-drink market or a total equivalent to about 2 percent of the world's daily fluid intake.

In December 1993, McDonald's joined hands with supplier Coca-Cola to venture into the Middle East, opening the first *McDonald's* restaurant in Riyadh, Saudi Arabia. The following month, a two-story outlet opened its doors in the country's western region. For Coca-Cola this venture was in fact a resurfacing in the Saudi market after an absence of several years. It had been doing business in the Middle East since the late 1940s before introducing its soft drinks as "The Real Thing" to thirsty Moroccans.

McDonald's opened its first franchise outlet in neighboring Bahrain a few weeks later. About the same time, 15,000 customers—some waiting in a drive-thru line seven-miles long—participated in opening day ceremonies at the first McDonald's restaurant in Kuwait City. Not one to rest, the company soon opened two franchises simultaneously in different sections of Egypt's capital, Cairo.

HEY, IT'S ONLY A FLAG...

Despite their heavy reliance on overseas sales and a symbiotic supplier-buyer relationship dating back to the 1950s, both McDonald's and Coca-Cola skyrocketed to the top of the list of all-time international marketing faux pas when an oversight almost turned into a "Super Size" international incident. The problem started when both companies innocently enough decided to reprint the flags of the 24 nations participating in the 1994 World Cup Soccer competition in Los Angeles on pieces of throwaway packaging.

Muslims from Europe immediately reacted with public aversion to the use of the Saudi flag, which carries a sacred passage from the Koran: "There is no God but Allah, and Mohammed is His Prophet." The flag first appeared in Spain on disposable aluminum cans of *Coke* soft drinks, and next in Great Britain on carryout bags for McDonald's hamburgers and french fries. The response was immediate—and explosive. Quoted in newspapers and on media outlets on three continents, outraged Muslim leaders and scholars lambasted the fact that not only was the holy inscription used to sell soft drinks and fast food, but the image was presented only to be crumpled up and trashed.

The Saudi government—which neither company had contacted before using the flag—released a succinct statement that put the entire matter into the proper perspective. "As the Saudi flag contains the Muslim Shahada [declaration of faith], the Saudi government never allows its use for commercial or promotional activities, or in any way that is not consistent with the respect due the Shahada."

Disney's Mickey Mouse: N'est Ce Pas...Faux Pas

A classic example of how *not* to market internationally is *EuroDisney*, according to Dr. Paul Herbig, assistant professor of marketing at the Graduate School of International Trade and Business at Texas A & M University. Dr. Herbig's analyses of international marketing issues are highly regarded; several of his books are standard texts in international business programs at colleges and universities across the US. His review of Disney's flawed entry into the European market is regarded as one of the best international marketing studies ever produced.

Without a doubt, the name Disney, and all it conjures up, is a preeminent global icon. For the past 70 years, the mystique that first began in the film cartoon *Steamboat Willie* has spread from the jungles of South America and the streets of Rome to the Australian outback. In peace and war, depression and prosperity, Mickey Mouse and company have been nearly omnipresent, but as Dr. Herbig asserts, that ubiquitous symbolism can lead to unintended results.

Since opening its gates in 1983, the Tokyo *Disneyland* amusement park has been visited by millions of Japanese who wanted to capture what they perceived as the ultimate US entertainment experience. Its ambiance and attraction rival the country's other hot spots, much to the chagrin of both traditionalists and those inured to all things Disney.

THE TRANSCENDENT, MYSTICAL *MICKEY*

I can personally attest to this phenomenon. When I visited Japan in 1985, I was the only person to remain seated on the bus when it passed by the Tokyo Disneyland park. The bus actually swerved, its balance thrown off by dozens of excited Japanese, Brazilians, Canadians, and Germans who lunged to the left-side windows for a better view of the shimmering "Magic Kingdom of the East."

For me, a Southern California native, this new amusement park held little excitement because I'd already visited the original Disneyland—the "real" Magic Kingdom—a good 27 times since my sixth birthday. Disney along with Lockheed Aircraft employed about 60 percent of the workforce in the city where I lived. It had been, at least subconsciously, such a significant part of my youth that it had become a casual part of my life.

Not so for those bus passengers. The magical experience that awaited them was so alluring that it seemed they might explode through the bus windows in a race for the entrance gates.

MISTAKES (ALMOST) NEVER TO BE REPEATED

While the Tokyo Disneyland amusement park was a great success, Disney admitted making a major error when the park was launched. It had licensed its name and image to another company that still actually owns and operates the park, as well as the land where it sits. Disney collects only a small fraction of the revenues generated—which run into the hundreds of millions of dollars every year. That was the price the company was willing to pay for its first international foray. It vowed never to repeat that experience, never to have its hands tied again.

Plans were already in the works for a new EuroDisney amusement park, and Dr. Herbig says the company was "fanatically intent" on owning and controlling the park, as well as enough adjacent property for its own exclusive hotels. From the outset, Disney's strategy was to transplant an American-style park to Europe. After rejecting several possible locations in Spain, the company settled on a 2,800-acre site 20 miles east of Paris. It invested a total of $160 million in the $4 billion project while the French government assumed the remainder of the risk.

According to Dr. Herbig, the initial problems that Disney encountered were unambiguous. French intellectuals lambasted the project as a Neanderthal attack on French culture, while farmers claimed their land had been condemned by the French government for sale to Disney. Conservative dress codes angered French workers, and regimented training programs and the company's decision to ban alcohol from the park infuriated French trade unionists, free-thinkers, and traditionalists simultaneously. To top it all off, the company decided to export its American-brand management system *en masse* for the simple reason, says Dr. Herbig, that "they were Disney and it had always worked in the past."

But, as they say, the best (or rather, worst) was yet to come. The list of gaffes at the very highest levels is staggering, but a few examples are in order. From the day the gates opened at EuroDisney in April 1992, it was clear that Disney, confident in its own success, hadn't bothered to do its homework.

- One of the first surprises was that attendance was highly seasonal. It peaked in the summer when most Europeans take long vacations—often a month or two—rather than on the year-round "long weekends" common in the US. Then the dismal European winters inhibited attendance for at least four months of the year.

- Europeans who had experienced Disney amusement parks in California and Florida visited the EuroDisney park expecting to find US-style "customer-based" service. Instead they found sometimes surly, young French employees who protested company grooming, service, and deportment policies.

- The company further failed to consider the European custom of enjoying leisurely meals at particular hours, complete with wine and beer. The park lacked sufficient seating at its highly priced restaurants, while it was full of fast-food establishments, which Europeans tend to abhor.

- In addition, Disney fixed an admission price 30 percent higher than is charged at its park in Orlando, Florida. In doing so, it neglected to consider Europe's lower per capita disposable income, an ongoing recession throughout Europe, and the culturally conservative vacation and spending habits, says Dr. Herbig.

- Perhaps most blatant was Disney's mistake in not adapting the park's attractions and content to local tastes and culture. Quite simply, Europeans wanted more Euro-based content in their park. While the Japanese are fond of US pop culture, Europeans tend to value detail and craftsmanship over gut-wrenching rides.

In 1994, Disney and its European partners restructured their agreement. Among its provisions was an agreement to change the park's name to *Disneyland Paris*, in somber recognition of the fact that the original "Euro" branding of the venerable Disney name had been a costly failure.

Whether the hard lessons learned in France will have sobered the company's upper-level management to the realities of going global remains to be seen, but it appears that future opportunities will present themselves one way or the other. In addition to expanding the size of its original park in California, Disney is building a second Japanese park—*Tokyo DisneySea*—at a cost of $3 billion with an expected opening date at the end of 2001. It is planning a second park in France to be built adjacent to Disneyland Paris the following year, and a "mega-park" in Hong Kong is slated to open its gates by the middle of 2005.

A quote in a July 2000 edition of the *Los Angeles Times* newspaper from Richard Reed, an analyst with Credit Lyonnais Securities in New York, says, "Over the next 25 years, I could see Disney opening a half-dozen parks internationally. Brazil, India, Mexico—anywhere there are enough people with a high enough income to make it work."

Wal-Mart Strikes Out in Brazil

When Wal-Mart Stores, Inc. decided to go global in 1991, the company carried a long-standing tradition of jumping into a market head first.

The foundation of the company was poured right after World War II when Sam Walton came home after service as an Army MP (Military Policeman) and borrowed $25,000 from his father-in-law to buy his own Ben Franklin Variety Store in the small town of Newport, Arkansas. Shrewd management and Walton's investment of irrepressible energy paid off when he forged out on his own. Over the next four decades, he created the most successful retail chain in the country—virtually revolutionizing the way Americans shop.

Wal-Mart's first overseas store (actually a super-discount *Sam's Club* outlet) opened in Mexico City in partnership with Cifra, the huge Mexican retailer. (It was in 1991, the year before Sam Walton died.) Within two years the company had created a full-blown international division, and by 1999, Wal-Mart had founded more than 600 *Wal-Mart* and *Sam's Club* retail and discount stores in Argentina, Brazil, Canada, China, Germany, and Puerto Rico. International operations in 1998 generated $7.5 billion, a 50 percent increase over the previous year. Earnings were posted at $62 million, a 10-fold increase over the prior year.

The company's official Internet website proclaims, "Wal-Mart has transferred not only its retailing concepts and strategies globally, but also its emphasis on adapting to local cultures and to community involvement. Across the globe, Wal-Mart associates [employees] respond to the local needs, merchandise preferences, and local vendors of individual foreign towns, just as they do in the United States."

Based on a corporate philosophy that expected the company's strengths and retail know-how to translate into an axiomatic certainty in any foreign environment, top management at its headquarters in Bentonville, Arkansas decided that the best blanket entry strategy into any given overseas market should be through partnerships with or acquisitions of local companies.

GO AHEAD, IGNORE YOUR FRIENDS

The problem was that Wal-Mart utilized its foreign partners less for marketing know-how than for simple local store management and distribution, according to Dr. Masaaki Kotabe of the Graduate School of Business at the University of Texas. For example, the company's initial overseas foray into Mexico was fraught with problems that centered around the US management's insistence, contrary to its stated policy, of importing US-made goods instead of selling products from local sources. Quite simply, it failed to foresee that Mexican consumers would prefer buying Mexican-made goods rather than items imported from the US. In addition, the company couldn't fathom that Mexican housewives have a comfortable habit of purchasing food in small grocery and specialty stores rather than in giant supermarkets.

Wal-Mart also erred in entering the Canadian market, says Dr. Kotabe. There, the company acquired an entire retail chain instead of developing more localized partnerships. While Canada has proven to be the company's most successful "overseas" market, the fact remains that of the 134 Wal-Mart stores in Canada in 1997, 122 were originally operated by Woolco, the Canadian retailer that Wal-Mart bought.

Wal-Mart's joint venture relationship with Pokphand Co. Ltd. of Hong Kong lasted only 18 months after the company decided to go its own way and establish its own network of stores in both China and Hong Kong. According to the *Asian Wall Street Journal*, "analysts noted that the dissolution of the joint venture could adversely affect Wal-Mart's expansion in the two areas." Lehman Brothers had predicted that sales at Wal-Mart stores in China could have reached as high as $35.7 billion by 2008, or about 5 percent of China's total retail market.

In Argentina in 1994, the company entered the market on its own, locating two Sam's Club warehouse stores and a pair of Wal-Mart super retail outlets in Buenos Aires. Local competitors reacted quickly to neutralize the company's big entry with a barrage of new store openings and a blitz of discount pricing promotions that led to two straight years of heavy losses.

In Brazil, problems quickly arose for other reasons. In the beginning, the company's entry had all the earmarks of the typical Wal-Mart "D-Day" policy: hit the market hard and fast to overwhelm the competition. Its initial investment amounted to $120 million to build five stores in São Paulo, Brazil's largest city, and overtake the largest market in Latin America.

According to Dr. Kotabe, Wal-Mart's intention was to displace Carrefour, Brazil's leading low-price retail food chain, which although based in France, has acclimatized itself so well to the Brazilian market that the average consumer in Rio de Janeiro doesn't even know the company is foreign-owned. The plan, cooked up in Bentonville, called for opening no fewer than 80 stores in the Brazilian market within just a few years, targeting the country's most populous areas.

REALITY RAISES ITS UGLY HEAD

Wal-Mart's initial success in Brazil—a company-record $1 million in sales in one day at one of the new stores—seemed to validate the company's strategic plan. But reality soon reared its ugly head in the most innocuous way: management failed to anticipate the long waits at the stores' check-out lines and chronic sell-outs of advertised products with virtually no timetable for when new stock would arrive at the store.

Added to problems within the stores was the admittedly tepid advertising campaign and products that were often not available when customers arrived. Some had traveled hours over less-than-well-maintained roads to spend their hard-earned *reals* and had fought for parking spaces, only to enter overly crowded stores. It was later discovered that many managers were setting prices below cost to increase sales and get high performance evaluations. Meanwhile, Wal-Mart's Brazilian competitors didn't waste any time in counteracting the Bentonville Blitz, blanketing the country with advertising promoting new store openings and, most effectively, offering lower prices. Perhaps most effective of all, they offered better customer service.

Schwinn Nearly Coasts Into Oblivion

My first experience with company oblivion came with my very first job in international business as a steamship schedule editor for a small daily newspaper in Los Angeles. It was the precomputer era. Every day, I'd cut-and-paste the previous day's schedules by hand, updating and revising the arrivals, departures, and destinations of the cargo ships. These ships were operated by more than 80 ocean carriers sailing into and out of every port on the US West Coast. After a couple of years of finger-slicing on knife blades and exposure to smelly glue, I learned a few things: for one thing, the correct geographic location and spelling of nearly every deep-water port in the world; and perhaps more important, that passion and foresight aren't inherited.

The paper had been in business reporting on global trade and transportation developments in Southern California for almost 70 years. Over time, it had developed quite a loyal regional readership, drawing off the vision and energy of its founder to survive not only the Great Depression, but also the restrictions on news coverage and ship movements during the two world wars, several economic downturns, and even the McCarthy era and the birth of Rock n' Roll.

After the baton was handed off to the founding publisher's son, the paper prospered, achieving a level of respectability based on providing its readers with "news they could use:" everything from new air cargo and ocean services to staff appointments and organization meeting announcements, as well as interviews with the new Consul General from France—that sort of thing.

But by the time I joined the staff, something was becoming increasingly wrong. The reins of the paper had passed to the founder's grandsons. Neither of them was really interested either in investing the time themselves to make the business grow, or in staffing the paper at the highest level with people who could make it successful. Within a few years, the world literally passed the paper by. Seen only as a revenue generator by a family that no longer cared about anything but the short-term bottom line, the paper eventually folded for good. The passion that compelled the founder and the foresight that drove him to see the global growth potential of a nascent Los Angeles faded over the years until mediocrity caused the once-proud enterprise to fade into obscurity.

The scenario is timeless. Indeed, the ancient Chinese called it the "Three-Generation Curse." It's a story all too common, particularly in the United States, and is played out in countless movies: the first generation—usually immigrants from "the old country"—works hard and sacrifices to create the business (scrimping on meals to save money, and working long hours, determined to make the business work); the second generation begins the downward slide to the temptations of affluence (wherein the somewhat disillusioned children join the country club that never would have admitted their immigrant parents); then the third generation flushes it all away in a tidal wave of indolence, wanton abandon, and sometimes even alcohol or drugs.

SELF-DESTRUCTION IS EASY: ALL YOU HAVE TO DO IS...

Leave it to the kids. The Schwinn Bicycle Company, which first came to life as Arnold Schwinn & Co., is a prime example of a family company that didn't survive to the third and fourth generations. The brainchild of Ignaz Schwinn, a German immigrant, the company began in 1895 in a Chicago storefront "factory" where Schwinn oversaw a handful of workers taking parts purchased from suppliers and assembling them as bicycles. Schwinn sold them to walk-in customers as well as through hardware and variety stores throughout the city.

From the beginning, the little company was a success. A keen businessman, Schwinn managed to survive several economic rough spots by intelligently joint venturing with other manufacturers and suppliers and acquiring smaller competitors. The company eventually grew to the point where it held between 15 and 20 percent of the entire domestic US bicycle market during any given year through World War I.

By 1920, drawn by his interest in other business ventures, Ignaz Schwinn left control of the company to his eldest son, Frank W., who many considered to be a tougher businessman than his father. Through the Depression and another world war, the company creatively designed and marketed its bicycles to the point that by 1970 the *Schwinn* brand name was the second most widely recognizable in the country after *United Airlines*. Schwinn boasted an unsurpassed reputation for quality and dependability. Most middle-aged American men today can remember with a smile the heady days when owning a Schwinn *Stingray* bike was the first step that would inevitably land them in the driver's seat of a *Corvette* convertible car next to a stunning blonde.

In the 1970s, the company's Chicago manufacturing facility churned out one million bikes a year. Clean, well-lighted and well-sited Schwinn dealerships dotted the landscape from Seattle to Miami. At this point, two critical events took place: first, the business passed to Ignaz Schwinn's grandchildren, and second, the company decided to enter the international field.

"Few family-owned businesses survive to the third generation," wrote Judith Crown and Glenn Coleman in their 1996 book, *No Hands: The Rise and Fall of the Schwinn Bicycle Company, An American Institution*. "The grandchildren enjoyed golf, alcohol, Las Vegas, and sailing on Lake Geneva. They had little interest in manufacturing, and even less interest in bicycles." According to Crown and Coleman, both reporters for *Crain's Chicago Business*, the Schwinn Bicycle Company missed the adult bike boom of the early 1970s because the controlling management was convinced that its production of children's bikes would be the continuing key to its success. Some people say, though, that the more pressing reason that the company dragged its feet was the Schwinn clan's unwillingness to invest the money needed to upgrade the company's aging manufacturing operation in Chicago. The results were disastrous.

Unwilling to spend money on its own domestic operations, Schwinn was forced by a strike at the Chicago plant to overcompensate quickly—too quickly, said analysts at the time—for the work stoppage by buying bicycles made in Japan, Taiwan, and eventually China. It made these purchases rather than improving the working conditions that forced the strike in the first place or taking a more clear-headed approach to going global.

According to industry observers at the time, the company should have partnered with manufacturers in both Japan and Taiwan to develop and manufacture jointly the lightweight bicycles growing in popularity in the lucrative US market. Instead, it "sold off the farm to pay for a new paint job on the barn," as the saying goes. Schwinn, which had in the past been the teacher who wrote the book on how to make bicycles, panicked and had that same book revised, reedited, and republished by students.

The company's decision to buy bicycles from, rather than work as an equal partner with, its Asian competition eventually sealed its doom.

THE STUDENTS UPSTAGE THE TEACHER

Schwinn's Japanese supplier was Shimano and within a short time the Japanese company was using technology and manufacturing techniques pioneered by Schwinn to turn the tables on the US company. Over time, Shimano became the largest exporter of bikes to the US.

In Taiwan, Schwinn invested in a tiny manufacturer, incongruously named "The Giant Manufacturing Company Ltd." Giant opened its doors in 1971 with a staff of three and assets totaling $100,000. With Schwinn's transferred expertise, Giant became huge by producing bicycles under more than a half-dozen brand names, exporting them to the US, and undercutting Schwinn in both price and availability. In 1972, imports—mainly from Japan and Taiwan—accounted for one-third of the almost 14 million bikes sold in the US.

Within a few years, Schwinn ranked fourth among US bike manufacturers and produced only 1.5 million bikes. Quietly, it began importing from both Shimano and Giant more than 200,000 bikes a year and selling them under its own name. By 1979, Frank V. resigned as chairman of Schwinn. He handed over the reins to the third generation in the person of Edward V. Schwinn, who, author Robert Sobel writes, "did not possess either the temperament or the skills required for such a position." Edward V. led the company into blunder after blunder—the most eloquent being the construction of a smaller second manufacturing facility in Greenville, Mississippi, to "pull up the slack for the Chicago plant." The Greenville factory was staffed by underpaid, unskilled workers and located more than 75 miles from the nearest interstate highway; it finally closed in 1991 after losing more than $30 million.

By 1984, despite the unionization of the company's Chicago facility, Schwinn had become so increasingly dependent on its foreign suppliers that Giant (which had been supplied with Schwinn dies, plans, and technical personnel) was supplying it with half a million bikes annually. Here was an opportunity to make up for a major past blunder. "This was the time," Sobel writes, "for Schwinn to demand the right to purchase a minority stake in Giant." But Giant countered the proposal by offering to buy Schwinn outright. The matter was dropped immediately, and Schwinn began to search for another supplier.

It was becoming increasingly clear that Schwinn had become less a manufacturer of bicycles than a wholesaler. Schwinn floundered on the "mountain bike" craze of the late 1980s, thinking it was merely a fad and fearing potential product liability lawsuits because of the risks of injury inherent in the type of use anticipated for such bicycles. Another slam hit home when Giant, using Schwinn technology and know-how, penetrated the European market to become a dominant bicycle supplier there—undercutting British, French, and Italian manufacturers as it had done to Schwinn in the US.

The failure to export, says Sobel, carried other costs as well. He quoted one competitor who said, "Schwinn was obsessed with cutting costs instead of innovation." When the company finally decided to take its brand name overseas, it could do so only by buying bikes that actually had been made in Taiwan by Giant, exported to the US, and then re-exported to Europe under the Schwinn name. This led European consumers to ask the obvious question: "Why should I buy a Schwinn when I can buy an identical Giant bike for ten percent less?"

TOO MUCH, TOO LATE

Stunned by Giant's success in the European market, Schwinn began a frantic search for the right overseas partner to provide an overseas market for Schwinn and pull up the slack for the company's shrinking US domestic market share. Perhaps most important, the Schwinn family wanted to reduce the pressure they were feeling to make the company perform up to its historic potential.

A fling with a Hungarian joint-venture partner in 1989 resulted in only more grief. The pressures on the Hungarian economy following the collapse of the Soviet Union conspired with low productivity, major quality-control issues, and the specter of communist-style management to eventually render the operation all but impotent.

Around the same time, in a frantic attempt to keep the company from unraveling altogether, Schwinn approached Hong Kong magnate Jerome Sze, owner of China Bicycles Company (CBC), with a proposal. Still limping badly from its experience with Giant, Schwinn wanted to make sure its bases were covered. Schwinn proposed to acquire an equity position in CBC in return for giving the Chinese company its exclusive business. (CBC was, at the time, a major supplier of bicycles to Sears Roebuck and several other mass market retailers in the US.) A deal was struck giving a one-third stake in CBC to Schwinn. Repeating its "Giant blunder," Schwinn sent a team of engineers, designers, and technicians to reorganize the CBC factory in Shenzhen province.

Schwinn may have seen the relationship with CBC as a godsend, but it turned out to be a death knell for the company. "CBC came light years in a short period of time because of a lot of technology transfer from Schwinn," said one industry writer at the time. Sze, voicing his decision not to become a subsidiary of Schwinn in the US, used what he had learned from Schwinn to increase his market share in Europe. At the same time, he acquired a US-based importer-distributor to start selling his own bikes on the American market under the *Diamond Back* brand name.

This was the final blow, and—after 97 years in business—Schwinn filed for Chapter 11 bankruptcy protection in October, 1992. The company had lost $50 million the previous year and had seen its domestic US marketshare shrink from a high of 28 percent in the late 1960s to a low of 8 percent when the bankruptcy papers were filed in Chicago. Reorganized today as Schwinn Cycling & Fitness, Inc., the company has passed to new management, but remains a shadow of its former manufacturing self. While it has begun manufacturing in the US with joint partners again, particularly in the bike fitness area, the company has changed largely into a marketer of bikes manufactured by its former overseas partners.

On a cold Saturday morning a few weeks after the bankruptcy filing, James Hurd, curator of the Schwinn Museum, opened the doors to a warehouse on Chicago's North Side. Stacked in boxes from floor to ceiling were crate after crate holding artifacts and memorabilia that chronicled the history of the company. There, too, was a treasure trove of old bicycles, one dating back to 1820. By 9 a.m., Hurd had sold off some $30,000 worth of calendars, old catalogs, decals, signs, framed advertisements, and posters.

The bicycle collection, valued at more than $1 million and considered to be one of the best in the world, was not among the assets the company's creditors were to fight over in court. The collection became the centerpiece of a fight between the 13 members of the Schwinn family. They battled it out—both in and out of court—for control of what was left of a once-proud American icon. It is said that the shouts could be heard echoing down the halls of the half-empty company headquarters at the corner of Jefferson and Fulton Streets echoing and re-echoing the blame for what went wrong.

Qualcomm: Murphy's Law Goes Wireless

In the summer of 1998, I wrote a piece for the magazine *Pacific Coast Trade* centering on an incident that underscores the toxic results of bad planning combined with the inherent vagaries of doing business internationally.

Richard Bliss, a field technician for Qualcomm Incorporated, and his five-man team were in Russia to do basic survey work on a modest $5.8 million cellular communications system in Rostov-on-Don, about 600 miles southeast of Moscow. The project wasn't Qualcomm's first in Russia; the company had already completed a pair of projects there over the prior two years and was working on another two in addition to the Rostov system.

Bliss used a sophisticated array of GPS (Global Positioning System) equipment, "testing and measuring the performance" of the region's existing wireless telephone network, according to a Qualcomm representative. That's exactly how Bliss saw it...that is until a squad of grim Russian military police toting AK-47s surrounded him and his group. The police arrested and hauled them off to jail after confiscating their equipment.

According to the Russian FSB (the post-Cold War successor to the Soviet KGB), Bliss was using satellite receivers that had been brought into the country illegally to survey highly "sensitive sites." Under Russian law, they said, any survey that is accurate to within 30 yards is considered a state secret. While the other team members were released after questioning, Bliss—who had been a Qualcomm employee for only five months—was charged with espionage.

All the work done by Bliss and his team had been "conducted in accordance with the statement of work specified in the contract" that Qualcomm had reached with Electrosviaz (the Rostov region's telecom IDSA communications company), said a company spokeswoman at the time. But that, apparently, wasn't good enough for the authorities. Having lived in Moscow for four years, Elaine Carey of Kroll & Associates, the New York-based international business intelligence and security company, says it plainly: "You see a lot of official documents festooned with a lot of seals and signatures that really mean nothing because they're issued by mid-level bureaucrats with no real authority to make decisions. A lot of time can be wasted by talking to the wrong people."

REALITY IN THE NEW "WILD WEST"

The incident made headlines all over the world.

At the time of his arrest, Bliss had been planning to return to the US for Thanksgiving as soon as the job was finished. Byzantine negotiations followed, involving Vice President Al Gore, the entire California congressional delegation, the US State Department, and the office of then-Russian Prime Minister Viktor Chernomyrdin. Twelve days after his arrest and after a $5 million "bail" shakedown by Rostov officials, Bliss was released and finally allowed to return to the US. He arrived on Christmas evening.

"In Russia, it's vital to know who you're dealing with because of the multiple levels of bureaucracy and the fact that communications between those levels is so poor," says Carey of Kroll & Associates. Qualcomm simply failed to deal with the right people at the correct levels of authority. Management in San Diego assumed that, because the company had some experience in doing business elsewhere in Russia, the bureaucracy was the same everywhere and could be dealt with in a "cookie cutter" fashion.

Qualcomm thought that getting Bliss out of the Rostov lockup and back to the US would be the end of the story, but that wasn't how it went. In 1998, a year after his arrest in Russia, Richard Bliss resigned. He charged that the company failed to secure the correct permits for the GPS equipment he was using, which the company had told him to transport into the country in his own suitcase. He filed a lawsuit with the company, asking for $1 million in compensation.

Some three years later, the books in Moscow still carry espionage charges against Bliss. However, Washington, D.C., authorities have gone on the record saying that Bliss will not go back to Russia to stand trial as no extradition treaty existed between the US and Russia at the time of his arrest.

Firestone's Not-So-Happy Birthday

The Firestone Tire & Rubber Company was planning to celebrate its hundredth year in business in July 2000.

A subsidiary of Japan's Bridgestone Corporation, the company had faced difficult issues in the past. It was accused of dominating the rubber production of both Malaysia and Liberia. It suffered a humbling recall of its entire production of *Firestone 500* tires in 1978. By and large, however, it had built itself into a global player supplying major automakers with a constant stream of quality tires.

The grand celebration, however, was not to be. "Rarely has a leading global company faced such an extraordinary confluence of problems," read *The New York Times* story (reprinted in the September 1, 2000, issue of the *Los Angeles Daily News)*. The company was having to deal with "its flagship product blamed for scores of deaths, its biggest customer (the Ford Motor Company, a longtime partner) undermining its every defense, its stock price plunging along with consumer confidence, and its top executives summoned before an angry Congress." According to writer Keith Bradsher, "some industry analysts say" the centennial celebration "has turned into a death watch for one of America's most familiar brand names." Few companies have ever taken such a firm grip on their own undoing.

MISERY LOVES COMPANY

Government regulators in Washington, D.C., were investigating charges that Bridgestone/Firestone concealed its knowledge of defects in tires produced at its US facilities. One day before the article appeared, they added 26 deaths to the 62 previously attributed to auto crashes caused by tire failures at high speed.

In Venezuela, one of the 18 countries where Firestone tires have been recalled, the country's national consumer safety agency petitioned Venezuela's state prosecutor to bring criminal charges against Firestone for "its failure to recall the Wilderness brand tires in a timely fashion." The agency also called on the city of Caracas to bring charges against the Ford Motor Company, claiming that the actual design of Ford's popular *Explorer* sport utility vehicle (SUV)—all equipped with Firestone tires—contributed to dozens of auto accidents and at least 10 deaths in the country. It appeared that Ford would be joining Firestone at the stake.

On the day that Washington and Caracas turned up the heat on Bridgestone/Firestone, Ford chief executive officer Jacques Nasser, who had stood shoulder-to-shoulder with Firestone throughout the entire recall ordeal, told a press conference, "This has been an extremely difficult and disappointing period in our relationship and we're going to take it one day at a time." The next day, Ford officials said they had "unilaterally shouldered the responsibility for protecting consumers" by handling the tire replacement situation in Venezuela.

According to press reports swirling around the eye of the Firestone storm, Ford executives stated publicly that the first report of problems with Firestone tires on its Explorer SUVs in Venezuela was forwarded in 1998. That was a full two years before Ford—not Bridgestone/Firestone—began replacing tires for customers there. The Associated Press (AP) reported that Ford executives in Venezuela began recalling the tires in May [2000] "only after waiting for Bridgestone/Firestone to act."

The automaker, said the AP, "categorically denied charges that it withheld information about defective tires...and also said that the design of the Explorer did not contribute to tread separation and blowouts of Firestone tires." Ford claimed that it had asked Bridgestone/Firestone for an explanation of the reported poor performance, and the tire manufacturer responded with two reports blaming the accidents on incorrect tire pressure, badly repaired punctures, and damage to the tires' surface "from the country's poorly maintained roads."

The state of Florida fired its own barrage at both companies, announcing in late August that both companies would be the target of a civil racketeering investigation. The state's attorney general's office said it would seek company records on everything from research and tire design to training records and the number of factory workers assigned to each shift.

That same month, Ford ordered the replacement of 6.5 million tires used mainly on its Explorer SUVs in an effort to fend off a developing flood of public outrage and government anger. The company closed three of its assembly plants in New Jersey, Missouri, and Minnesota for two weeks starting August 28 to free up 70,000 tires for the recall effort, with Michelin, Goodyear Tire & Rubber Company, and several other tire makers increasing output to help meet the demand. "We expect these actions to reduce revenues and increase costs," said a company spokesman.

WHERE'S THE BOSS WHEN YOU NEED HIM?

In the meantime, a member of the congressional committee who was looking into the entire affair expressed his anger at the fact that Ford chief executive and president Jacques Nasser sent several subordinates in his place to testify before the consumer protection panel. The Ford chief had, over the preceding two weeks, appeared in a pair of television commercials viewed in both the US and Venezuela aimed at restoring consumer confidence and "clearing the air." Pointing to the fact that Bridgestone/Firestone chief executive Masatoshi Ono would travel all the way from Tokyo to appear, Louisiana's Congressman Billy Tauzin commented, "A lot of people are going to find it curious that [Nasser] has the time to cut TV commercials, but won't take the time to testify."

Ono appeared contrite before the congressional committee. "I come before you to apologize to you, the American people, and especially to the families of those who have lost loved ones in these terrible rollover accidents," he said. "I also come to accept full and personal responsibility...for the events that led to this hearing."

A chastened Nasser, feeling the pressure of intense media scrutiny and an increasingly angry public, did appear. After waiting through more than seven hours of testimony before he was called to face the committee, Nasser declared, "we can't let this go on," as reported in the *Los Angeles Times*. He pledged to work on developing an industry-wide early warning system for safety problems and to share information "in the future" with government agencies around the world. "From now on, when we know it, so will the world."

But the initial response wasn't what either company wanted or expected. The explanations of both companies "strained credulity," said one committee member. Congressman Tauzin, chair of the proceedings, made the outspoken statement, "We have to ask ourselves why we're in this mess and what we can do to make sure it never happens again," which served to produce complaints from Ford dealers dating back to 1996 about problems with Firestone tires on their Ford Explorer SUVs.

Bridgestone/Firestone wasn't spared the heat aimed at Ford. The day of the hearings, Tauzin's office issued a statement commenting on an internal Firestone memo dated in January 2000 that "severely undercuts the company's claims that it was unaware of any potential defects." The statement said that the document "confirms our suspicion that Firestone officials knew they had a serious problem long before they began a recall [in August]."

At the second round of hearings the following week, Nasser fired a heavy broadside against longtime partner Bridgestone/Firestone. In no uncertain terms, he told the Congressional committee that the entire problem was with Firestone tires rather than defects in the design of Ford's best-selling Explorer SUVs—most of which were sold new with Firestone *Wilderness* tires as standard equipment.

Following Ono's acceptance of personal responsibility "for the affair" at the initial committee hearing, Bridgestone/Firestone executive president John Lampe stood in for Ono, who had returned to Tokyo. Lampe angrily responded that, while Firestone "had made some bad tires," the real problem was in the Ford Explorer SUVs. "We have seen an alarming number of serious accidents from roll-overs of the Explorer after a tire failure," he angrily told the committee.

SPREADING THE BLAME AROUND

Unbelievably, the Firestone-Ford debacle expanded even further. In mid-September 2000, Ford said that it was investigating tire tread separation problems on tires manufactured by Continental-General Tire used on its *Lincoln Navigator* SUVs. The company stated that it was launching the investigation based on reports of problems with the tires coming from Saudi Arabia. A representative of Continental-General Tire denied the statement, however, saying "There is no such investigation. What's transpiring here is a result of the Firestone situation."

The claim by Ford, said *USA Today*, has significant implications. "If tread separation problems are noted on other brands, Firestone could get less blame. If tread separation shows up significantly on other vehicles, it helps Ford's argument that [the design of] the Explorer isn't part of the problem."

Ford took another hit when an internal company memo was turned over to congressional investigators. It cast a shadow over the company's claims that its recommendation to consumers in Venezuela to reduce tire pressure to "improve the ride" had nothing to do with safety concerns in that country. The memo (dated July 8, 1999) was circulated 10 months before Ford issued its tire recall in Venezuela, and more than a year before a recall was ordered in the US. While citing other possible causes, the memo specifically stated that "low tire pressure might have contributed to tread detachments." A second memo dated May 24, 2000, and also turned over to the government was "identical to the earlier memo, except the paragraph alluding to tire pressure had been omitted," said an investigator. Ford's recommendation was to lower the tire pressure to a level below that recommended by Bridgestone/Firestone. Investigators said this "was being investigated as a move by the company to try to limit the possibility of rollovers among certain Ford vehicles that come with the tires, notably the Ford Explorer."

The investigation into both Firestone and Ford promises to be a protracted ordeal for both companies as the ponderous investigative machinery in Washington, Caracas, and Orlando (Florida) creak toward their own conclusions. Many questions will be asked and responses given, but the real issues revolve around which questions will in fact be answered. It's those answers that will provide the greatest lessons on both how, and how not, to do business.

It Must Be Something in the Water (Source Perrier SA)

James Ward's first thought was that it had to be the lab equipment. As head of the laboratory at the Mecklenburg County Environmental Protection Department in Charlotte, North Carolina, he oversaw the routine testing of various products sold in the US. From gasoline to paints, he had to ensure that they conformed to a variety of environmental safety and quality-standard rules.

It was late January 1990. For the past several months, staffers from the lab had traveled to the local supermarket to buy two or three bottles of *Perrier* water, a leading brand of imported sparkling water. They used it as a diluting agent in their lab tests for hazardous chemicals. It was simply cheaper to buy the Perrier water—which was noted for its purity—than to have the laboratory staff produce and purify its own water.

According to *The Economist,* which chronicled the story as it developed over the next several months, a routine test on a sample that the lab was processing turned up an unusual reading on a mass spectrometer. The reading indicated that something was corrupting the test sample.

Ward, confident of the purity of the Perrier water used as a medium during the test, spent two days testing and retesting every piece of equipment in the lab. He also rechecked the sterility of every utensil—from petri dishes to slide covers. Unable to turn up anything amiss, Ward sent out an assistant to buy more Perrier water. Eight bottles were brought back to the lab and each was tested.

Each bottle was discovered to contain minute quantities of benzene, a carcinogenic industrial solvent. Drafting a report, Ward immediately contacted both the North Carolina state environmental office in Raleigh and the US Food & Drug Administration (FDA) and passed on his findings. Perrier Group America (the US subsidiary of Source Perrier SA of France) heard about the problem only after both the state and federal authorities had been notified. *The Economist* reported that the company felt "there was no need for haste." According to the company, the concentration of benzene, which varied between 12.3 and 19.9 parts per billion, was a ratio well within the acceptable limit of 5 parts per billion specified in FDA guidelines, and at the same time, was well below the levels that would endanger a consumer's health. "A cup of non-freeze-dried coffee contains more benzene," the magazine said.

Nevertheless, Perrier Group America decided independently to recall more than 70 million bottles of Perrier water from restaurants and markets in both the US and Canada. Before it had taken the time to study the scope of the problem, the company announced that the problem was no longer an issue and that the benzene contamination was limited only to Perrier water sold in North America.

THE WRONG TURN

In France, however, *The Economist* stated that parent company Source Perrier SA's rapid actions to allay consumer skittishness were more far-reaching. At first, *The Economist* reported, the company reacted decisively by ordering its bottlers around the globe to halt the bottling of the sparkling water, which at the time accounted for 14 percent of the company's total worldwide sales of $2.5 billion in 1990. Then, two days after word of the contamination broke in the press, Source Perrier made a decision that would come back later to haunt it. The company quickly issued a statement to the press saying that the source of the contamination was a benzene-based cleaning fluid that had been used on a bottling line serving the North American market at one of its bottling plants. The offending bottling machine, the company said, had been broken down and disinfected.

In truth, Source Perrier apparently had no idea yet what the source of the contamination was when it made its initial statement to the press. Just three days later, employees discovered the actual cause: failure to replace the charcoal filters that screen out impurities in the natural gas present at the natural spring that is the source of the company's water supply. All of the Perrier water produced during the preceding six months was affected—covering virtually the company's entire global market.

Source Perrier found itself having to change its story. What followed over the next few days exacerbated the entire problem and sank the company even further into a morass of recriminations and media scrutiny. On February 14, 1990, just three days after learning the truth about the contamination, Source Perrier held another press conference in Paris. Representatives of the worldwide press who had flocked to Paris to cover the story were crammed into a room too small to accommodate half their number. Incredibly, they served chilled Perrier water as Gustave Laven, the firm's chairman, cracked jokes and announced the worldwide recall of the product. When asked why the company had decided to expand its recall from North America to include its entire global output, Laven (in reference to one of Source Perrier's popular French television commercials) responded, "Perrier is crazy!"

President Frederik Zimmer meanwhile quipped, "All this publicity helps build our brand renown." Unbelievably, Zimmer went further saying that Perrier water "naturally contains several gases, including benzene. Those have to be filtered out." A reporter observed, "If the company is actively filtering benzene, surely the filtration plant would be the obvious place to look for contamination?"

Zimmer's revelation that Perrier water contained benzene proved to be a total disaster. According to one analyst, "Mineral water is an odd product. As with petrol, most consumers have difficulty telling one brand from the another. With such weak product differentiation, the strength of the brand is everything." Source Perrier's brand, wrote the magazine, like those of its rivals, was "built on purity. In the health-conscious 1980s, the supposed purity of mineral waters was the main reason why the world market for bottled water grew at 3040% per year [over that period]." In 1990 alone, Americans spent more than $2 billion on bottled mineral water, according to *Beverage World* magazine. One beverage industry consultant, commenting at the beginning of the Perrier water affair, put it this way: "The last possible thing Perrier can afford to have happen is for the public to think there is benzene in their spring, whether it gets filtered out or not."

NOTHING TO JOKE ABOUT

Source Perrier's global withdrawal of its product was the first of its kind that didn't involve the malicious tampering of a product. Only a few years earlier, Johnson & Johnson had been forced twice to order a worldwide recall of its *Tylenol* pain reliever medication after some capsules had been deliberately laced with cyanide. But the contrasts between the two incidents "made all the difference," said Stephen Greyser, a professor at Harvard Business School in Cambridge, Massachusetts. The key issue was that Source Perrier's problem "was of its own making. In that sort of situation, consumers are a lot less forgiving, and second, the Tylenol incidents resulted in eight deaths, while Perrier's posed no real health threat."

Greyser said that, to a drinker of Perrier water who didn't read the newspapers, watch television, or listen to the radio, "Perrier's response to the crisis would have seemed perfect. It withdrew the product swiftly, cleared up the problem, and reintroduced the product within weeks. But because Source Perrier fumbled its initial explanations so badly, the company got rotten press worldwide." Like the benzene residue that caused the problem in the first place, the fallout from the contamination incident and the company's mishandling of the entire situation lingered on and on.

In Britain, the company's subsidiary, Perrier UK, was left on its own to allay consumer fears about product quality. The subsidiary received no direction or coordination from parent Source Perrier, SA, for any concerted attempt to either explain the situation honestly, or more important, apologize to its customers. Perrier UK launched its own campaign with advertisements in newspapers across the country stating there "was no hazard to the public's health."

To add to matters, the British subsidiary found itself with 40 million unwanted bottles of Perrier water for disposal. The company decided to dump the water—after giving assurances to government officials concerned about the possibility of ground water contamination—and recycle the distinctive pear-shaped, green bottles. This proved to be a tall order because the UK had virtually no market at the time for recycled green glass. When the company announced that half of the bottles would be recycled, it drew loud criticism from several environmentalists who chastised Perrier UK for not recycling the entire lot, and all expectations of a positive public response were dashed.

A FIZZLED RELAUNCH

Within a few weeks of the recall, Source Perrier's staggered product relaunch was also mishandled. In early March, the company began to lay plans to get Perrier water back on store shelves around the world. A month later, just a week before Perrier sparkling water was due back on sale in the US, the FDA ruled that the claim printed on the mineral water label that it was "naturally sparkling" was false. The judgment was made on the grounds that the water and the gas used to make it "sparkle" were taken out of the ground separately—therefore, the federal agency said, the carbonation was artificial. The FDA also objected to the company's claim on the label that Perrier water was "calorie-free." Water, the agency said, "usually is."

Not wanting to make an already sticky situation go from bad to worse, Source Perrier acquiesced and changed its labeling. But there was more to come. The day before the scheduled US relaunch, the New York State Center for Environmental Health went public with its objection to the term "sodium-free" on the Perrier brand label. The Center claimed that it had conducted its own tests and had concluded that the Perrier water in a number of bottles it analyzed had sodium levels marginally exceeding FDA limits.

To top it off, the company's $25 million relaunch advertising campaign in the US came in for heavy criticism. The offending component of the campaign, crafted by advertising giant Burson-Marsteller, were radio commercials featuring Jill Purity, a fictional news reporter for the "Perrier News Network," who joked about the benzene scare. An executive from the New York-based agency added insult to injury when, quoted in *Adweek* magazine, he quipped, "This is just not serious. It's nothing that's going to cause widows."

THE COSTS OF AVOIDANCE

In the days before the benzene scare, Source Perrier was in the enviable position of literally having created its own market. The company name, like *Xerox* and *Coca-Cola*, was used almost generically. True, the company was being squeezed by a flood of longtime competitors as well as newcomers; but, before the benzene scare, it had established itself as the global product standard and its sales were growing steadily in an increasingly crowded market.

It was a different story after the dust settled. With Perrier water deprived of a place in the market for a full six weeks, consumers already disaffected by Source Perrier's self-abuse and mishandling of the entire benzene issue began to turn to the competition. In 1991, sales in the US—the company's largest overseas market at the time—dropped from a pre-crisis market share of 13 percent to less than 8 percent. In the UK, its share of the market dropped from a commanding 49 percent to less than 30 percent. Even in France, Source Perrier's cut of the market slipped from 40 percent to 34 percent.

To the company's credit, after the fallout from the benzene scare settled, it instituted a coordinated crisis-management plan to be implemented globally from headquarters in Paris. The company recognized that its biggest mistake was the inconsistency of the stories that it had disseminated to the media and the lack of credibility that situation evoked. In the words of one of its executives, the company was "staggered by the speed at which the whole situation spiralled out of control." He was citing the fact that many of the company's distributors and overseas wholesalers found out about the benzene problem only through their local and national press. That, he admitted, had allowed rumors to spread, compounding the situation even more.

Quoting from *The Prism,* a journal published by the management consulting firm of Arthur D. Little, *The Economist* concluded, "Managers tend to be wrong-footed by corporate crises because they are used to shaping events, not to having events grasp, control and shape them. Once it had regained control of the affair—a week-long struggle—Perrier did most things right. But it would have all been a lot easier had each part of the company been pouring from the same bottle at the outset."

Ten years later, in September 2000, the spectre of contamination raised its ugly head again. Source Perrier, now a unit of Swiss-based Nestle, SA, found itself as the focal point of another product-quality scare. The company hit the headlines in New York after as many as 7 people in New York City and in Westchester and Suffolk counties—including an 18-month-old boy—were hospitalized after drinking *Perrier*, *Poland Springs*, and *Aquafina* bottled water. The beverages had been tainted with ammonia or lye.

The damage to the company could have been enormous. At the time, New York ranked fourth in the US market for bottled water. California, Texas, and Florida were the top three customers for the 4.6 billion gallons of bottled water valued at $5.2 billion sold in the country in 1999.

Perrier reacted quickly, saying it would cooperate "fully and completely" with the Federal Bureau of Investigation, the Food & Drug Administration, and the New York state agencies investigating the incidents. The company pledged to "do everything [it] can to help the authorities get to the bottom of this situation." To Source Perrier, "everything" centered on a new quality program instituted after the 1990 benzene scare. It called for an "archived" sampling of every lot of bottled water produced by the company. In effect, the new program permits Perrier to keep a "file" on its product so it can be accessed to monitor quality issues.

In a statement released to the press, Perrier Group president Kim Jeffrey said the company had examined its manufacturing and distribution operations and found no evidence suggesting that the contamination occurred in their processes. He stated, "We will continue to monitor our facilities and cooperate fully...with the investigation." Within a few days, the possibility that the source of the contamination was within Perrier evaporated, as evidence began to build showing that the tainted water was the result of tampering. The International Bottled Water Association said the incidents "appear to be local and isolated criminal actions involving products sold in New York City alone." He added, "There is nothing to indicate that the contamination originated in the manufacturing or distribution chain." PepsiCo, parent of Aquafina, acted in concert with Perrier, saying it had "rigorously checked" its production facilities to make sure that its water was untainted "at the source or during any bottling or distribution operations."

But despite attempts to focus the investigation on a criminal act "by a person or persons unknown," a residue of sorts remained. As the investigation continued, the number of poisoning reports increased. Virtually all of them, according to authorities, were classified as either hoaxes or unprovable. According to the New York City police, many of the new reports were filed by people motivated by "everything from allergic reactions to medication to pathetic attempts to get their names in the paper." According to a Cornell University psychiatrist, some New Yorkers who reported unsubstantiated poisoning may simply be suffering from anxiety. "People have grave concerns about contamination or tainted stuff," he said. "When people get anxious, they can get every symptom known to mankind."

Lessons Learned

Why does company management that should know better blindly craft blunders that damage reputation, alienate staff, confound partners, lose precious market share, flush hard-earned operating capital down the drain, and sour and frustrate new and potential customers?

The answers are numerous. Like the tendency to create blunders in the first place, those answers lie dormant in the fabric of every company and surface during a crisis when—because of some inherent flaw—the company is unable or unwilling to take a good long look in the mirror to see what is really there, rather than what their egos tell them is there.

PRIDE COMES BEFORE A FALL

Narcissism and actions borne out of its skewed perspective can be crippling—if not fatal. It's like seeing a classic Greek tragedy play itself out. Pride turns into arrogance, which in turn develops into hubris. Hubris then drives the otherwise innocent hero to destruction—with a Greek chorus that should be heard, but isn't, warning of impending doom.

Qualcomm's frightening misstep in Russia, Disney's European faux pas, and Wal-Mart's slog though foreign markets share a common trait with the marketing gaffe of Coca-Cola and McDonald's. Each was benign in nature from the viewpoint of a wildly successful domestic company. But each also indicates what can happen when a company assumes that its past achievements will automatically ensure its future accomplishments.

As a result, a company neglects its homework, whether for reasons of cost-saving, immediacy, lack of resources, or otherwise, and relies on what it perceives as a forgiving marketplace. Then suddenly, instead of a solid span, the past success proves to be a raised drawbridge. Unable to jam into reverse, the company falls into the raging waters simply because its assumptions were based on its proud perceptions of who it *was* and it forgot about the vulnerabilities inherent in every business.

THE MORAL: Markets are not stable but undulate like the sea, and rogue waves are unpredictable. Regardless of how grand the ship, the captain always knows its vulnerabilities. A decision made out of arrogance without regard to the power of the ocean can sink the entire vessel, or at least leave its crew and decks in shambles.

GLOBAL MEANS DIVERSITY NOT UNIFORMITY

The international success of companies like McDonald's and Coca-Cola has been built in large part on management awareness of consumer diversity, albeit an awareness that sometimes has been forgotten with disastrous results. Whether a company expands within a single country or overseas, consumer diversity—the result of cultural, historical, religious, political, geographical, and other such factors—is ever-present. A company must have the ability not only to adapt initially, but also to continue to account for that diversity as changes occur in the make-up of the marketplace and in the company's own projects and policies.

In Disney's case, Dr. Herbig of Texas A & M University says that the company "failed to take the time to understand its customers better and, in essence, it assumed...that what had succeeded in the United States (and presumably, in Japan) would also work in France." It forgot to make a list of the essential traditions of a European lifestyle, and it learned the hard way that the American way is not everybody's way—even on the pathway to a *Magical Kingdom*.

Management at Wal-Mart made a similar wrong turn. The company, heady with its firm grip on the domestic US market, couldn't move fast enough to achieve its inviolable expansion goals. It faced a dual challenge: to sell mainly American products the American way in diverse foreign markets, and also to export a fundamentally American corporate culture. It failed at both, unnecessarily experiencing mediocre results across the board internationally for years because of a feeling that if Wal-Mart can sell it in Abilene, it can sell it in Kowloon. David Glass, Wal-Mart president through the turbulent 1990s, encapsulated the company's attitude at the time: "Everything that is done in Arkansas or Kansas can also be done in Brazil or China."

THE MORAL: Ships of different countries had a tradition of dipping their flags in respect to each other as they passed. In the best nautical tradition, recognize the diversity of the world around you by gestures of respect. Insisting that your way is best is an imposition, while recognizing the ways of others is an invitation.

KNOW AND APPLY THE RULES—OF THE OTHER GUY

Failure to know and apply rules can sink a business as fast as it can sink ships. Just like the captains on the Andrea Doria and the Stockholm, a company must know the rules, apply the rules, but never assume that the other guy plays by the same rules. Many of the examples in this chapter are of companies that failed either to comprehend or to apply the rules.

McDonald's and Coca-Cola knew the rules of international trade and had a long history of successfully infiltrating diverse markets worldwide. Yet despite all of that experience, they forgot a simple rule: government emblems, flags, official seals, and similar political signs often have great meaning to nationals, let alone religious adherents. While much of the world's population may be desensitized to what could be offense in today's consumer world of disposal products, there still are many who could well take offense. Throw-away packaging is not the best place for displaying symbols that carry so much emotional meaning.

Disney and Wal-Mart both neglected to learn the rules and practices of the places where they wanted to do business, assuming instead that they could simply transplant a piece of America overseas. They compounded the problem by failing to recognize the early warning signs of restless natives. By the time they regrouped, they were on the defensive and had to take evasive action to save their investments.

Richard Bliss's headline-making, unintentional plunge into the world of spies was a result of his company's failure to understand that the rules of doing business in Russia differ from state to state, and even city to city, within the Federation. In fact, such differences are also seen in Qualcomm's own country, the USA, where the laws and practices of both local and national authorities must always be considered when doing business. However, Qualcomm forgot that the Russian government is at present less centralized, assuming instead that the rules would be the same throughout the country and that local levels of authority would recognize federal ones as in the US.

Fortunately, Qualcomm learned from the Bliss episode and has extensively modified the way it conducts its surveys. A company representative says that in Russia the clients now conduct the tests while Qualcomm employees merely supervise and advise without handling any of the equipment. In the year following Bliss' arrest, the company—posting $3.94 billion in sales in 1999—inked a $10 million contract in Krasnador, Russia, and similar telecommunications projects in Bangladesh, Nigeria, and the Congo. It also clinched a deal on a $200 million wireless system in the Ukraine. To add to that, the company has operations throughout Latin America and Asia.

Driven by a breathtaking glibness, Perrier neglected the Golden Rule that is a guideline for all companies of any size that offer products or services to the public: do not lie. By treating the 1990 benzene scare with flippant humor, the company failed to relieve the very real concerns of its consumers, eventually casting Perrier as being almost completely out of touch with them. Quite simply, Perrier stood mesmerized at the helm believing that its reputation was pure and secure while failing to take immediate decisive action to meet its obligations to those customers that positioned the company in the first place. It flew down a path of least resistance until it was trapped in a web of disinformation it had spun for itself.

Fortunately for Perrier, no one paid for the company's folly with their lives. Sadly, the same can't be said for Ford and Bridgestone/Firestone. When push came to shove, these two long-time partners were more concerned about saving their own reputations than working together to honestly address a growing tidal wave of public- and private-sector objections. Faced with allegations of defective product design and manufacture, these two companies failed to address the issues with immediate and sincere concern for the consumer, and instead turned on each other in a frenzy of finger-pointing and recriminations in the press that left the public thinking that its trust had been misplaced.

THE MORAL: No one is above the rules of the game. If you want to play a winning hand, you must know and use the same rules as the other players in the game. No matter what reputation you bring to the game, it is your conduct at the table that counts.

KEEP YOUR EYES ON THE ROAD

The evaporation of the family-owned Schwinn company can be tied directly to lack of attention by the dynasty heirs. The controlling element of the company's hierarchy sold out its birthright through decisions that were short-sighted and, ultimately, fatal. By demanding cost-saving policies and refusing to invest in necessary self-improvement, Schwinn missed opportunities in a changing market and lost its competitive edge. The company could have retained its identity if it had carefully built a watertight collaboration with its overseas manufacturers rather than giving them the shop and allowing them to run off with what Schwinn taught them. Schwinn's destiny eventually wound up in the hands of family members, who didn't care what became of the company, and shrewd competitors adept at taking the offensive when the defenses had not been secured.

THE MORAL: If you don't stay on board, the circling sharks will get you.

BUILD MISSION CONTROL BEFORE LIFT-OFF

When an earthquake, hurricane, flood, or other disaster strikes a populated area, public and private organizations rush to the devastated region and implement well-rehearsed emergency plans. A command post is established to coordinate actions in the field and centralize communications. Every business should take a lesson from such emergency response teams.

McDonald's and Coca-Cola forgot about the purpose of mission control: to check that all systems are "green" before launch. Their failure to recognize the impact their joint World Cup marketing strategy would have on the deeply held beliefs of adherents to one of the world's largest religions is troubling. Both companies had spent years cultivating the Middle East with a flurry of activity in the year just preceding the World Cup blunder. What happened? The explanation given is that because companies are so large, neither knew what the other was doing and both assumed the other would make corrections. Despite being partners for so long, the companies quite simply failed to run their plans through the checklist at mission control—whether their own or a joint team.

Source Perrier, Bridgestone/Firestone, and Ford ended up mired in public disbelief because of a failure to implement a centrally controlled response in a crisis situation. Different limbs took different paths, the bodies falling with arms and legs akimbo. Product recalls were authorized by local divisions without central coordination, and explanations were given without proper research and verification. Source Perrier's management tried humor in a potentially life-threatening situation. Ford and Bridgestone/Firestone showed more interest in saving their own skins and pointing blame at each other than working jointly to address with high-profile concern the public's fears and find a solution to why customers were dying on shredded tires and rolling over in SUVs.

THE MORAL: The launch button is likely to blow up the rocket if mission control has not first completed its checks. Systems and policies must be set and practised in advance to ensure immediate and appropriate centralized response if the rocket develops a problem.

A WOUND LEAVES A SCAR

The customer is the final judge of any company's plans and actions, no matter how noble or venerable the company might be. Once consumers have come to trust in the quality and reputation of certain brands, they form high expectations of the companies that produce and sell those products. If consumers merely feel their trust has been betrayed—regardless of the actual situation—customer confidence is likely to fall.

Sometimes wounds are not too deep and the scars fade in a short time. For Coca-Cola and McDonald's, their World Cup mistake caused a mere bump in their road and is seen as a history lesson learned, but it tarnished their otherwise explosive entry into the Middle East markets. Disney's kingdom lost some luster and Wal-Mart's market plunge turned into a slow slog when these companies failed to elevate local diversity over the American Way, resulting in slow investment returns and lukewarm customer reception. Qualcomm still feels a little stung by its spy episode, and it now moves with greater caution.

Deep wounds leave severe scarring, if the company survives at all. The Schwinn family no longer heads its one time trend-setting company, and the company that exists today is very different in focus and market position. Source Perrier has lost substantial customer confidence in the purity of its mineral water, and has had a slow come-back. In perhaps the most tragic example, dozens of people in the US and abroad have died in tire separation and SUV rollover accidents involving Ford and Bridgestone/Firestone products, with the result that customer confidence in both companies hit a record low in Fall 2000.

THE MORAL: Public trust takes a long time to build and seconds to destroy, and consumers tends to be short on forgiveness and long on memory. A wound should never be left to fester in today's highly competitive markets. It should be cleaned, dressed, and tended carefully so it heals with hardly a mark.

CHAPTER 2

Language and Translation Blunders

Say What You Mean and Mean What You Say

"Then you should say what you mean," the March Hare went on. "I do," Alice hastily replied; *"At least...at least I mean what I say...that's the same thing you know."* "Not the same thing a bit!" said the Hatter. *"Why, you might just as well say, 'I see what I eat' is the same thing as 'I eat what I see!'"*
—Lewis Carroll, Alice in Wonderland

A RECENT SURVEY OF AMERICAN BUSINESSES that compete globally concluded that their number one problem area is communications, both internal and external. This is brought into startling focus when you realize that, by the most recent count, at least three thousand languages exist in the world, each with its own regional and ethnic dialects and subdialects.

While many countries such as the United States, France, Germany, and Japan have a primary language for both written and oral communication, a large number of countries are bilingual, while still others are multilingual. For example, many African nations use the language of their former colonial overseers (French and Spanish, even German, Portuguese, and Italian) and also speak English, as well as their native languages and dialects. Communication in South Africa remains a mélange of Afrikkans, English, and a score of native African languages.

Several centuries ago, Dutch was the language of trade in many parts of Asia—including Japan—because of the strong presence of merchant traders from Holland who did business there. Portuguese, as well, was widely understood because Portugal vied with Spain, Holland, and numerous city states for the lucrative Far East markets. In large parts of Southeast Asia, French and Chinese are as common as the native languages, again because of former colonization.

Multiple languages are also used in more developed countries where history has played a strong role in both linguistic and economic development—for example, the Flemings and Walloons in Belgium, the small pockets of German-speakers in eastern France, and the German/Italian/French linguistic montage in Switzerland.

But despite the Tower of Babel that this global hodgepodge might appear to be, most countries have evolved an acceptable lingua franca—that is, a generally accepted language used to communicate and conduct business between people who have that language in common, even though they also have their own preferred language. In other words, most countries have found a common language for conducting economic affairs that transcends cultural differences.

The broad palette of languages that interplay in world trade can make for some serious—and sometimes humorous—mistakes.

There's "No, No" On Your Lips, But "Yes, Yes" In Your Eyes

Language is "the mirror of culture...and multi-dimensional in nature. This is true not only of the spoken word but also of what can be called the nonverbal language of world trade." So say Michael Czinotka, Pietra Rivoli, and Ilkka Ronkainen in their book *International Business*. These authors add that language serves four distinct roles in international trade:

First, language is important in information gathering and evaluation efforts. Rather than rely completely on the opinions of others, the manager is able to see and hear personally what's going on for himself. The best market intelligence is gathered by a manager willing to become part of the market rather than observing it from the outside. Second, language provides access to local society. Although English may be widely spoken, and even be the "official" company language, speaking the local dialect can make a dramatic difference. Third, language capability is increasingly important in company communications, whether within the corporate family or with channel members; and, lastly, language provides more than the ability to communicate.

Communication can take many forms—from spoken words and body language to inference and innuendo. The subliminal message of an advertisement, a commercial, a business conversation, or a business letter can speak unintended—and sometime intended—volumes. All communication, particularly spoken language, occurs within cultural and linguistic contexts. It extends beyond mechanics to the interpretations of contexts.

Each culture, over time, has developed its own subtle, and not-so-subtle, nuances of meanings and images. Each has its own sanctioned and forbidden modes of behavior. In all cultures, all people perceive themselves, the others in their culture, and the outside world, in light of nuances based on their own individual experiences. All this works together to make communication between persons of different cultural backgrounds and perspectives extremely difficult and fraught with potential pitfalls.

Language, then, is considerably more than the spoken word. It encompasses all manner of communication, both verbal and nonverbal, overt and covert.

BEAUTY, WORTH, AND VALUES

Communication between peoples is molded by a tremendous variety of factors: the aesthetics that mold a culture's values and concepts of beauty; the spiritual beliefs that help shape its sense of morality, place, and worth; the social structures that determine how people relate to one another; and the ethics that clearly delineate the borders that separate the socially acceptable from that which is not.

To traverse the communication minefield successfully, anyone doing business in the international marketplace must not only know, but also understand, the cultural environment of their company's international customers and partners. This understanding is an essential key to survival because every culture leaves its own indelible imprint on organizational structures, personnel policies, marketing strategies, advertising, interpersonal relationships, distribution channels, and a host of other components affecting any successful international business venture.

American Demographics covered in depth the issue of intercultural communications in an article in their May 1988 issue. "Reading from left to right or vice versa seems like a harmless cultural distinction between North American and Middle Eastern nations—at least until marketers get involved," wrote Stephen Karel. He was alluding to an ad for detergent that featured dirty clothes piled on the left, the detergent in the center, and clean clothes neatly stacked on the right. Reading left to right, which is the custom in the US, Canada, or Mexico, would have logically communicated the message—even without words—that using the detergent would convert your clothes from soiled to clean. Not so in the Middle East or other countries where messages are read right to left. The message told those potential customers that the soap would make their clothes filthy.

"Language can play tricks on marketers who don't respond to cultural differences," said Karel. "As more businesses go global, the chances for misunderstanding may increase." He quotes from a business study asserting that business people must examine "not just the spoken word, but all the elements of a culture that form a barrier to mutual understanding."

A good illustration might be British companies looking across the Channel to find consumers in France. They have often been advised to "speak the language" of French consumers. In a story in the magazine *Marketing*, the writer asserts that, "As a country with enormous pride in its heritage, an unrivaled understanding and appreciation of food and drink, and an ancient history of poor relations with the UK, it does not perhaps look like the most willing recipient of UK brands." However, he added, "the French consumer is not inherently unadventurous; he is a complex animal who has a number of perceptions about the UK." As an example, he suggest that "the French believe that English people eat dreadful puddings, jam with meat and mint with everything, all under perpetually grey skies." His advice: "Tap into a natural source of positive cultural heritage—the Great British Tradition. Products that can demonstrate a clear craftsmanship rather than an outright style are indicative of 'positive Britishness' and are appreciated by the French," who receive that "Britishness" in a positive light "when it offers no real threat to French cultural 'superiority'," he concluded.

DIVIDED BY A COMMON LANGUAGE

Some interesting problems can arise when attempts are made to reach what are thought to be single-minded markets supposedly speaking a common language. Spanish is probably the most vivid example of a language that, while it has many commonalities throughout its use in different places, certain words have marked variations in meaning. As a result, the message that's meant to be conveyed isn't necessarily the message that's received.

To illustrate, according to Philip Cateora in his book *International Marketing,* the word "ball" translates in Spanish as "bola." Bola means ball in several countries, a lie or fabrication in several others, while in yet another, it's a vulgar obscenity. *Tropicana* brand orange juice, he writes, was advertised as "Jugo de China," in Puerto Rico, but when marketed to the Cuban population of Miami, Florida, it failed to make a dent in the market. To the Puerto Rican, "China" translated into orange, but none of the Cubans in Miami were interested in buying what *they* perceived to be Chinese juice.

The assumption that all Spanish-based cultures are similar if not the same is even transcended by what is thought to be the most universal of all "languages"—music. "Even though we have a common language, there are many different cultural preferences," said Anibal Torres in an article published in the March 1995 edition of *Management Review*. The Torres family owns Top Ten Hits, a record company specializing in tropical Latin music and located both in New York City and Winter Park, Florida. "Our music has a very strong market in Puerto Rico, the Dominican Republic, Colombia, Venezuela, the Caribbean Basin, and the eastern part of the United States. We don't expect a huge response to our records in Los Angeles, because the majority of Hispanics in that area are from Mexico, and the Mexican market likes a different kind of music."

Cultural dissonance was driven home to me when the plumbing in my rented house decided to back up and flood the kitchen one Saturday afternoon. I called a local plumber, and in the course of conversation he shared with me that he had emigrated to the US from Argentina. As he worked on the pipes, he found additional problems that needed repair. So, I telephoned my landlord, who asked to speak to the plumber. An animated conversation in Spanish followed. The plumber at times narrowed his eyes, and other times he nodded his head in qualified agreement. After about 10 minutes, he hung up, sighed, and asked, "He's Cuban isn't he? I can always tell. I could only make out some of what he said. Their Spanish is very different, but don't worry, everything will be OK." I have to admit I did worry. But, fortunately, everything did work out.

A GLOBAL COMPANY "CULTURE"

Effective communications are critical not only for determining the market viability of a country or region, but for the viability of a company itself. According to Peter Pribilla, executive vice president of Siemens AG in Munich, Germany, "Ultimately, a company's culture is its personality. It reflects common values, and shapes employee behavior and affects how people work together. It influences the openness of communications and receptiveness to new ideas...coloring our expectations, overall aims, priorities, and how we work to attain our goals. In effect, it is the spirit behind company strategies and programs, ranging from a focus on customer needs to creating company value."

Quoted in the December 1999 issue of *Management Review,* Pribilla said, "The goal is not to develop one 'mind' in every part of the world, but rather to achieve a meeting of the minds. That's what distinguishes companies with a truly global culture from those without." Employees and divisions "across borders can work together because they all operate from the same basic beliefs." A transplanted culture won't guarantee success, he said, but "the lack of unifying corporate beliefs can only lessen a company's chances of being a major global player."

SAY WHAT YOU REALLY MEAN AND WATCH THOSE FINGERS

Raphael Baron, founder of Polyglot International, a San Francisco-based translation service, was interviewed for a story in the July 17, 2000, issue of *Industry Week* magazine. He said that while more companies have recognized language translation as a necessary part of doing business abroad, "their understanding of the real nature and true value of translation lags behind." He clarified in further comments that his business keeps "running into large, large corporations, and certainly into emerging companies, that simply do not include translations as a budget item. The industry truly does not understand how much translation costs...and that it isn't a machine process, but a very labor-intensive process."

Baron added, "When I say translation, I truly mean more than just language conversion...It's also a cultural phenomenon...more than simply customs and traditions." He recalled a situation where negotiations between an American construction company and the Russian government continued for months because neither party realized that the other was using a different measurement system for proposed earthquake-safety specifications. Although the numbers were accurately translated, "The Americans assumed they [the Russians] were talking Richter [scale]. The Russians assumed they [the American engineers] were talking 'modified Mercali,' which is the scale that is used in Russia."

Another example: In the 1980s, a group of American businessmen started a campaign to promote American-made products around the world. Part of their task called for the design of a "Made in America" symbol or logo. They felt that would help establish a sense of pride in US-made products. The symbol was based on the "OK" hand sign, which has been widely used in the US for generations—an open hand with the thumb and forefinger forming a zero. They failed to realize, however, that the hand sign had obscene or insulting connotations in a number of countries overseas. In Brazil, Greece, Ghana, and Turkey, the sign is a vulgar sexual invitation. In southern Italy it is an insult with an anal connotation. In Malta, this hand sign was used for a time as a signal between male homosexuals, and, in France and Belgium it still connotes—innocently, perhaps, but no less evocatively—that a person is a "zero" or "worthless."

It's a Big—and Small—World After All

Let's take a world tour, then, of verbal and nonverbal language blunders, both big and small. Keep in mind the haunting words of Blaise Pascal, the 17th century French philosopher, "There are truths on this side of the Pyrénées which are falsehoods on the other."

EUROPE

The world's second smallest continent, Europe stretches from Iceland in the northwest to Turkey in the southeast, from Portugal in the southwest to Finland in the northeast. Dominated by the European Union—the trade, economic, and political bloc headquartered in Brussels, Belgium—Europe covers one-sixth of the world's land and is home to 508 million people. In the late 1980s and early 1990s major events transpired, causing the political and economic makeup of the continent to explode: The Soviet Union disbanded, the two Germanys were unified, Czechoslovakia split in half, and Yugoslavia was subdivided.

More than 50 separate languages are spoken in Europe. Despite the ongoing move toward economic and monetary unity, each country remains its own separate entity with its individual cultural matrix. Some vignettes of communications missteps can illustrate this:

- BACARDI The beverage company attempted to cash in on French chic when it created a fruity drink and tried to sell it in both France and Germany under the name *Pavian*. A little research would have determined that, not only are there sections of France where German, not French, is commonly spoken, but "Pavian" happens to be the German word for "baboon."

- PROCTER AND GAMBLE A lack of understanding of the nuances of doing business in Europe provided a fair share of hilarity when a major marketing effort to sell *Puff* tissues in Germany flopped. It was discovered that, in some parts of the country, the term "Puff" is a colloquialism for "house of prostitution." The company fared no better in the United Kingdom, where the term "Puff" is widely used to refer to homosexuals.

- CLAIROL Did you know that the word "mist" in German means "manure"? No? Well, apparently neither did Clairol when it tried to market its *Mist Stick* curling iron in Germany. Needless to say, few ladies saw the glamour in the idea of running a hot stick of cow dung through their hair.

- GENERAL MILLS Commenting on a new General Mills snack food called *Fingos*, *Fortune* magazine ran a tongue-in-cheek brief commenting that, "Since you're supposed to eat the fingers manually, the company probably thought the name was a cute play on 'fingers.' Just as well there aren't any European export plans. In Hungarian, the name sounds like 'flatulate'."

- ELECTROLUX Scandinavian vacuum cleaner manufacturer Electrolux raised more than a few eyebrows when one of its most expensive marketing efforts in the US market was spearheaded by an ad claiming that "Nothing Sucks Like an Electrolux!" In the US, 'sucks' means bad or terrible.

- SCHWEPPES Mistranslated advertising copy in Italy for UK-owned Schweppes Tonic Water enthusiastically encouraged thousands of Italians to mix their gin with "Schweppes Toilet Water."

- OTIS Similarly, the Otis Engineering Company found itself in for more than just a bit of embarrassment. A sign appeared in Moscow that was supposed to read "Completion Equipment," but it had been translated to read "Equipment for Orgasms."

- MARKETING IN RUSSIA The Center for Russian and Eurasian Studies in Moscow reports how in the early 1990s some advertisers went astray by assuming that the appropriate language for an ad would be easy to come up with in a country where the population had only one brand of particular items anyway—and in limited supply, no less. For example, the slogan "Fly Aeroflot" was meaningless because the country only had one airline. The assumption, the Center said, proved true for some goods, like disposable diapers and Coca-Cola soft drinks, but in other cases, Western manufacturers would have done better had they taken a closer look at the Russian market. "Even giants like Procter & Gamble weren't able to avoid language and translation gaffes in their Russian marketing and promotional campaign," the Center said. Such an innocent product as "shampoo and conditioner in one bottle" was mistranslated into "shampoo and air conditioning in one bottle" simply because the Russian word "kondisioner" meant "air conditioner" before the free-market era. The Center conjured up the vision of a Russian consumer trying to figure out the relationship between air conditioning and hair care, and whether it meant the shampoo was enriched with freon.

- **JOHNSON WAX** The Johnson Wax Company successfully marketed its *Pledge* brand of furniture polish in Germany under the brand name *Pronto*. Correctly determining that a leap into the Dutch market would require a change of name, the company invested a lot of money in repackaging, relabeling, and advertising the polish for customers in The Netherlands under the name *Pliz*. Unfortunately, it was discovered too late that the Dutch pronunciation of "Pliz" sounds awfully close to "piss." Housewives, it turned out, were embarrassed to ask salespeople for the product, so sales stagnated.

- **CALVIN KLEIN** Several years ago, a western marketer conducted a consumer test on the streets of the Lithuanian capital, Vilnius, asking passersby to sample a perfume. After about an hour, she was surprised to discover that the brand name elicited a rather stiff response from 70 percent of the women she surveyed. The reason? The brand name, *CK*, happened to be the acronym for the Central Committee of the defunct Lithuanian Communist Party.

- A US-based hosiery manufacturer's attempt to use humorous advertising in Spain fell flat when its ad copy claimed that anyone who didn't wear its product "wouldn't have a leg to stand on." When translated, the ad said that customers who bought another brand of product would "only have one leg."

- **ANHEUSER-BUSCH** Anheuser-Busch, the US producer of *Budweiser* beer, has used the slogan "King of Beers" for many years, but it ran into a problem in Spain when an overeager copywriter used the wrong Spanish word and translated the company's tag line into "The Queen of Beers."

- **COLGATE PALMOLIVE** One of the largest pharmaceutical manufacturers introduced *Cue* toothpaste onto the French market before someone in the marketing department accidently discovered that Cue is also the name of a popular French pornographic magazine.

- **VITAMINIC** The European music website "Vitaminic" encountered difficulties when it tried to market itself to English-speaking users. The company had an established identity with German, French, and Italian users—they had no problem with the site name, readily identifying it with popular music. But the company quickly found that the name caused problems for potential web site visitors in the UK, Canada, and the US, who "couldn't say it, couldn't spell it, and thought it was a web site for health products like vitamins," according to one observer.

- An advertising program to promote a telephone system called the *Chat Box* in France caused nothing but confusion. The company thought the term would carry over effortlessly from English to French, failing to realize that it became the unintended equivalent of "Cat Box."

- COLGATE-PALMOLIVE A unique advertising campaign in Great Britain for the Colgate-Palmolive Company was so successful that the company decided to take it across the English Channel to the European continent. The ad, developed by advertising giant Foote, Cone & Belding, featured the company's *Ajax* liquid household cleanser. The commercial's "hook" was a puzzle that the television viewer needed to solve: The bottle of Ajax cleanser was seen as a reflection in gleaming bathroom tiles and faucets with the reflected, or backward, tag line reading "Xaja diuqil, nomel ro etihw." ("white or lemon, liquid Ajax"). The clever commercial was a rousing success in Austria, Switzerland, and The Netherlands, but fell on its face in Greece. The reason? "Xaja" means "silly" or "stupid" in Greek.

- STUDEBAKER In the late 1920s, Studebaker marketed one of its cars as the *Dictator*, but found sales slacking off, particularly in Europe, as time passed and the developments in Nazi Germany and Fascist Italy became the first things people thought of when the word was mentioned. The company produced its last Dictator in 1938, the year before World War II started.

- RICOH The Ricoh Corp. inadvertently created a major faux pas when it launched a series of blanket advertisements for its photocopy machines in Europe. One of the advertisements featured a demure young man with tousled hair and lipstick kisses covering his face. It carried the tag line, "Guess who ordered the Ricoh copier?" Meanwhile, another of their ads showed a young woman arriving at work to discover a dozen red roses on her desk. The tag line for that particular ad read, "The girl who insisted on the Ricoh copier." Ricoh's mistake was that they took a pan-European approach to the marketing campaign. The advertisements were a hit in The Netherlands, but they bombed in Great Britain and Denmark where socially active feminist groups succeeded in forcing Ricoh to pull the ads, which they considered "insensitive" and "blatantly chauvinistic."

ASIA

Nearly half of the sun's daily journey across the face of the earth—nearly 11 hours—is spent crossing the world's largest continent. Asia is so huge that it could hold all of both North and South America, as well as most of Australia. It is home to almost four billion people, nearly 60 percent of the world's total population. Asia's centerpieces are China, one of the world's most rapidly expanding economies, and India, the world's most populous democracy and a hotbed of high-technology enterprise. Staggered by the monetary crisis of 1997, Singapore, Hong Kong, South Korea, Taiwan, and Japan have found themselves in direct competition with the region's new up-and-coming economies of Indonesia, Thailand, Malaysia, and most recently, Vietnam.

The region has a history of business relations with the rest of the world that goes back centuries. Low-cost labor, particularly in the developing countries of Southeast Asia, now produces many of the world's consumer goods—from computers to children's toys. Trade with every part of the world moves in and out of the region. Asia is a classroom that teaches hard lessons to those who don't study and learn the ways of business there:

- **JAPAN** Japanese language and cultural nuance have, over the years, provided many examples of both what to do and what not to do when using language to convey a desired impression. Japanese consumers will react even more than their US counterparts to a brand solely on its modern or foreign-sounding name, rather than on any deep content or hidden meaning. Thus, two of the most popular beverages in Japan are *Pocari Sweat* and *Calpis*, sports-type drinks that convey to young Japanese, in particular, a positive, "healthy" image. Needless to say, the names just wouldn't fly in the US—they'd evoke images of perspiration and cow urine. Nor would it work in the US to sell a chocolate candy in a tin box advertised as "Hand-Maid Queer Aids," a takeoff on Band-Aids adhesive bandages. Two other Japanese product names that blundered in the US were a baby soap named *Skinababe*, and a hair-care product called *Blow Up*.

- **EXXON** The trouble with language translation put Exxon "in the tank," when the company discovered, much to its chagrin, that *Esso*—its brand name in Japan—meant "stalled car" when phonetically translated into Japanese. Hastily trying to correct the mistake, the company settled on the replacement name "Enco," which, it was later learned, phonetically translates into "sewage disposal truck."

- **SUMITOMO** Sumitomo, the Japanese steelmaker, spent a lot of money and time developing a steel pipe of great durability for export, intending that the US would be a primary market. The steel pipe—called *Sumitomo High Toughness*—was marketed in industry publications with the acronym "SHT" displayed in bold letters on all promotional materials and advertisements. Totally oblivious to the implied meaning ("SHT" when spoken sounds like "shit," slang for excrement), the company featured the acronym with the tag line, "It was made to match its name."

- One of the largest tourist agencies in Japan began receiving an unusually high number of inquiries from customers in the US, Australia, Canada, and other English-speaking countries interested in "sex tours." They only needed to look at their own business card to understand the reason for all the calls—the company's name? Kinki Nippon Tourist Company.

- **EMU AIRLINES** EMU Airlines never got off the ground when it tried to do business in Australia. As anyone who's been to a zoo knows, an emu is a bird that can't fly.

- **KENTUCKY FRIED CHICKEN** Chinese, with more than a dozen dialects, is a difficult language to work with in any case. This was made abundantly clear when Kentucky Fried Chicken's surefire "Finger Lickin' Good" ad campaign in China invited consumers there to, literally, "Eat Your Fingers Off!"

- A manufacturer in China reportedly wanted to market a sewing machine with the brand name *Typical*. When told by some Western observers that the name meant ordinary or undistinguished, they replied that several successful companies in the US had similar names, like Standard Oil.

- CHINA A US company reportedly negotiating a sale of technology to a buyer in the People's Republic of China found the talks grinding to a halt. The Chinese complained that the cost of the electricity necessary to operate the machinery for the project would be too high. The Americans were perplexed because neither electricity nor power costs were mentioned anywhere in the contract. Referred by the Chinese to Article 10 of the contract, the Americans saw that, indeed, a line in the offending article read, "The current [electrical current] value of the machinery is $1 million."

- COLGATE-PALMOLIVE Colgate-Palmolive spent a lot of money marketing *Pepsodent* toothpaste in Southeast Asia; the company's marketing plan focused on promoting the product's ability to enhance white teeth. The slogan "You'll wonder where the yellow went" hardly made an impression in two target markets in the region where locals deliberately chewed betel nuts to achieve the social prestige associated with dark, stained teeth. The slogan was also seen by many in Asia as a racial slur.

- TOKYO GAS & ELECTRIC COMPANY Literal translations are among the most humorous. I actually drew a small crowd of concerned passersby when I started laughing uncontrollably after first seeing a giant neon sign towering over the Ginza District in downtown Tokyo. It carried the slogan of the Tokyo Gas & Electric Company, "My Life, My Gas."

- CATERPILLAR The marketing people at one of the world's largest manufacturers of earth-moving equipment were more than a little upset when they found that a business magazine in Tokyo had fiddled with the company's trademarked logo in one of its ads. The company, Caterpillar Inc., discovered that some enthusiastic graphic artist, cum translator, had changed its signature machines to "Bugs that Crawl" tractors.

- RJ REYNOLDS TOBACCO COMPANY "Salem—Feeling Free" was a slogan that has sold a lot of cigarettes over the years, but the product never really caught on until the manufacturer came up with another catch phrase. It seems that the slogan hadn't enticed consumers as much as it confused them. Literally translated into Japanese, it read, "When smoking Salem, you will feel so refreshed that your mind seems to be free and empty."

- COCA-COLA In Taiwan, "Come Alive with the Pepsi Generation" was looked at askance when it stated, unequivocally, that drinking "Pepsi will bring your ancestors back from the dead." Not to be outdone, The Coca-Cola Company invested millions in rendering the company's name on thousands of signs and billboards around the country only to find out that the characters used to sound out the name phonetically—"Ke-Kou-Ke-La"—could mean either of two things: "A Female Horse Stuffed with Wax" or the more profound "Bite the Wax Tadpole." Scores of frantic staffers in Atlanta burned the midnight oil to research more than 40,000 Chinese characters to find the most accurate phonetic equivalent. They finally landed on "Ko-Kou-Ko-Le," which loosely translates to a much more benign "Happiness in Your Mouth."

- A good example of non-spoken communication was a television commercial for an American-made underarm deodorant that ran on Japanese television. The commercial showed an animated octopus applying the deodorant under each of its eight arms. The ad was a total failure because the producers failed to realize that an octopus doesn't have arms—it has legs.

■ PHILIP MORRIS COMPANIES INC. For years, the Marlboro Man rode the plains of the US Southwest touting the masculine attributes of smoking that particular brand name of cigarette. Highly successful in its heyday, the promotional campaign—more recently curtailed because of restrictions in the US on cigarette advertising—fell flat in Hong Kong. The reason? Consumers in Hong Kong are highly sophisticated and urbane. Few saw any appeal in riding around on a horse in the hot sun, and even fewer could see the link between the perceived US concept of cowboy individuality and smoking.

■ UNILEVER International business writer David Kilburn wrote a story in *Adweek* about Unilever's attempts to promote its *Timotei* shampoo in Asia. The product was successfully marketed in Japan in 1985 with advertising that depicted a young blond woman washing her hair and touting the product's reputation for mildness. In Taiwan, however, the same advertisements failed to attract business because raven-haired Taiwanese women simply couldn't relate to blonds. Some even wondered if the product would actually change the color of their hair.

■ In the 1960s, an American manufacturer of toothbrushes was very pleased to find that its sales figures in Vietnam were much higher than they had projected. The pleasure faded, however, when the company found out that its product was eagerly acquired from Saigon to Da Nang by agents of the Viet Cong, who were using the toothbrushes to clean their weapons.

AFRICA AND THE MIDDLE EAST

Centuries ago, traders from the Arabian Peninsula moved goods between trading posts as far apart as China and East Africa. The nations of the Middle East, with their economies now based largely on oil revenues, are struggling to redefine themselves as manufacturing and regional distribution centers. Many African countries are still attempting to stabilize their ruling governments. At the end of World War II, only four countries in all of Africa were independent of colonial rule. Today, virtually every nation on the continent is self-ruled, but Sub-Saharan Africa remains largely underdeveloped and embroiled in regional conflicts that have sapped its strength and diverted precious manpower and wealth from more productive pursuits.

Post-apartheid South Africa reigns as the continent's most robust industrialized economy, while to the north the developing nations of Kenya, Uganda, Zaire, and Nigeria continue to labor amid tribal animosities and poverty for a footing in the rapidly globalizing world economy. The extreme north of the continent, bookended by Morocco and Egypt, is seeing increased development as both countries have acted to privatize much of their state-owned enterprises to make themselves more attractive to international investment.

Some 850 million people populate both regions. Speaking more than 880 languages and dialects, they present some of the most compelling marketing challenges in the world:

- In the 1980s, a European-made brand of tomato paste was marketed in the Middle East but failed to catch consumers. Afterwards, it was discovered that the phrase "tomato paste" had been literally translated into Arabic as "tomato glue."

- PILLSBURY The Jolly Green Giant has been an advertising icon for 75 years since making his debut as a product trademark for the giant green peas produced by the US-based Minnesota Valley Canning Company. He reappeared as the star of a new advertising campaign for his parent company, Pillsbury. The new campaign featured such tag lines as "Give peas a chance" and "I stand for goodness—In fact I haven't sat down in 75 years." But in the 1960s, the company created an inadvertent laugh when it marketed its brand in Saudi Arabia. "Jolly Green Giant" translated literally into Arabic as "Intimidating Green Ogre."

- The story is told of an American bank that was given a 30-day option on the purchase of another financial institution in the Middle East. A negotiator for the US bank proposed in French—a language widely used in the region—that the loans be put into an escrow account. The local sellers called off the negotiations, embarrassed by the suggestion that they would "create a reserve for cheating." The misunderstanding arose from the incorrect use of the word "escrow," which, in French means "cheat" or "gyp."

- On several occasions, international business educator David Ricks has written on the importance that sound tone and pitch can have in conveying a message. In some languages two words are spelled identically but are differentiated by sound. This is a major issue in many countries in Africa where people communicate in a dizzying variety of harmonic languages and dialects. Ricks tells the story of the Igbo people of Nigeria, who were taught by Christian missionaries to sing the second verse of "O Come all ye Faithful." The missionaries thought they had taught their flock to sing, "Very God, begotten not created," while the actual meaning of the verse (using the traditional European version of "O Come all ye Faithful" as a base) tonally translated into "God's pig, which is never shared." The befuddled Igbos faced another theological conundrum when a verse from another hymn, "There is no sorrow in heaven," was musically translated into "There is no egg on the bicycle."

- MONT BLANC PENS Religious sensitivities came to the fore when Mont Blanc pens found its high-quality writing implements all but banned in Arab countries, until it was clearly explained that the trademark white marking found on the ends of its pens is not the "Star of David," but the representation of a snow-capped Alpine mountain peak. In a similar incident, shipments of bagged sugar to Iraq were banned by the government there until the company removed its logo from the bags. The reason? The logo resembled the "Star of David," Israel's national symbol.

- Rioting broke out in Bangladesh when Moslems protested the importation of a particular brand of slippers from Canada after a rumor spread that the company's logo resembled the Arabic characters for Allah. The only way the government could appease the rioters was to prohibit the sale of the rubber slippers and confiscate all shipments of the slippers that had already cleared Customs.

- An airline serving the Middle East almost lost its authority to provide service to the region when its magazine and newspaper advertising showed an attractive female flight attendant serving champagne to smiling first-class passengers. The ad was deemed "offensive" because it violated two primary principles of the region's Islamic-based culture: first, Moslems are prohibited from drinking alcoholic beverages; and second, unveiled women are prohibited from mingling with men who are not their relatives.

LATIN AMERICA

Comprised of three separate regions—Central America, South America, and the island nations of the Caribbean—Latin America stretches from Guatemala southward to the tip of Tierra del Fuego, and from Chile in the west to the Windward and Leeward Islands of the eastern Caribbean. Brazil, which spreads across nearly half the continent of South America, is the business centerpiece of the region and one of the world's most rapidly developing economies. Mercosur, or the Southern Common Market (the regional trade alliance formed by Argentina, Brazil, Paraguay, and Uruguay), dominates the continent's business in the south, while the Adean Pact promotes trading in the northwest.

In early 2000, the US legislature approved a trade pact that would allow duty-free access to US markets for many products manufactured in the island nations of the Caribbean. The intent is to help the Caribbean nations reduce their historic reliance on agricultural exports. The pact promises to boost trade with the region and undoubtedly will also provide ample opportunities for interesting lessons on both how to—and how not to—conduct international business. Some of the lessons already learned:

- PERDUE One of the best examples, a classic blunder that's made its way into dozens of magazine articles and business books, was US chicken king Frank Perdue's attempt to communicate that "It takes a Tough Man to Make a Tender Chicken" to customers in Latin America. The fairly straightforward statement conveyed another picture entirely when it translated, literally, into "It Takes a Sexually Stimulated Man to Make a Chicken Affectionate."

- THE PARKER PEN COMPANY Roger Axtell, author of *The Do's and Taboos of International Trade* series, once served as vice president of worldwide marketing for The Parker Pen Company. Later, while a special advisor to the governor of Wisconsin, Axtell reported that Parker's trademark *Jotter* pen had to be renamed before it could be sold in parts of Latin American where the word "jotter" means athletic supporter.

- FEDERAL EXPRESS Federal Express, the Memphis, Tennessee-headquartered expedited air carrier, ran into some initial difficulty when the company started to serve the Latin American market. Because of the word "Federal" in the company's corporate name, consumers in the region initially thought that the company was government-run. The company found itself trying to overcome an expectation that it would be as medievally bureaucratic and inefficient as the governments of many of the countries it planned to serve.

■ FORD MOTOR COMPANY In the mid-1970s, Ford released its design-flawed *Pinto*—an underpowered economy sedan that featured a poorly designed carburetion system, a dangerously positioned gas tank, an overstiff suspension system, and as much storage space in the trunk as a cigar box. The car generated only mediocre sales when introduced in the US, but it didn't measure up at all when it was marketed in Brazil. At the time, Ford was using names related to horses for several of its car lines, such as *Mustang* and *Maverick*. The thinking in Detroit was that if it worked in the US to identify innocuously an economy sedan with a piebald Southwestern Native American pony, what problem could there possibly be in using the same name in the largest Portuguese-speaking country in the world? Well, the problem was that "Pinto" is a Portuguese street-slang expression casting derision on the size of a man's "appendage." It took just a few days for the company to perform one of the fastest marketing turnarounds on record— moving at the speed of light, it reformulated its advertising strategy and changed the name of the Brazil-bound Pinto to *Corcel*, which is Portuguese for "horse."

■ In Brazil, a major American air carrier advertised its "rendezvous lounges" aboard its Boeing 747 jumbo jets flying between the US and Rio de Janeiro. The company was abashed to find that the term "rendezvous" in Portuguese implies an illicit sexual liaison.

NORTH AMERICA

Three of the world's most powerful economics make up North America— Canada, Mexico, and the United States; their combined Gross Domestic Product is $7 trillion. Trade negotiators from the three countries concluded the North American Free Trade Agreement (NAFTA) in August 1992, setting in motion a mechanism that over time is intended to minimize or altogether reduce restrictions on goods moving between the trio.

Even before the agreement, bilingual Canada and the US enjoyed the most lucrative trade relationship in the world. In the mid-1990s, Mexico overtook Japan to become the United States's second-largest trading partner. Yet, despite their proximity to one another, some companies from all three countries still blunder their way across both borders to find that they can't assume that what works in Veracruz will necessarily work in Halifax.

■ COORS Any beer aficionado in the US can recall the days when *Coors* beer, produced in Golden, Colorado, could only be found in the western US. Urban folklore tells of visiting easterners and foreign visitors shipping home cases of the brew—known as "Colorado Kool-Aid"; they stockpiled it as though it were some particularly rare Chateau Rothschild wine. The company's "Turn It Loose!" advertising splash sold a lot of beer in the US but had a less-than-enthusiastic reception in Mexico. There the literal Spanish translation predicted that anyone drinking Coors would "Suffer from Diarrhea." Not very inviting, one has to admit.

■ BRANIFF AIRLINES The now defunct Braniff Airlines wanted to appeal to first-class travelers when it promoted its leather upholstery to customers in Mexico. The trouble is that the company's advertising agency literally translated its "Fly in Leather" tag line into "Vuela en Cuero"—or "Fly Naked."

- MCDONALD'S McDonald's, Inc., got into hot water in 1988 when it included an illustration of the Mexican flag on the paper placemats used at its franchises throughout the country. The company didn't anticipate the outcry: after government officials expressed their anger that ketchup might be splattered all over a national symbol, the placemats were recalled.

- FORD MOTOR COMPANY Ford's economy-class *Fiera* pickup truck may have conjured up visions of hot sales in Mexico, but unfortunately no one bothered to find out that the word translates to a slang word meaning "ugly, old woman." The same can be said for the company's *Caliente*, the export version of the automaker's popular *Comet* car sold in the US. After an expensive advertising campaign yielded few sales, Ford discovered to its dismay that "Caliente" is Mexican-Spanish slang for "prostitute."

- An American T-shirt maker wanted to capitalize on the visit of Pope John Paul II to Miami, Florida. Instead of displaying the desired "I Saw the Pope," or "El Papa," the incorrect Spanish on the shirts proclaimed that the wearer had seen "la Papa," or "the potato."

- In another shirt-related gaffe, a magazine advertisement of an American manufacturer of men's dress shirts was supposed to read, "When I wore this shirt, I felt good." This fairly straightforward message took on a whole other meaning when the literal translation read, "Until I wore this shirt, it felt good."

- PANASONIC Matsushita Electric, Japan's electronics giant, promoted a new personal computer targeted for use with the Internet in 1996. Panasonic, Matsushita's partner, developed a web browser to make the computer system "user friendly," and licensed the US cartoon character Woody Woodpecker as its animated Internet guide. But the day before advertisements were scheduled to run, the company piqued the interest of a puzzled media by inexplicably canceling its product launch indefinitely. For good reason: The ads featured the slogan "Touch a Woody, the Internet Pecker." After an American staff member of the marketing team in Tokyo explained to "stunned and embarrassed" upper-level Japanese managers that "Touch a Woody" and "Pecker" held sexual connotations in American slang, the company decided to reorganize its marketing effort for the computer system.

- The manager of a US supermarket who wanted to impress a visiting delegation of businessmen from Japan at least deserves some credit for trying. Laying out a repast of sushi and tea, he found out later, much to his disappointment, that sushi should be served raw, not deep-fried. He also learned by error that serving Japanese green tea would have made a much better impression than offering dark tea imported from China.

- THE HYUNDAI MOTOR COMPANY Hyundai of Korea entered the US auto market in 1986 only to find its marketing efforts stymied because of confusion surrounding the correct pronunciation of the company's name. Many people confused the name with "Honda," one of Hyundai's biggest Japanese competitors. The Koreans tried mightily to get Americans to use the Korean pronunciation ("High-Yoon-Day"). But failing, they finally "bent with the wind" in a promotional campaign that encouraged customers to say "Hun-Day as in Sun-Day."

- Several years ago, a group of angry American auto union members used sledge hammers to destroy a compact Japanese car in protest of what they felt was a "flood of foreign imports" responsible for the loss of their jobs. The incident received tremendous play in the media and elicited some sympathy for the participants—until a reporter discovered that the sledge hammers were imported from India. A similar anecdote is told of an auto worker in Detroit who was so upset with the successful sales of Japanese-made cars in the US market that he decided to produce and sell shirts displaying the message "Buy American-Made!" in both English and Japanese. The wind disappeared from his sails when someone informed him that, while the English was on target, the Japanese line urged patriotic Americans to "Buy an American Maid!"

- The nuances of doing business in French-speaking Canada can present their own set of pitfalls. For example, an automaker marketing its vehicle in Quebec found that the tag line telling potential customers that its car "Topped them all" had been translated into "Topped by them all."

- An American manufacturer of laundry detergent tried to sell its product in Quebec, claiming that it was "the best one to use on especially dirty parts of the wash." The phrase was translated into colloquial French so the phrase "the dirty parts" came out as "les parts de sale." This proved to be a handicap as that particular phrase is French-Canadian slang for "private parts."

- HUNT-WESSON Hunt-Wesson found itself in a similar situation when it attempted to market its *Hungry Man* line of TV dinners in Canada under the name "Gros Jos" only to find out that in slang it means "large breasts."

- An advertisement for an American brand of canned fish caused no end of trouble when it ran in newspapers in Quebec. The advertisement featured a woman wearing shorts and playing golf with a man. The intended inference was that a woman could take the time to play golf with her husband and then serve the canned fish for dinner. If the company had done its homework it would have learned that women in Quebec don't play golf with male partners, nor do they wear shorts on the golf course. More importantly, canned fish generally is not served as a main course in Quebec.

- HEINEKEN According to *Brandweek* magazine, executives from Heineken USA, the US subsidiary of the Dutch beer company, "were in for a shock…when they convened a Florida meeting to introduce distributors to a 'teaser' campaign that played off the brand's trademarked 'Red Star' logo." Miami wholesalers were not amused, telling the visiting executives that the Miami area's numerous Cuban emigrés would take the logo as an inflammatory reference to the Communist regime that so many of them had fled from. The ads were immediately shelved.

Lessons Learned

GET ON THE INSIDE TRACK

Most companies who have had to retract and revise their names, advertising, symbols, and marketing strategies because of communication defects simply failed to research their targeted markets in sufficient depth. Sometimes the answers are quite easy to find. Many books, seminars, and other educational resources are available to teach would-be global marketers about the values, tastes, beliefs, and social structures of various cultures and countries. A quick look in a translation dictionary can bring immediate, eye-popping revelation.

However, a first glance is generally not enough. "Third sources" of information—someone else's books, lectures, opinions, etc.—may not reveal that the design on a pen resembles the Star of David, that Japanese tea is green and sushi is raw, or that a *Red Star* logo, the abbreviation *CK*, or the words "Federal" or "Dictator" can have unwanted overtones among populations that have sought to overthrow certain regimes. Nor may they state the unobvious facts that gum cleaners might become gun cleaners in Vietnam, that canned fish is not a sought-after delicacy in Canada, and that it is taboo in some places for men and women to consort on planes or golf courses, let alone wear shorts or drink alcohol.

The first rule of effective communication is to use your own personal senses to gather and evaluate the values, tastes, beliefs, politics, and social structures of your target markets. Access to local society begins with your commitment to understanding—truly comprehending—the culture and environment of that society. Personal visits and interviews, cultivation of friendships with resident and overseas nationals, and joint marketing with local companies (not imposing your own management, staff, policies, and systems) can be very helpful in avoiding cross-cultural linguistic gaffes.

THE MORAL: If you rely on someone else to tell you what they think you should know, you will have only yourself to blame when what you know is not what you should have known. Personal time in the market is as important as personal time with the product or service.

MEANING IS IN THE EYE AND EAR OF THE BEHOLDER

Whether trading globally or within a country, every company must recognize that diversity in communication is a key issue. A language faux pas might seem hilarious after the fact, but it can be disastrous to a company's bottom line, affecting not only sales but also the company's hard earned reputation.

Language diversity across country borders seems fairly obvious, and the preconception of a common language within a country's borders is certainly out-moded, and has been for centuries. Populations everywhere have shifted with the sands of time. Country borders have sometimes been remapped, resulting in residents changing their homeland without ever leaving home. And hundreds of enclaves of diversity exist within countries because migrating peoples often retain their own historical roots.

Nevertheless, language diversity has been forgotten on occasion by companies that should have remembered two important facts: first, sounds and words have different meanings in different languages; and second, a common language does not equate to a common meaning. It seems that a check with a dictionary or a native speaker might have kept Bacardi from making a monkey of its *Pavian* fruit drink in Germany, Clairol from fertilizing the German hair care market with *Mist Stick* curling irons, and the Johnson Wax Company from embarrassing Dutch housewives with *Pliz* furniture polish. Similarly, Electrolux might have avoided offering the American public vacuums of poor quality because they "suck" and Spanish-speaking populations might not have been flooded with Tropicana brand juice that was "orange" in Puerto Rico but "Chinese" in Miami.

THE MORAL: A word or sound does not always have the same meaning for one beholder as it does for another. In fact, it may have no meaning to one ear but be downright offensive to another.

FLOUNDER IS NOT ALWAYS A FISH

Language translations that are intended to be straight often turn out to be crooked. The problem usually tends to arise from language conversion without language comprehension. Any person can pick up a dual-language dictionary and convert a word or phrase from his or her language into the other one. But that conversion may not have accounted for the nuances of meaning, common usage, or slang, and in fact, it relies on the editor of the dictionary to "get it right" in the first place.

With a little more effort, blunders in language conversion can generally be avoided before being released to the public. This effort certainly would have been preferable to selling shirts proclaiming "the potato" in Spanish instead of "the Pope," to labeling containers bound for the United States with the acronym "SHT," or to offering to bring ancestors back from the dead by sipping a Pepsi soft drink. Large and small companies alike are not immune from language gaffs, and although many might be hilarious after the fact—such as "Buy American Maid," "Touch a Woody," "tomato glue," "Gros Jos" frozen meals, and "Fly Naked" leather, to name a few—the expense involved in developing and implementing a market promotion makes it important to get it right in the first place.

THE MORAL: A wise person says it not only with finesse and panache, but also with a clear understanding of exactly what is being said.

SAYING IT WITHOUT WORDS

Innuendo, association, and nonverbal communication can be at least as potent and poignant as an explicit verbal message. Pictures, colors, and shapes, as well as words, convey messages to viewers, who then apply their own interpretations. It is at this point that messages sometimes go awry because the meaning of the message will depend highly on the beliefs, culture, education, sex, age, and other characteristics of the receiver.

Many companies have learned a hard lesson when the photographs or pictures displayed in their advertising said more than words. A quick flip of a photograph from left to right would have made clothes clean for consumers who read from right to left. The choice of a softly curled brunette would have made a shampoo more alluring in a culture unaccustomed to blonds. A modern urban setting would have attracted more cigarette buyers from among the sophisticated and citified gentry than photos of a leathery cowboy on horseback under a hot prairie sun.

In the hunt for undesirable innuendos and associations, an understanding of common language usage and slang in the targeted markets is essential. Some companies no doubt wish they had done more research before going public with their choices. Most likely, EMU Airlines actually intended its planes to fly, while the Chinese *Typical* sewing machines were probably not as mediocre as the name would suggest to Americans. Intimate encounters were no doubt the farthest things from the minds of those who named the rendezvous aircraft lounge, and most likely the French developer of the *Chat Box* didn't know any American cat lovers. Companies using names or symbols that evoke a government presence—such as "Federal," "CK," or a "Red Star" logo—may have a tough time gaining market share where a population is particularly sensitive to government control.

THE MORAL: Sometimes thoughts are louder than words. Nonverbal messages can seal the fate of a product or service.

WE ARE ONE AT HEART

There are, of course, hundreds of examples of what separates us all—comically and poignantly. Sometimes, though, it's easy to get so caught up in the differences that segment us ethnically and linguistically that we become focused on the contrasts and forget to look for the similarities. If anything has become evident as the world shrinks and its collective economy continues to globalize, it is the fact that we are sometimes more "in tune" with one another than we realize.

International marketing consultant Richard Miller was speaking at the Direct Marketing Symposium in Bangkok, Thailand, when he made what he acknowledged was an "arrogant cultural slip." While conducting a session in multicultural marketing, Miller held up a copy of the *Asian Wall Street Journal,* an English-language publication that had the headline, "Chinese Politician Makes Hay." Miller told the class that he "was appalled that the WSJ would use such an obviously American idiom in an Asian publication." But, he got his "come-uppance when one of the students said, 'But Mister Miller, we understand the expression. We watch American television all the time.'"

In fact, focusing on similarities can be the best way to success. Just as English products that emphasize craftsmanship quality in the "Great British Tradition" might be more appreciated in France, so they will also be more desirable to the world's population as a whole, because quality is valued by consumers everywhere. Global companies that strive for a meeting of the minds among the many distinctly different individuals that make up the company should also emphasize the similarities—not by imposing a single mindset, but rather by recognizing and encouraging the loyalty and beliefs of its employees in its corporate values. People worldwide appreciate sincerely interested and courteous visitors, while sensitive issues—politics, religion, sexual references, and the like—are generally taboo in conversations among culturally aware travellers, and likewise should be avoided in marketing and promotional campaigns.

THE MORAL: An awareness of the core values of all people is as important as knowing the differences.

CHAPTER 3

Product and Service Blunders

"IF THE SHOE FITS, WEAR IT"

THE SUCCESS OF A PRODUCT in any given international market is directly proportional to the amount of effort invested to determine how appropriate the product is for the intended market. Some firms face a serious quandary on this question: Are they willing to compromise and market a product overseas in a way that might undermine what is perceived as the company's core competency if that will meet the needs of that particular market? Or should they attempt to actually "sophisticate" the target market by raising its level of both taste and expectation?

To some this is one of the key issues that success in the global marketplace rests on, while others see it as a blend of corporate and cultural arrogance—a choice between "dumbing down" or "lifting up."

There's a story told about a multi-million-dollar defense project aimed at designing the ultimate combat aircraft. Engineers and designers were assembled and given carte blanche to design an aircraft that could meet every possible tactical requirement. At the same time, they were to utilize all the existing technology to make it the fastest, "stealthiest," most technologically advanced, and combat-worthy "super plane" in the entire world.

About a year later, the plans were unveiled and a computer-graphic mock-up of the aircraft was created. Experienced test pilots were called in to test-fly the aircraft, but every attempt to get it to perform to design specifications ended with the pilot crashing at high speed into the "ground." Pilot after pilot tried to take advantage of the airplane's obvious attributes, but none was able to master it.

The problem soon became evident. The design team had labored for months to engineer a plane that ended up so sophisticated that no human could fly it; the capabilities of the "super plane" exceeded those of any of the pilots attempting to master them. Their reach had exceeded their grasp.

Iridium Calls, But Nobody's Home

If there was a poster child made to order for the telecommunications industry boom in the 1990s, it was Iridium. Backed by international giant Motorola, the Washington, DC-based wireless "telecom" company was on the cutting edge in the development of wireless satellite communications.

The idea for the company was conceived in 1987 when a Motorola engineer and his wife were planning a vacation on a remote island in the Caribbean. The wife, a real estate executive, was leery of traveling to a vacation spot where she'd be out of telephone communication with her home office. Just what would happen if traveling businesspeople had the wherewithal to "stay in touch" from anywhere in the world with a single, fit-in-your-briefcase telephone unit? The proverbial light bulb clicked on, the vacation was canceled, and Motorola found itself on the threshold of wireless communications—an industry that, just 13 years later, would have a global value in the hundreds of billions.

Four years later, Schaumburg, Illinois-based Motorola rolled-out Iridium, the "new kid on the block" ready and willing to take on the competition with the entrepreneurial, "open field" mindset that had come to typify the rapid evolution of technology fueling the light-speed growth of the telecom industry. (The company's name itself evoked a "new age" mentality. Iridium is a rare metallic element, number 77 on the Periodic Table, which was the same as the number of telecommunications satellites the company originally planned to put into orbit to support its global wireless system. Although the number was eventually reduced to 66, the original name stuck.)

WASTED POTENTIAL

According to Standard & Poor's, the international potential was enormous. The industry analyst forecasted that an estimated 250 million subscribers around the world would be using wireless technology by 2001, with wireless penetration in the European Union pegged at 35 percent in 1998, while fully five out of every ten people in Norway, Denmark, Finland, and Sweden either owned or had direct access to a wireless telephone.

But like many of its competitors, Iridium saw the true growth potential in supplying wireless telephones to multinational companies that not only have operations in more sophisticated markets like the US and Europe, but also in regions around the world that lacked the infrastructure to support traditional land-lined, or "wired," telephone communication systems. They were looking at regions like Africa, the Middle East, Southeast Asia, Eastern Europe, and Latin America—where poor-quality telephone service is the rule, not the exception.

Iridium's first-of-its-kind plan to utilize low-level satellite technology (called LEO, leap-frogged over the competition, which rely on more traditional high-altitude satellites requiring comparatively huge dishes. Iridium's satellites—each, with its lightweight solar panels extended, measuring about the size of a compact car—would orbit the earth at an altitude of about 420 miles.

BLINDED BY THE LIGHT

John Richardson, Iridium's chief executive officer, commented on the company's target market in a 1999 *Washington Post* article: "We had a blind spot in identifying customers. Did we want to talk to the man on the street or to multinational companies like Shell Oil who push people all over the earth?" He added that, "This [an Iridium phone] is not a product for the guy who walks into Radio Shack and wants to make a phone call on the way home."

Rendered starry-eyed, the Iridium hierarchy allowed the glare of market dominance to blind it to the radical changes of the portable telecommunications industry in the mid-1990s, namely, the huge market niche carved out by cellular service providers in Iridium's primary target business market: the mobile global business traveler or worker who spends more time on the road or in isolated areas than in an office. Cellular technology, which relies on land-based dish systems rather than on distant orbiting satellites, had come to dominate that niche market faster than anyone had predicted.

The company's approach toward applying its basic technology was first-rate and should have resulted in a truly portable product that was inexpensive to use. (In fact, a prototype of one of Iridium's first satellite designs now hangs in the Air and Space Museum at the Smithsonian Institute in Washington, D.C.) But exactly the opposite occurred. In November 1998, Iridium unveiled its first handheld satellite phone, after spending $140 million on an international advertising blitz and setting a goal to sign up 500,000 customers within six months. By April, however, only 10,294 people had signed up—and they were to pay $3,000 each for the clunky, oversized telephones and up to $5 per minute to talk on them.

The company had, simply, pulled the wrapping off the package before it could offer completely workable telephones for customers to use and a fully functioning support system. "We're a classic MBA case study in how not to introduce a product," Richardson said. "First we created a marvelous technological achievement. Then, we asked the question of how to make money with it."

Right out of the gate, the company ran into problems. Iridium customers who had signed on during the prelaunch advertising campaign or during the first few weeks after the unveiling were unable to get phones because its two suppliers—its parent, Motorola, and Kyocera Ltd. of Japan—were way behind in their production schedules. "They were selling a phone service, and they didn't even have the phones," said one analyst in the June 1999 issue of *Businessweek*. "That kind of mistake is unfathomable." In addition, when the supply finally met the demand, already frustrated customers found out that the phones ate a lot of power and had to be recharged two or three times a day.

Another major flaw in the Iridium system design was that its low-level satellites required that every individual telephone call be routed from satellite to satellite via a complicated series of computer transmissions. As a result, subscribers—that is, those who could get hold of an Iridium phone in the first place—were chronically plagued by cut-off calls, blocked access, and ear-piercing interference.

If this wasn't enough, Iridium's phones would only work in areas with open sky. Meanwhile, its ubiquitous cellular competitors offered small, inexpensive, and highly portable telephones that were usable both indoors and in cities.

BANKRUPTCY AND OBLIVION

Iridium struggled on through a many-months-long fusillade of recriminations and firings. Then in August 1999, the company—once the golden child of the global telecom industry—filed for bankruptcy. It sought protection after failing to meet its obligations on $1.5 billion in loans; the company had taken out the loans to fix problems that everyone now agrees should have been fixed before the first telephone was ever distributed.

Iridium stumbled along through July 2000. Finally, rejected by one prospective buyer (a "last resort" investment concern from New York who balked at the company's $50 million price tag), parent Motorola made the decision to pull the plug on the entire Iridium operation. In August Motorola passed the word to Iridium to activate its "decommissioning" plan. Iridium was told to issue orders to its 66 LEO satellites—now effectively "space junk"—to, individually and over a period of several months, fire their thrusters, and alter orbit to a new course that would send each into the earth's atmosphere to burn up. For a moment it would blaze like a shooting star.

"A lot of engineering went into making Iridium possible," said Herschell Shosteck, a Washington, DC-based analyst. A specialist in the wireless telecommunications industry, the *Washington Post* quotes him saying, "Iridium can serve as a reminder to the entire wireless industry in the future...a reminder not to let technological exuberance override business prudence."

When Hip, Wow, and Cute Don't Cut It (DaimlerChrysler)

The marketing gurus decided to call it the *Smart*. The name was perfectly suitable for a micro-compact car designed for a new generation of young, status-conscious businesspeople who were looking for an alternative to the mass-produced cars turned out like sausages by the competition. When the first Smart car rolled off the assembly line in October 1998, expectations were high and success was all but guaranteed.

DaimlerChrysler AG (DCAG) had made an unprecedented effort to position the car as a trendy alternative for "hip urban professionals." Within seven months, however, DCAG realized that the $1 billion it had sunk into the Smart mobile had been flushed down the drain. It only took that amount of time for the company to find out the hard way that the car was not only overpriced for savvy and cost-conscious European auto buyers at $11,000 per unit, but also left an awful lot to be desired in terms of basic design.

QUIRKY IS AS QUIRKY DOES

The car was, according to one description, "quirky and unusual, akin to two bucket seats on four wheels powered by a small engine in between."

Designed by a team from both DaimlerChrysler and the developer of the Swiss *Swatch* concept car, the Smart mobile was equipped (or one might say, unequipped) with an anemic 45-horsepower engine, space for only two passengers, no back seat, and storage space equivalent to a large shoe box. A two-tone paint job made the car look like a bloated Tylenol capsule.

"You can't put anything in it—a box of franks, maybe and that's it," said a Lufthansa flight attendant interviewed for an article in the May 1999 edition of *The Detroit Daily News*. His wife—pregnant with their first child—agreed. "It's only for two persons. It's too small. You have no place behind you or in front of you. It's good for singles."

Well, in a sense the marketing team was right, the reaction to the Smart car was overwhelming. Potential buyers were staying away in droves.

NOT SO SMART AFTER ALL

Desperate to make the best of what was turning out to be one of the most expensive blunders in European automotive history, DCAG decided to reverse the tide and generate interest in the Smart mobile by "taking the car to the people." The plan?—open a network of 110 so-called Smart Centers in eight European countries: Austria, Belgium, France, Germany, Italy, the Netherlands, Spain, and Switzerland. The centers would be configured as scaled-down dealerships and would be located at shopping malls and other popular business locations heavily dependent on pedestrian traffic.

The company had projected very ambitious sales goals for the Smart mobile. Plans called for 130,000 of them to be whizzing down European highways by the end of 1999, the first full year of production at DCAG's automated, modular manufacturing plant in Hambach, France. The target was later cut to 100,000 cars when it became apparent that sales wouldn't come even close to meeting the original goal. By the end of March 1999, the specially trained and highly aggressive sales teams at the Smart Centers had sold a meager 39,700 units.

At that rate, the company figured, only 80,000 Smart cars would be sold by the end of the year—far short of even the new reduced target. Germany led the sales through the first three months of 1999 with 9,000 cars. France and Switzerland tied for a distant second at 2,000 each. At the bottom of the list was Belgium with only 500 cars sold.

PUTTING ON A HAPPY FACE

Attempting to steady the nerves of a roomful of cynical shareholders, DCAG chairman Robert Eaton said, "The market launch of this ambitious project fell short of our expectations, but we are making tremendous efforts to reinvigorate this process." Co-chairman Juergen Schrempp quickly added, "We have no trouble admitting that we are possibly ahead of our time. Whatever is necessary will be done."

The Smart mobile "is doomed," Steven Hagerty, an auto industry analyst in the London office of Schroder Securities, told *The Detroit News*. "It's not a practical product. By definition, it will always miss the mark. Aside from sitting in it and driving it, it's useless."

One observer called it "The product for which there was no market." Underdesigned, overpriced, and poorly marketed, the Smart became an embarrassment to the company. DaimlerChrysler—the proud inheritor of the Mercedes Benz cachet—should have known from the beginning that hip, wow, and cute can't replace a generations-old, hard-earned reputation for quality, and for designing the right product for the right target.

Sony and PowerStation 2

In 1998, sales of video and computer games in the US alone grew by more than 35 percent over the previous year. Sales hit 181 million units—the equivalent of almost two video games for every household in the country.

According to the Interactive Digital Software Association (IDSA), the 181 million games, laid end to end, would stretch 34,000 miles.

On a dollar basis, interactive entertainment software sales during 1998 reached $3.7 billion, with computer game sales reaching $1.8 billion, a 25 percent hike over 1997. For the third year in a row the industry experienced double-digit growth. The IDSA predicted even greater growth through 2002 and beyond. The University of Oklahoma and the National Institute on Media and the Family released a study showing that in 1999 a full 84 percent of all teens regularly play video/electronic games, on average, about one-and-a-half hours a day.

This is the world Sony lives and operates in. As the second largest manufacturer of consumer electronics on the planet (Matsushita is larger), Sony developed a reputation for its cutting-edge application of technology. Sony's founder, the legendary Akio Morita, created the company out of the pile of rubble that was post-World War II Tokyo. Known for its innovation, the company churns out flat-screen televisions, computer monitors, DVDs, *Walkman* and *MiniDisc* stereo systems, video and computer hardware and games that accounted for nearly two-thirds of the company's $63 billion in sales in 2000.

The star of the company's pantheon of electronic hardware is the *PlayStation (PS)* game console, a highly sophisticated unit that permits a player to transform a television set into a personalized video arcade. The console applies digital technology to present a wealth of colors and extremely realistic graphics.

REACHING FOR THE VIRTUAL BRASS RING

At the height of the video revolution in the late 1990s, Sony found its PlayStation—which utilizes compact disc (CD) technology—in direct competition with the Nintendo Corporation's *Nintendo 64* console. The Nintendo 64 is similar to the *PS*, but many "video gamers" favor it because it has faster loading game cartridges and brighter color tones. Both consoles are equipped with 64-bit processors, nearly four times more powerful than the consoles produced by competitors Sega and Neo-Geo. Each has developed its own loyal customer base. Sony aficionados lean toward "shoot-em-up" and sports games. Nintendo fans prefer strategic and more cartoon-based activities.

In September 1999, Sony—reportedly pressured by large US retailers eager for the revenues the system would generate —upped the ante and put to rest all the rumors circulating through the industry about its expected contribution to the next generation of game consoles. The company announced that it was developing a new console: named the *PlayStation 2* (PS2), it came equipped with an unheard-of 128-bit processor, a combination audio CD and Digital Video Disc (DVD) player, as well as a high-speed modem to allow direct downloading of new games and real-time game-play between multiple gamers.

The PS2 console made its debut in Japan in March 2000 with a staggering 3 million units shipped to retail stores throughout the country before the launch date. Within a week, more than 1 million PS2 consoles were sold. Sony estimated that by the end of the company's financial year (March 31, 2001), more than 10 million PS2 consoles would be shipped to retailers around the world.

The response in Japan far exceeded the company's original estimates, but there was a downside. The sales boom in Japan and the anticipated volume of demand in the US, where the PS2 console was to be launched seven months later, forced Sony to push back its original release date in Europe and Australia by a full four weeks. The original schedule had called for the PS2 console to be released simultaneously in the US, Canada, the EU, and Australia in late October.

And, to top it all, the reaction to the PS2 console itself wasn't nearly what Sony had expected. While the demand in the US was high (several large retailers stopped taking preorders early in the year), enthusiasm for the PS2 was, to say the least, lacking. According to one online import retailer in the US, one of the first to test the Japanese version, "The software is absolutely awful and so are the load times. The games look like they spent five minutes putting it together to get it out." His company, he added, "had lots of sales at first but when people realized how awful the product was, sales died off. Our customers are horribly disappointed."

"They rushed, they made promises, they didn't use even fifty percent of PlayStation's power," said another. A New York-based importer commented that, after the initial frenzy, "sales dropped off ninety percent. You got no buyers because there was no software of any value." Beyond "the initial splash," he said, "I really don't see the thing taking off unless they really improve it. Sony should have taken the time to make sure it was right from the start, but [Sony] felt it had to move fast, and it shows."

In short, Sony undercut itself by moving too rapidly. By releasing a product that it hadn't taken the time to develop fully, Sony sacrificed market share for expediency.

General Motors Steps in It, Again...and Again

Sometimes a company can create nothing but grief for itself by targeting competition from overseas rather than sticking to its core competency and fine-tuning the basic product that put it on the map.

NOSE TO NOSE WITH THE GERMANS AND THE SWEDES

In the mid-1970s, General Motors (GM) found itself going "nose to nose" with BMW, Mercedes Benz, and Saab in the ongoing battle for the hearts and minds of the US high-end auto market. Driven by oil shortages, a trend toward fuel efficiency, and federal regulations mandating high emission standards, the company's flagship Cadillac Division was looking to reestablish its image by offering the public smaller, "smarter" cars.

One would think that GM, still the biggest automaker in the world, would have a distinct hometown advantage in the fight and that jousting with the foreign competition would be something the company could take on in style. But, no...

The honor of taking the first shot at the competition fell to the company's Cadillac Division because GM was seeing a lot of its longtime "Caddy" customers deserting to Mercedes. GM studied the situation and came to the conclusion that, as luxury *Mercedes* cars are smaller than *Cadillac* sedans, it would counter the German import upstart with a smaller, truncated version of its venerable *Fleetwood* model.

Cadillac presented the *Seville*. But, people couldn't equate the name "Cadillac" with the concept of "small." GM discovered that the new design wasn't attracting buyers away from Mercedes. It was merely shifting its own faithful customers from the Fleetwood and *Brougham* models to the *Seville* sedans. The car "stalled," teaching the company that the very Cadillac cachet was based on the concept of "big." Mercedes and BMW were never threatened by the Seville sedan, even after it was redesigned to a larger scale for the US market and also redesigned specifically for the Japanese market. It was remarketed then with some success for both markets.

GM followed the Cadillac Seville sedan with a second stab at the competition, producing another small car, the *Cimmaron*. This car also failed because, as one observer said, it "didn't even look anything like it was even distantly related to a Cadillac. It sort of looked like a Chevrolet with delusions of grandeur."

Restudying the problem, General Motors decided to take the battle to Europe, in a fashion. The company's design team came up with the *Allanté* automobile, which it marketed as an American luxury car with European—specifically Italian—flair. The car body and interior furnishings were manufactured in Italy and then flown to the US, where the final body, frame, and engine assembly work was done at the GM plant in Hamtramck, Michigan.

The first Allanté cars, priced around $55,000, rolled off the assembly line in 1987 to acidic reviews: the overall quality wasn't up to the hype. Its deficiencies were typified by a manually operated convertible top that made raising, lowering, and latching it into place a major headache. GM put plans to sell the car in Europe on ice ("in the competition's own backyard") when *The Automotive News* delivered the heaviest blow—it named the car its "Flop of the Year" for 1987. Sales staggered on until production of the car was discontinued in 1993.

THE GHOST RETURNS

But the ghost of the failed Allanté luxury vehicle would not go quietly into that good night. Five years later, buyers of the Allanté model that was produced between 1987 and 1990 were angered by the spotty performance of the car's diesel engine. After a number of Cadillac dealers refused to honor a promotion that offered the current value of a Mercedes Benz *560 SL* on a trade-in of an Allanté auto for another Cadillac sedan, miffed customers filed a class-action lawsuit against General Motors. The company was compelled by the US District Court in San Francisco to carry out a three-part plan to placate its customers, and found itself having to pay some $1.3 million in legal bills to put the matter to rest.

JUST BUY ME A CADILLAC

According to one auto industry observer, "Cadillac forgot that its best weapon was its own cachet. In taking on the European competition the way they did, the company lost sight of the fact that it had a faithful following of buyers who had come to expect a certain level of quality—an image of luxury—that they'd be willing to pay for. If I want to buy a Cadillac, I want to buy a Cadillac that looks like one, not a Cadillac that looks like an imitation Mercedes or BMW."

Peugeot Runs Over Its Own Feet

It's quiz time: what is the key to maintaining market share and meeting the needs of potential customers in what is probably the world's most competitive market? If you guessed it might be to develop a strategy crafted specifically for that market, adapt your product to meet the needs and expectations of potential customers, and treat your in-market management team like family instead of lepers, you'd be off to a great start.

Good for you; too bad for Peugeot. The French automaker had sold its cars in the US for 33 years before it formally closed up shop and took its business back to France in 1991. The largest car manufacturer in Europe in the 1970s—selling a respectable average of 20,000 cars per year in the US in the 1980s—saw its market share eventually dwindle to just 5,000.

THEY LIKE US...REALLY? WHY?

The reason for Peugeot's success in the US among its faithful middle- and upper-class consumers was quality construction and engineering, European-style design and handling characteristics, and refined "traditional" comfort. The company, however, didn't take the time to fathom this. Instead, it opted to sacrifice its reputation on the altar built in lockstep by the US auto industry, an altar built on the foundation of cookie-cutter mass assembly techniques, mundane design, and high-cost "deus ex machina" engineering schemes.

In the mid-1980s, Peugeot was at the top of its form. The company found itself, if not "king of the hill," at least in the competition when high oil prices sparked intense consumer interest in its diesel-powered cars. Sales were at an all-time high, and the company couldn't have been stronger, according to Francis Wolek, a professor of management at Villanova University, and Jean-Loup Archawski, president of MCDS Inc., a management consulting company based in Ardmore, Pennsylvania. Writing in the May-June 1995 issue of *Business Horizons* magazine, the pair concluded that Peugeot's success in the US wasn't due to a finely tuned strategic marketing strategy, but rather to not having one at the start.

Walek and Archawski commented that the company's initial entry into the US market in 1958 "was the result of pressure from the French government," which "wanted Peugeot to export to a market that would bring hard currency back to France." The government, they said, "even insisted that Peugeot distribute its cars through the system used by Renault, a government-owned company." The pressure was actually welcomed by certain executives in the company who felt that it would motivate some in the company who weren't wholeheartedly in favor of exporting Peugeots to foreign markets. One of the most intransigent was Maurice Jordan, the company's operating head until 1965, who felt that exports would be "unprofitable," seeing them only "as a means to keep production lines working and bring greater economies of scale."

Grudgingly supported by the management in France, the company entered the US market with no long-range strategic plan and with only the resources to distribute the cars that its French manufacturing facility was already making. At best, the pair wrote, "the company was betting that American sales would provide the resources and exposure needed for a strategy to emerge out of involvement with American allies and customers."

Peugeot managers in the US saw the need to produce a car that was fashionably French and practically American—paté de foie gras on a hamburger bun, so to speak. The strategy paid off, and, in 1971, Peugeot placed a respectable second in the running for *Motor Trend* magazine's "Car of the Year" award. Favorable reviews continued into the 1980s.

LITTLE CRACKS IN THE PAINT... AND THE REPUTATION

But then the company, aiming at higher-end customers, failed to include in its newest designs the standard features that those American drivers have come to expect—air conditioning, automatic power windows and seats, a sunroof, and controls placed to American, not European, tastes. In addition, Peugeot cars were acquiring a reputation for frequent equipment break-downs: nothing major like the transmission, engine or brake systems, but small, annoying problems with leaking seals, temperature controls, rusting, and poorly applied paint.

Why didn't Peugeot take the lessons to heart, address the issues, and redesign the cars it was selling in the US to American tastes? Such modifications, say Wolek and Archawski, would have been expensive. Adding air conditioning alone, for example, would have meant significantly redesigning the entire engine compartment. Providing acceleration for high-speed passing would have meant altering a suspension system especially designed for the snappy road-handling practiced by French drivers.

French and American government safety standards were also an issue. French safety standards are based on crash avoidance and stress road-handling capabilities, while US standards stress a strong passenger compartment and the ability of a car to absorb damage. Peugeot figured that it would cost the company more than $90 million to re-engineer cars specifically for the US market.

SETTING UP A "COMPLAINT DEPARTMENT"

The complaints generated in the US were something new to Peugeot's upper management in Paris. So was the system set up in the 1970s by Peugeot Motors America (PMA), the company's US subsidiary, to collect and package consumer feedback. Peugeot simply wasn't used to complaints: since the end of World War II the company had a relatively captive market in France—demand actually far outpaced supply. About the time capacity and demand leveled out in the early 1980s, the company was focusing its time and effort on its acquisitions of Citröen and Chrysler Europe to create what was at the time Europe's largest auto manufacturing concern. This "Europe First" diversion was to be Peugeot's undoing in the US.

PMA had formed a "Dealers Council," a working group of Peugeot dealers throughout the US that would pool customer feedback. The information would be evaluated, analyzed, and then sent on to corporate headquarters in France.

THE SOUNDS OF SILENCE

The minutes of the Dealers Council meetings through the end of the 1970s showed that they were very concerned "that Peugeot was not seriously following through on positioning [as an affordable, total luxury automobile]...especially in its failure to adapt product and practices to US expectations in the luxury market." The Council threw down the gauntlet in December 1979 by unanimously passing a strongly worded resolution "demanding that Paris make a commitment to the US market."

"The Council," the resolution said, "wishes to point out to Automobile Peugeot that the US market...is the most competitive in the world. Any major automotive manufacturer who is unable to successfully merchandise his product in the US market today must be deemed to have an inferior product and organization. The Council has extreme concern over what it perceives to be a 'not give a damn' attitude on the part of...those in France responsible for the success of the US market.... Put in simple terms, the Council recommends that Peugeot either get totally involved in the US market or get out altogether."

In their research, Wolek and Archawski discovered some of the rationale behind the attitude of Peugeot's French management toward the US market. Cars made in France for export to the US in the late 1970s and early 1980s were produced by modifying an assembly line ordinarily used to make cars for the European market. The modification of the line required a fairly steep set-up cost, so US-bound Peugeots were produced only twice a year. As a result, cars delivered to the US reflected market intelligence that would be six months or more out of date.

The PMA tried to counter Paris's intransigence with a well-crafted advertising campaign, improved customer service, a US-style leasing policy, and a specially designed turbo-charged engine for its workhorse *Model 505*. Although they saw some sparks of success through the 1980s, Peugeot sputtered until it died in the US. The core of the company's indifference to the American market, the writers say, was the lack of "what one Peugeot executive describes as essential for overseas success: headquarters champions who translate market feedback and use it to fight for adaptations in corporate policy and auto design." The top management of Mercedes, for example, "believed that the US market was critical to its success from the earliest days of the company. One reason Peugeot had no American champions was that every executive sent from France either entered a new business in the US, or left the company on returning to Europe. This pattern was so striking that an assignment to the US was taken by Peugeot's best and brightest as a prelude to a career eclipse."

And how did Peugeot's management in Paris react to the acidic Resolution passed by the US Dealers Council? It's been 31 years, and whichever members of the long-defunct Dealers Council are still around are still waiting, no doubt some breathlessly, for a response.

Failed "Aspire"-ations (Acer)

During the past decade, the United States has firmly ensconced itself as the world leader in information technology and personal computers use. In 1998, the European Information Technology Observatory (EITO) determined that the US spent 4.5 percent of its Gross Domestic Product on information technology, versus 2.6 percent for Japan and 2.3 percent for Western Europe. The US market for personal computers (PCs), specifically those used in the home, was awesome: $69.4 billion-worth were sold, up more than 14 percent from the preceding year. In 1999, more than four out of every ten personal computers produced in the entire world found a final home in the US.

The market growth outlook for home-use PCs over the next several years in the US was the kind of long-term growth forecast that makes marketers cast their eyes heavenward in thanksgiving —11 percent growth predicted annually through 2002. It reflected the kind of growth potential with deep roots firmly planted in a booming economy, a trend toward telecommuting, better and cheaper software, and a growing interest in the Internet. One private sector industry analyst, the Cahners In-Stat Group, actually predicted the US home networking market will grow more than 600 percent to $1.4 billion by 2003. This staggering growth would be fueled, in no small part, by cheaper, more powerful PCs.

While a price drop cut into revenue growth for PC manufacturers and suppliers, the overall outlook held tremendous opportunities tied to the promise of steady market expansion. Expansion, that is, for those companies with a firm grip on what the market requires.

EVERYWHERE BUT HERE

Enter Acer, the Taiwan-based manufacturer of personal computers, which in 1998 held the top slot as the number one PC supplier in both Southeast Asia and Latin America. In just five years, the company's global revenues had skyrocketed from $1.8 billion to $6.5 billion—largely because of the appeal of the company's unorthodox way of doing business.

That unorthodoxy was personified in Stan Shih, chairman and chief executive officer of Acer America (Acer's North American spin-off) who practiced an uncommonly democratic and, some might say, Western way of managing the business. Eschewing the traditional pattern of family-owned businesses, Shih shocked the world of Taiwanese business by making employees shareholders. He went even further by demilitarizing the company's work environment—no more uniforms, no more company song, and no more morning salutes to the company flag.

The company—capitalizing on its "Global Brand/Global Touch" slogan— ranked as the third largest PC maker in the world for both branded and Original

Equipment Manufacturer (OEM) models. (OEM goods are computer hardware components packaged for and sold in bulk to professional users with multiple workstations. For example, customers might be other computer companies and system builders with multiple-user systems to maintain such as schools, hospitals, and large corporations with multiple work stations.)

Acer America touted itself as being the market brand leader in 30 countries with significant market share in 90 others. A large part of the company's success Shih attributed to what he called its "fast food business model"—the distribution of parts and components by air and sea from its 17 manufacturing sites around the world to more than 30 local assembly plants. In turn, subsidiary distributors in each country "localize" the product for internal distribution and sale. The model has been used in graduate school courses as a case study on logistics and distribution. It demonstrates success in reducing inventory costs and overhead, as well as drastically cutting the amount of time it takes to get a finished product to market. The approach maximizes use of the latest in manufacturing technology.

Acer, said one source at the time, had all the hallmarks of a company that would fit right into the American computer market—entrepreneurship and a distinctly non-Asian business attitude. Its success in other markets should have been a platform for the company to slice off of a significant part of the highly competitive PC market in the US. The company seemed to have everything going for it, except that is, a product that American PC users wanted to buy. Successful everywhere else in the world, Acer just couldn't get it right in the US.

ALL DRESSED FOR THE PARTY, BUT...

In 1990, the company acquired the Altos Corporation, a California-based maker of minicomputers. It happened to be just when the bottom fell out of the US market for that narrow-niche type of micro-PC, but Acer salvaged the operation by molding the debris into Acer America. Shih took over Acer America just two years later. Despite several thorough—some say severe—reorganizations and critical reappraisals of its US marketing strategy over the next several years, the company was faced with a startling reality: although the US accounted for a full third of its total business, the company itself ranked ninth in the US. More telling was the remorseless bottom line seen in black and white: After a combined loss of $120 million in both 1995 and 1996, the company had posted a loss of more than $141 million in 1997.

A large part of the failure was due to Acer pushing its *Aspire* computer into the branded US market without the company investing the time, effort, and money to establish a brand name in the country. In an article in The *Electronic News* at the time, technology reporter Carolyn Whelen wrote, "The company needs to understand its American audience better, and the fact that the best product doesn't always win. To improve brand recognition, it should link its overseas success to locally-known companies like Texas Instruments and Siemens."

Behemoth competitors like IBM and Compaq were utilizing Acer's Asian manufacturing capability and selling Acer-made products in the US under their own brand names. Meanwhile, Acer's established beachhead in the US market was operating based in large part on the lucrative "Original Equipment Manufacturer" business—which at the time accounted for more than half of the company's total global sales.

Realizing it lacked the brand-name recognition necessary to establish a customer base in the US, Acer made the decision to concentrate on its US OEM business—despite heavy competition from Apple, IBM, Dell, Hewlett-Packard, and Compaq. Acer all but abandoned any hope of gaining greater market share in the intensely competitive US retail PC market.

Over time, the company was able to penetrate the US market with the Aspire computer. Until then, the company found itself a victim of its own success—a company aspiring to great things, but finding itself, like the small child looking longingly through the toy store window, on the outside of the glass.

Promises, Promises (Daihatsu Motor Company Ltd.)

In March 1992, Daihatsu Motor Company Ltd. announced that it would withdraw from the US market—only five years after it sold its first car there.

The company was the first Japanese automaker to pull out of the highly competitive American market since the early 1960s, when Toyota temporarily withdrew to reorganize its North American operations. Daihatsu found itself in a tight, recessionary economy, trying desperately to establish an identity with an American car-buying public reticent to spend money—even for low-priced cars. It was treading water in a market pool filled to the brim with a flood of imports.

The company was in the same position that Toyota (which owned almost 15 percent of Daihatsu) and Nissan had been in three decades earlier when they were trying to establish toeholds in the US. Daihatsu started selling its *Charade* compact car in the US in January 1988. It was the last of nine Japanese carmakers to enter the postwar American market.

From the beginning the company was at a distinct disadvantage. Initial shipments were limited to only 12,000 cars to comply with Japan's voluntary US import limits. Meanwhile, on the horizon the spectre of increasing protectionism, rock-bottom gas prices, and a soaring yen cast an ever-widening shadow.

In business since 1907, Osaka-headquartered Daihatsu held respectable market share in 130 countries. At the time of its foray into the US, the company had a campaign underway in Japan to expand its plant and boost production by 10,000 cars a month, to almost 1 million cars and trucks annually. In the US, however, the company remained a virtual unknown. But despite the signs, Daihatsu decided to forge ahead with its plans.

PLANNING AND DREAMING

Daihatsu America's executive vice president, C.R. Brown, was quoted saying that the company's US debut was "well-timed" (in the November 1987 edition of *Ward's Auto World*). One result of extending the retail financing for cars in the US, he said, to three-, four-, and five-year terms, "will be more car sales and Daihatsu America will be well-positioned to meet this trend with small cars to be proud of," he said, adding that the company had plans to establish more than 750 dealerships across the US within three years.

According to Brown, the company's target market for the three-door, front-wheel-drive Charade was to be "30- to 35-year olds with a college education and an income of $30,000 to $50,000 annually." This was their aim despite the fact that a cursory study of the target US demographics of Daihatsu's competition—namely Toyota, Nissan, Subaru, Hyundai, and Suzuki—would have shown that virtually all the players were married to the same game plan. But, Brown said, Daihatsu had a product that the competition couldn't offer—a well-designed, economy car with standard fuel injection, four-wheel independent suspension, power front-disc brakes, and lots of legroom.

TOO LITTLE, TOO LATE

The first Charade model, Brown was quick to add, was just the beginning. The company plans included a "second and then a third wave" in the US market. The grand scheme included a four-door Charade model (equipped with a more powerful engine) and the introduction of two new cars—the compact *Applause* and a newly designed subcompact car, *Leeza*. The Leeza car had been clocked at 95 miles per hour on a recently completed test track in Japan, which the company had built to handle cars at speeds 40 percent greater than Japan's most restrictive speed laws.

At the time, press reports of discussions between Daihatsu and Bombardier Inc. (the Canadian manufacturer of snowmobiles and railcars) also surfaced. There was reportedly some talk to build a plant in Canada to produce as many as 200,000 Charade vehicles—primarily for the US market.

The company sank almost $18 million dollars into an advertising campaign that put what it called "an unusual spin" on auto advertising. In its desperate attempt to set itself apart from the competition and gain a foothold in the US, Daihatsu tried to turn the tables to capitalize on its relatively low profile. Soon, national magazines like *People, Sports Illustrated, Discover, Newsweek,* and *Cosmopolitan* were displaying full-page ads for Daihatsu featuring only half of one of its *Rocky* sports utility vehicles (SUVs). The point was that "the vehicle isn't being noticed yet," said a spokesman for the Southern California advertising agency that created the ads. Another print ad, a two-page color spread, showed a nighttime, elevated view of Daihatsu's headquarters building at Los Alamitos, California. The building was flanked by two massive skyscrapers topped by signs that read "Gigantic Motors" and "Titan Auto." Significantly, all the lights in the Daihatsu building were shown blazing, while the two skyscrapers were dark.

"Our advantage is not the volume of car sales; it's the quality of engineering," said one ad agency executive. "That simple fact resulted in the slogan, 'It's not how many we make. It's how we make them.'" But it was too little too late. The company sold only 15,118 Charade compact cars and only 295 Rocky SUVs in 1989, when it had dealers covering 35 percent of the total US market.

Adding to Daihatsu's problems, the producers of the "Rocky" films featuring Sylvester Stallone threatened a lawsuit. The filmmakers charged the company with trademark infringement. The suit was eventually settled out of court.

By the following June, even C.R. Brown's exuberance of the preceding two years had begun to wane. "I'm keeping a low profile these days," he told *Ward's Auto World* magazine. Reiterating his belief that most Americans were "lumping Daihatsu with Hyundai, Suzuki, Subaru (and other car makers whose sales had 'hit the wall') because its name is vaguely similar," he postulated that there's a common perception "that we're a Korean company."

Toyota and Nissan never boasted about their national origins in their advertising during their early years, but now every Daihatsu print advertisement and television commercial carried the words "From Japan," the magazine observed. Brown said that the ads were especially targeted to audiences in the Midwest and Northeast—two regions where the company was still virtually unknown. Plans to expand there had been shelved "for several reasons"—such as a lack of adequate product availability, a restricted model range, and an overall softness in the US small-car market. "Even so, we're buying that [television commercial time] for 40% less than it would cost us for a national campaign." But, he added, the core issue remained "our lack of brand awareness." That proved to be Daihatsu's undoing.

TOO MANY PROMISES

"Daihatsu's first mistake was a failure to enter the US market earlier and establish brand recognition before the market tightened up," commented one auto industry analyst. "You can't promise dealers that you're 'saving the best for last' when your competitors, who already have a beachhead established, are able to exploit their advantage and ride out any economic or political storm." The company, he adds, "made promises it couldn't keep. Daihatsu deluded itself into a Scarlett O'Hara-like 'tomorrow is another day' mindset. Months went by without anything being accomplished."

Daihatsu, he says, "felt that it could mask its lack of a viable marketing plan by making the competition—and the public—think that 'something better' was about to come along. You can't market promises, and think you can drive the situation in the direction you want when you're the newest player in the game. Daihatsu was a classic example of too little, too late, and too many promises made and not fulfilled."

Life in the Fast Lane (Yugo America Inc.)

Up until the 1980s, most Americans axiomatically associated inexpensive, imported cars with Japan. Of course there were exceptions—the most notable was the classic Volkswagen *Beetle* of the 1960s. But, by and large, Americans felt that any car offering the mere basics (namely, a body, four wheels, an engine, and a suspension system) must have been produced by a Japanese automaker such as Datsun, Toyota, or another of their contemporaries.

In fact, in Toyota's first full year in the US (1958), the company sold only 288 cars; the following year it sold 1,028; and in 1960, only 821. In the years following, the Japanese quickly adapted their cars to the US market. The best of the lot was the 1984-1985 Toyota *Corolla* compact car, which set a standard for reliability, economy, and design.

While the Japanese were laboring hard to capture the US economy car market, another competitor appeared on the scene. In the fall of 1985, the first compact *Yugo* was driven off the ship at the Port of New York-New Jersey. Priced at $3,990, the Yugoslav-made compact car was the lowest-priced car sold at the time in the US—it cost $1,000 less than its nearest economy competitor, Chevrolet's Japanese-made *Sprint* model. *Time* magazine described the Yugo car as "boxy and jut-jawed...sheer utility on wheels."

Oddly, the idea for the Yugo car wasn't conceived in Yugoslavia, or even Europe. The company that spawned the car was Yugo America Inc., headquartered in Upper Saddle River, New Jersey. Automotive entrepreneur Malcolm Bricklin, who formed the company in the US in 1984, was best known for importing the first Japanese *Subaru* compact cars into the US in the late 1960s. Bricklin was convinced that an inexpensive car held promise in the US market (even though the market was flooded with compact and midsize imports). He concluded that US buyers who couldn't afford a new midsize import would be willing to spend their money on a new inexpensive compact, rather than wait to buy a three- or four-year-old import.

In the spring of 1984, Bricklin began talking to representatives of auto manufacturers in Brazil, the UK, Spain, Romania, and Czechoslovakia about producing an inexpensive car for export to the US. The following September, he awarded a contract to Zavodi Crvena Zastava (ZCZ), Yugoslavia's largest automaker.

POTENTIAL ON A PLATTER

The initial response was overwhelming. Even before the first Yugo compact was off-loaded, more than 3,000 orders were taken by Yugo America's 83 dealerships—each of which had to put up a $400,000 letter of credit. Most of the dealers were located in the Midwest and eastern US, where initially only 500 of the cars were available. One Ohio dealer reported more than 200 orders with deposits, "sight unseen."

The company announced that it expected to sell every one of the 40,000 models it was planning to ship to the US by the following summer. Several industry analysts predicted that the US market for a car like the Yugo compact could reach as high as a million units annually.

Positioned as "basic, reliable transportation at an affordable price," the Yugo compact was expected not only to appeal to first-time car buyers and typical used car purchasers, but to US households in need of a third, or even fourth, car. "We want the Yugo to be the '80s Beetle," said Yugo America president William Prior. "The car will be a very guttural basic car. Part of its audience will be those who can afford to buy a $10,000 car, but who want the least expensive car for all those back and forth trips to the commuter train station."

Yugo America conducted a review of 55 advertising agencies, finally settling on a New York-based firm that crafted an aggressive $15 million multimedia ad campaign. It featured the Yugo compact as the vehicle for America to drive to take the "road back to sanity," and portrayed the car as being as "classic" as the VW Beetle or the Ford Model-T. The materials downplayed the Yugo's country of origin, alluding to the car as a "European import."

The basic standard Yugo *GV* compact was a front-wheel-drive, manual transmission car with a small 1.1 liter engine. The car came without either a radio or air conditioning, but they could be installed later. The GV (for "Great Value") came equipped with a number of additional features, though— including four individual headrests, power disc brakes, a rear-window wiper, and metallic paint.

A VICTIM OF SUCCESS

From the beginning, dealers began voicing concerns that ZCZ wouldn't be able to keep up with the unexpected demand. When the first limited numbers of Yugo cars became available, dealers were put in the position of having to tell potential buyers they could only promise a Yugo compact the following spring. The dealers said this could cost the Yugo its distinct price advantage; meanwhile, Yugo America worried that the lack of supply would cause some dealers (who had been allocated a strict 50 cars per month) to jack-up the car's basic sticker price.

In an effort to prevent a meltdown, Yugo America petitioned ZCZ to nearly double its production schedule for Yugo cars to export to the US. The original projections called for 40,000 cars in 1986; 75,000 the following year; and 110,000 in 1988. To maintain enthusiasm, Prior of Yugo America announced that ZCZ had earmarked $431 million to upgrade and modernize its production capability. Also, plans called for a convertible model in 1988, and a two-seater, four-wheel-drive Yugo *TCX* sports model to roll off the assembly line in 1991.

The company's "anything goes wrong and we'll fix it" 12,000-mile/1-year warranty—called "one of the most generous" in the business—was extended to cover all 1989 Yugo models for 40,000 miles or 4 years.

But still, too few cars to keep pace with demand and a lackluster public relations campaign soon became the least of Yugo America's problems.

"HELL ON WHEELS"

In its second year on the US market, only 36,000 Yugo compacts were sold, partly because of ZCZ's inability to keep up with the demand, and partly because a widely quoted report in a 1986 issue of *Consumer Reports* magazine called the Yugo "loud, uncomfortable," and "unsafe at any price." The report criticized the car for poor performance in the federal government's 35-miles-per-hour crash tests, and also judged that the company poorly handled a recall for a seat belt defect. The report labeled the car's overall performance, particularly of its engine and transmission systems, "a disaster."

According to the magazine, "If $4,400 [the Yugo model's approximate final price tag] is the most you can spend on a car, we think you'd get better value from a good used car than a new Yugo." To top it off, the Yugo car received a rock-bottom score in consumer satisfaction from auto industry analyst J.D. Power & Associates after a survey showed that 80 percent of Yugo car owners reported problems with their cars.

According to J.D. Power, the Yugo compacts scored positively on only one characteristic out of the more than 30 that consumers were asked to rate: the Yugo, they said, had "old-fashioned styling." A car company is really in trouble, said an executive with the auto industry analyst, "if the best thing anyone can say about you is that your styling is out of date."

By late 1987, Yugo America finally acknowledged its basic lack of understanding of the complexities of the US auto market and saw that it needed more capital and better financial controls to become truly competitive. A search for financial backing paid off in mid-1988 when Malcolm Bricklin sold his stake in the company to Mabon Nugent, a New York-based investment broker, for $40 million. By that time, Yugo America had ironed out some of the major problems that had given it a black eye in the industry press—the company seemed to be on the road to recovery.

THE WORLD TURNED UPSIDE DOWN

Paul Lambert, former senior partner in Yugo America's marketing and advertising agency, Lambert/Dale & Bernhard, stated: "This story is about what happens when Wall Street comes in with money but lacks the level of experience and intuitiveness to run a car company." He blamed the intrusion by Mabon Nugent in Yugo's strategic marketing plan and advertising plan as a partial reason for the company's downward slide—a charge the investment firm vehemently denied.

In January of 1989, Yugo America Inc. suddenly announced that it was filing for bankruptcy—after only four years in business. The company reported unsecured debts of $35 million and secured debts of $16 million. In addition, dealers were owed more than $5 million for warranty work.

The company lingered on in an attempt to reorganize under the direct tutelage of its Yugoslav parent, which pumped $30 million into Yugo America to pay off outstanding debts and buy more time to market its newer models. The new models were equipped with electronic ignition systems, automatic transmissions, and other "improved" standard features. The company's new president, US auto industry consultant John Spiech, also earmarked $10 million for television and print advertising to transform the company's negative image and develop a loyal customer base.

One of the television commercials aimed at improving the Yugo's wheezing image showed a huge industrial forklift picking up a Yugo car, turning it upside down, and shaking it vigorously. Nothing came loose except some pocket change that dislodged from one of the front seats. "We wanted to do something that stands out," Spiech said at the time. He added that more than 350 improvements had been made to the Yugo since the first was sold in the US four years previously.

But, despite the last-ditch efforts, only 4,900 Yugo cars were sold through the third quarter of 1990, down from a year high of 48,800 in 1987. Humiliation piled on to humiliation. Comedians zeroed in on the Yugo compact and jokes about the hapless car abounded. (Riddle: Why put a rear window defroster on a Yugo? Answer: To keep your hands warm while you're pushing it. Comedy one-liner: They said the safest place to be during Hurricane Hugo was in a Yugo; even in a hurricane, the thing would only go 40 miles an hour.)

Despite the desire to make 1991 a "turn around" year for the company, it proved to be its last in business. The lack of supply, the poor public relations, the mismanagement by Mabon Nugent, and the quality issues all proved to be too much to overcome. Oddly, though, the coup de grâce that mercifully ended the Yugo compact's lingering death in the US had nothing to do with any of those issues. In April 1992, citing the ongoing civil war in Yugoslavia as a major impediment to production, Yugo America announced that it would cease importing the car and filed for Chapter 7 bankruptcy liquidation.

But some dealers who wound up with inventories of Yugo cars to unload after the bankruptcy were philosophical about the whole experience. "As it turns out, the car was actually getting better," said one dealer in Wisconsin, adding that the 1990 and 1991 models were "definitely improved" by the new five-speed transmission and the fuel injection. He said that the Yugo compact "had improved substantially. But was it a great car? Absolutely not."

Interviewed in the *Milwaukee Business Journal,* one Yugo car owner related that in her first year of ownership she had to replace the brakes, engine, and exhaust system. "The ones I've seen on the street all seem to have the same sound to them," she said. Another, asked what kind of car he wants to drive after his Yugo compact finally fell apart from a lack of spare parts, replied, "I'm thinking of going back to my Cadillac Eldorado."

THE PROTON SAGA

The demise of the Proton *Saga* mini-compact car is intimately interwoven with the life and death of the Yugoslav-made Yugo compact—both failed miserably at gaining a foothold in the US market.

In the late 1980s, the US market interest in his beleaguered Yugo car had begun a downward spiral, auto entrepreneur Malcolm Bricklin—almost surrealistically—sought out another car. He chose the Proton Saga model, a car in many ways a competitor to the Yugo compact for the US market. The Proton Saga car was produced in Malaysia by a joint venture operation formed between the Malaysian government and Mitsubishi of Japan. His plan: Market the two cars jointly, but take pains to differentiate between their individual characteristics. That way, Bricklin felt, Yugo America could gain market share by broadening its appeal. Part of the plan called for the company to ride on the coattails of success of the Japanese carmakers—to benefit from their already-established foothold in the crowded US market for compact cars.

"We need to package it [the Proton Saga car] so that it's perceived as comparable to a Japanese car," said William Prior of Yugo America. He projected that the company could sell 80,000 Saga cars in the US within three years.

GETTING POLITICAL

According to Jonathan Mantle in his book *Car Wars,* the Proton Saga car was the brainchild of the fiercely nationalistic Malaysian prime minister, Dr. Mahathir Mohamed. In 1985, Mahathir had opened the Proton factory (National Automobile Enterprise), declaring the government-owned company's first production model "more than just a quality automobile. It is a symbol of Malaysians as a dignified people." A car was thus "transformed into a vehicle for Mahathir's political ambition."

Bricklin had been recommended to Mahathir by former US Secretary of State Dr. Henry Kissinger, who had taught the future Malaysian prime minister when he was a student at Harvard University. The Proton Saga car was so highly thought of that it was named Malaysia's 1985 "Man of the Year"—the first time anywhere that a car had been awarded such an honor.

But it was almost doomed from the start: the manufacturing facility—designed and built by Mitsubishi of Japan—was obsolete before it turned out its first car, and the Malaysian economy was in a shambles. The government lost 35,000 ringgit (or about $15,000) on each Proton Saga car sold. In addition, the assembly plant was scrambling to source parts from Taiwan and South Korea because of the high yen in Japan—where half the car's components were made.

Despite the problems, at Bricklin's urging, Mahathir ordered that the first shipment of Saga cars be loaded aboard an oceangoing auto carrier for export to the US. The very first US-bound car was sent ahead by air freighter. According to Mantle, "The entire management team was assembled at Kuala's international airport. An Islamic cleric offered a prayer, and the managing director sprinkled blessed water on the white Proton Saga, over which was draped a banner reading, 'On to the USA.'"

Shortly after the first batch of Saga cars had been exported to the US, Bricklin announced that he hadn't secured the proper documentation from the appropriate authorities in the US. In addition, the car's engine failed to meet the most fundamental US government-mandated air emission standards. Soon afterward, the Saga car was withdrawn from the American market. Right in the middle of negotiations with the Malaysian government to reorganize the company's US marketing efforts, Bricklin sold off his majority share in Yugo America to New York investment banker Mabon Nugent. The fate of the two cars was sealed.

The result was a huge financial loss for the Malaysian government and a major embarrassment for Dr. Mahathir. Three years after the "glorious launch," Mantle wrote, the Malaysian management was thrown out and replaced with an all-Japanese management team. "The unfortunate Malaysian government was berated for the Bricklin fiasco by its own finance minister who said, 'If that happens to a Japanese, he commits hara-kiri.'"

Still wheezing along with government funding, the company began to export its Saga cars to Europe in the early 1990s. By 1993, the government felt that the company was healthy enough to revert back to Malaysian management.

The saga of the Saga car isn't over. According to *The Detroit News* of May 24, 2000, government-backed Proton "has made considerable advances in engineering, design and manufacturing capability with the assistance of Japan's Mitsubishi, which is a minority shareholder." According to the paper, the Saga car—renamed the *Iswara*—remains in limited production. The company "recently pull[ed] the wraps off its latest development, a relatively modern front-wheel-drive compact car called the Waja," billed as the first car of a purely Malaysian design. Well, not really. Proton, the paper reported, "relied heavily on technical assistance from Mitsubishi in developing the new car, which is said to use some components from the Volvo S40 and the Mitsubishi Carisma, both of which are built in The Netherlands."

According to Proton executives, the company had no plans to market the *Waja* car in the US. Plans do call for selling the new car in Europe and throughout Asia. The paper stated, however, "Proton officials have said they have been talking with several unnamed US automakers about collaborating on future small-car designs."

The Dishwashing Liquid Wars (Lever Brothers)

The last thing any company wants is to find itself the subject of a federal lawsuit, particularly a lawsuit in which two components of the same company wind up on opposite sides of the aisle.

In 1992, Lever Brothers—the American subsidiary of the venerable 100-year-old British manufacturer of a wide range of consumer goods—took the US Customs Service to court. The company said that Customs had allowed the importation into the US of British-made dish washing liquid and soap products carrying the same brand names as the American subsidiary's products that had different chemical contents and characteristics—to the detriment of the American subsidiary's business.

In other words, Lever Brothers sued the government for allowing products made by its parent company into the US for sale to American consumers. The case hinged on the question of "gray goods"—which by definition are products that possess a valid US trademark and are made by an overseas manufacturer, but are shipped to the US for sale without the permission of the US trademark owner. The move was a bold one; in fact it was the first time an American company had sought—and won—a summary judgment against Customs regarding the importation of "gray goods."

The genesis of the confrontation in court teaches an important lesson. Being blissfully unaware of your potential market's requirements can seriously damage any credibility your company might have with its customers.

BROTHER VERSUS BROTHER

Both Lever Brothers in the US and Lever Brothers in the UK manufactured a dish washing liquid called *Sunlight* and a hand soap called *Shield*. That's where the similarity ended. The UK-made products, produced specifically for the British market, had different formulations and characteristics, including fragrance and texture, from their US-made counterparts. The transatlantic squabble between the Brothers Lever arose when containers of the UK-made products began arriving at the Port of New York. The products had been shipped across the pond by third parties in England, who may have acquired the products from sources other than Lever itself somewhere along the UK distribution chain; ultimately they were selling them to others who exported them to the US.

In his ruling, the judge said, "The British and American versions, while having generally similar appearances, are physically different, apparently because of the different tastes of American and British consumers." He said the issue was covered by the Lanham Act, which prohibits the importation of goods that "shall copy or simulate" products of an American trademark holder.

The gray goods invasion took a heavy hit on the Lever Brothers US operations. "Lever's people in the United Kingdom should have exercised better control of its distribution chain," said one observer. "The whole thing seriously damaged Lever's reputation in the US for quality."

Between 1980 and 1986 the company had spent $178 million on advertising to promote its Shield soap, only to have the "poorer" quality of the illegally imported UK-made product generate thousands of letters from disgruntled customers threatening to switch brands. According to one source, gray market goods cost US manufacturers between $10 billion and $15 billion annually in lost sales.

The Custom's announcement that it would appeal the ruling prompted one attorney close to the case to comment, "When the government loses, it should come to its senses and admit it was wrong. Who on earth wants to defend a position that confusing consumers is a good thing?"

Where "Finger-Lickin" is Welcome (Kentucky Fried Chicken)

Of all the products sold internationally, perhaps the most susceptible to marketing mistakes are food products—subject to broad and sometimes vexing health regulations, environmental requirements, and often, religious prohibitions. To market food products successfully, a company must skillfully wind its way through a sometimes frustrating maze of vagaries. These run the gamut from individual taste (yes, not all Japanese like fish and not all Italians are enamored of pizza—at least the American version) to more broad cultural contexts (like Snapple and General Foods encountered as described in other chapters).

MISREADING THE LAY OF THE LAND

Kentucky Fried Chicken (KFC) provides a graphic example of what a company shouldn't do to penetrate unique markets abroad. The company's "finger-lickin' good" chicken was welcome (or so it seemed) everywhere in the world from the UK to Japan. Yet, when it attempted to set up shop in India, it unexpectedly faced an imposing phalanx of public- and private-sector opposition.

It was 1995 and the company had been one of the first fast-food franchisers ready to take cautious, yet deliberate advantage of the Indian government's loosening of its stranglehold restrictions on foreign investment. For years, the Indian government had equated foreign investment with unwanted foreign rule and influence, an attitude that was a direct holdover from the days of the British Raj. During an intense five-year period, widely divergent groups challenged each other in New Delhi. As a result, the door to foreign investment in India opened— just a crack to be sure, but opened nonetheless.

The government's deeply rooted attitude led to its regulatory infrastructure being almost totally unprepared for the wave of foreign companies that showed up, wanting to supply its 900 million consumers with everything from dish soap and pizza to frozen yogurt and submarine sandwiches. But it was the fast-food sector that many felt held the most promise. Pizza Hut, McDonald's, Dominos, T.G.I. (Thank God It's) Friday's, and TCBY (The Country's Best Yogurt) were in the running. They planned to enter the market with franchises in the country's largest population centers—Bombay, New Delhi, Calcutta, and Bangalore. That's where KFC's troubles began.

Located in southern India, Bangalore, with a population of 2 million, had been a center of commerce for more than 450 years before Kentucky Fried Chicken announced plans to open its first franchise there. KFC intended to open 30 more franchises in major metropolitan areas across the country.

KFC (then a subsidiary of Pepsico Inc.) couldn't have picked a more difficult venue for its maiden entree into the country. Bangalore was rapidly becoming the high-technology capital of India; it is also the headquarters of the Karnataka Rajya Raitha Sangha (KRRS)—one of India's most influential, vocal, and violently antiforeign investment farmer's association in all of India. Within a few weeks of the June opening of the two-story KFC franchise on Bangalore's fashionable Brigade Road, the organization warned the company to shut down the franchise within a week or "face direct action."

When he issued the warning, the president of the KRRS cited a US Senate investigation report saying that every seven seconds an American contracted cancer because of the processed meat and poultry sold by the American "junk food" industry. He charged that the industry used chicken that was inflicted with a form of cancer and processed with five times the amount of food grains needed daily for humans. Also at issue, he said, was the amount of water that would be diverted to grow the food grains and fodder to feed the animals. Joining forces with the KRRS, the equally vocal Karnataka State Farmers Association prompted the government of the State of Karnataka to post armed police to stand a 24-hour watch in front of the restaurant.

The opposition's most stinging charge came when both groups took KFC to court in September. A sympathetic Bangalore Municipal Corporation ordered the franchise to shut its doors. What was the charge? The company had violated India's Prevention of Food Adulteration Act by using three times as much monosodium glutamate (MSG) in its "hot and spicy" seasoning than the Act allowed. KFC denied the charge.

One inside observer said the company "could have diffused at least part of the problem by bending over backward to make sure it was well-known that its seasoning met the government standard." The company, he said, "could have actually cut back the use of MSG to well below the legal standard to emphasize its willingness to suit market tastes." More important, he said, KFC was guilty of "completely underestimating the deeply-held animosity against foreign investment in India at the time. If they had taken into consideration the political climate of the time, they would have seen that it would have been wise to wait a while before the door opened further than it was."

KFC, he concluded, "got caught up in the fever of the moment and wanted to make sure that it didn't get beat out by the competition. They moved too quickly, which signaled the incorrect message that the company was sweeping in just like the other big franchise chains with dollar signs in their eyes."

JAPAN BREAKS OUT OF THE MOLD

Just a few years earlier, Kentucky Fried Chicken Japan Ltd. (KFCJ) could claim success in staking out a respectable countrywide market niche by actually ignoring, or in some cases defying, operational directives issued from its parent company's headquarters (in far-off Louisville, Kentucky). Interviewed in a November 1988 edition of *Nation's Restaurant News,* then-president and CEO of KFCJ, Shin Ohkawara outlined several areas where KFCJ had insisted on product standards and practices that are still in place more than a decade later.

The first Japanese-style confrontation came when Louisville mandated a change in the type of cooking oil used in its deep-frying process to cut operating costs. Although Ohkawara was told that the chicken would taste the same, he refused. "If we had switched to palm or soybean oil, we could save 30 percent. But we continued to stick with corn or cottonseed oil, just as we have for 17 years." The company's customers, he said in another interview, had come to expect a certain standard of quality and "it was they who should be satisfied, not corporate headquarters."

Around that time KFCJ introduced a new type of packaging for use in Japan—flat, wide cardboard boxes that allow chicken to be packed in a single layer. Each package is fitted with a ribbed plastic lining to absorb grease. The move was an aesthetic one that created a polar opposite from the KFC packaging in use for years in the US, which would become opaquely transparent from soaking up all the grease. (Some of my fondest childhood memories come from the colorful language my father would use when the greasy bottom of a Kentucky Fried Chicken bucket soaked through the *Los Angeles Times*-cum placemat and left a giant ring on the kitchen table.) Needless to say, the move to more expensive packaging caused the folks in Louisville to have a fit. "Compared with the United States, packaging costs us more than twice as much, but we are doing it anyway," said a determined Ohkawara.

Another point was the way in which KFCJ's chicken was actually packed. In the US, the chicken is dumped into a box or barrel-shaped container fitted with a thin sheet of "absorbent" paper, or piled on a plate in no particular fashion. In Japan, where the people are truly as fussy about the way food is presented as about the way it's prepared, KFCJ insisted on packaging both its take-out and dine-in chicken in prescribed patterns.

Accompanying side dishes are smaller than those in the US and are specifically prepared to suit Japanese tastes—for example, a corn salad or green salad with cucumbers, corn, and shredded vegetables. The biscuits that accompany each meal are prepared with a lower salt content than those in the US, and served with a more palatable honey that has been cut with maple syrup to reduce its sweetness. Other innovations introduced by Okhawara include smoked chicken, fried fish, and green tea ice cream and sherbet cups.

To this day, KFCJ remains one of Kentucky Fried Chicken's most successful overseas franchise operations. In fact, at Christmas time, the company's chicken is so popular that the company has to take reservations—all of Christmas Eve's production is sold out a week in advance. According to Izumi Kamiyama, then-editor of *Gekkan Shokudo,* one of the country's largest restaurant industry publications, "Kentucky Fried Chicken would never have been successful [in Japan] by following American advice."

Come Prepared (Campbell Soup and Lipton)

JUST ADD WATER FOR HAPPINESS

Criticized for having some of the blandest food in the world, the United Kingdom nonetheless has provided one major US food producer with some interesting challenges. Campbell Soup discovered that, although the British reacted favorably to the quality of its products and were accustomed to buying canned soup, they were not used to buying it in condensed form. According to one source, it appeared to them that Campbell was offering them half the amount of soup they were used to at the same price. The company simply added water to its existing product and repackaged it, thus putting it on the same par with the local competition.

The lesson wasn't lost on the company. It has since built research facilities in Hong Kong, Mexico, Australia, and the UK to develop products adapted for local and regional tastes.

IT'S ALL IN HOW YOU DESCRIBE IT

In the early 1990s, Lipton, producer of a moderately successful line of instant meals called *Side Dishes*, found that the concept wasn't working in Latin America. The company had pegged a significant part of its future growth on this market. Unfortunately, the idea of "instant" food didn't strike the desired chord with housewives throughout the region who felt that the concept implied that they were lazy and unwilling to make the extra effort required to prepare more traditional, quality meals for their families.

Lipton created a new ad campaign that proclaimed, "Surprise your family with new and exotic tastes from around the world." That campaign at least partly dulled the edge of the perceived stigma. At the same time, it gave housewives in the region an excuse to try the product—who could turn down the opportunity to provide their families something unique and exciting?

Olestra—Stomachache for Frito-Lay and P&G

Probably the most blatant case of "product disconnect" occurred in February and March 2000 when Frito-Lay and Procter & Gamble began distributing throughout the US snack foods prepared with a newly developed fat substitute for cooking made from vegetable oil and sugar.

Called *Olestra*, the new oil was marketed, after more than a decade of research, as a calorie-free frying and baking alternative with the same texture and taste as real fat. What a boon to the snack food industry—Olestra oil could open up a virtually closed health conscious consumer market, and take a step toward removing the expression "a moment on the lips, a lifetime on the hips" from the national lexicon.

The problem with Olestra oil, though, is that—like bran—its molecules are too large to digest or absorb. In other words, it passes through the human body the way mineral oil does, causing some people gastrointestinal problems including abdominal cramping, diarrhea, and other symptoms best left to the imagination.

Approved by the US Food and Drug Administration (FDA) in 1996 (and reaffirmed two years later), the product resulted in a flurry of studies from Johns Hopkins University and the University of North Carolina (UNC). Those studies disputed the charges with claims of their own that people eating snack chips prepared with Olestra wouldn't have "significantly more stomach trouble than those who eat regular chips."

The studies were deemed credible enough to be published in the *Journal of the American Medical Association,* but weren't credible for the nonprofit Center for Science and the Public Interest. The nonprofit, Washington, DC-based health-care watchdog group released its own widely circulated counter report calling the two studies "junk science." The Center's report noted that both researchers who had conducted the studies had been consultants to Procter & Gamble on other projects.

The issue that caused the most public consternation was covered in neither the Johns Hopkins nor the UNC studies: a researcher at the Harvard School of Public Health claimed that Olestra oil retards the absorption of cartenoids, which help protect the human body from heart attack, stroke, cancer, and some eye diseases. In addition, Olestra oil supposedly counteracts the effects of the government-recommended daily doses of Vitamins A, C, and E.

Any plans to market abroad snack foods made with Olestra oil took their first hit in 1995 when Procter & Gamble (P&G) asked the UK to approve the product's use. The company was forced to withdraw the petition when the government in London quickly created a regulatory barricade to P&G's move. The second, and perhaps most telling, blow came in June 2000 when the Canadian government ruled that no products prepared with the fat substitute could be sold in the country—a decision that, in effect, left the US the only country in the world to approve Olestra oil as a food ingredient.

The move by Ottawa prompted speculation by Olestra oil foes that the FDA would reconsider its approval, or at least require a sterner warning label on every package of P&G's *Wow* chips and Frito-Lay's *Pringles* to warn consumers of the possible gastrointestinal problems that could result from eating the products. P&G, which alone had spent $500 million in developing Olestra oil, retorted that the label is "confusing as it is" and should be removed altogether in favor of listing Olestra oil—now called *Olean*—on the required list of the products' ingredients.

Frito-Lay and P&G have cooperated in the building of a $200 million Olean oil manufacturing plant in Cincinnati, Ohio. Both are sticking by Olean oil. P&G claims that it expects its brand name to pull in $400 million in revenues from its first year of selling snack foods prepared with Olean oil.

Lessons Learned

It's axiomatic that to succeed in either the global or domestic marketplace, a company has to offer something that the competition doesn't—a product or service with unique features or characteristics that a potential individual customer will be willing to buy, even possibly at a higher price than those of the competition. To do this, a company needs to understand that it is *not* all about its corporate requirements and needs, rather it *is* all about the consumer and his or her needs.

WHAT THE MARKET EXPECTS, THE MARKET ACCEPTS

Seven important words to remember: "what the customer is willing to buy." This concept implies an understanding of what consumers in a targeted market both need *and* want, which means developing a product that is not only unique and distinct from the competition, but also adapted to the tastes, preferences, and requirements of those intended to buy it. It is essential to consider not only such influences as culture, history, religion, and social structure, but also the temporal political, economic, and societal climate that will indicate whether market entry is likely to be successful at any given time.

Companies that have succeeded in inserting new products into new markets know the value of adapting their products to ensure customer satisfaction, even though increasing sales and market share came with a little extra cost and a bit less profit. Thus, Latin American housewives do not need or want easy-to-prepare food because they are supposed to labor lovingly to provide nutritious home-cooked meals to their hungry families, but they *do* need and want to offer a greater variety and more exotic repasts at the table. Likewise, British canned soup lovers do not need or want to add water, so pre-watered soup is more expected and accepted than condensed.

The tie between consumer expectation and acceptance became crystal clear to Lever Brothers when its goods specially formulated for marketing in Great Britain landed on shelves in America instead. On the other hand, this lesson came a bit harder to Kentucky Fried Chicken when it chose the wrong place at the wrong time to introduce American fast food in India.

THE MORAL: To compete with established brands, customer preference often must be won over with patient strokes, starting with the expected and the accepted and moving toward the unusual and innovative only as a brand gains recognition and reputation.

CONCEIVE FOR THE CONSUMER, NOT JUST FOR THE COMPANY

Well-established companies—Iridium, DaimlerChrysler, Sony, General Motors, and others—have sometimes failed when entering intended markets because of the inability to "look beyond their own noses." These companies were driven not by the needs of the consumer, but by their own need to turn their good names into instant success, at least until the initial excitement faded. Big, short-term market share equates to big salaries and happy shareholders.

The first thing they missed: products released before they are functional or tested for flaws tend to crack the veneer, if not fatally crush even the most venerable companies. Product defects, bad maintenance records, product unavailability, lack of parts, and poor customer service add up to companies that are so intent on being the first in the race that they forget to put on their track shoes.

As Iridium, Sony, and Yugo learned, paid orders need to be filled without too much delay. As Peugeot, Proton, and Proctor & Gamble found out, consumers may be health and cost conscious, but they won't buy products that they come to distrust or believe are unsafe. Companies that are committed to their customers have a responsibility to the market at large and will be respected for producing products and offering services that are well-considered and carefully designed, even if the competition gets there first on a few occasions.

The second thing they missed: although initially satisfied customers may not lead to immediate bottom-line gratification, when business is managed to satisfy the consumer, it generates happy, loyal customers who come back for more no matter what the competition offers. The first question should always be whether the product developer is working for the market or the marketer.

Japanese management of Kentucky Fried Chicken franchises stuck to this rule despite instruction from the home office, resulting in a highly successful overseas operation. Whether a company makes food products, cars, computer games, or satellite telecommunication equipment, there is more to competition than price. Scaled-down, under designed, and poorly marketed products are unlikely to satisfy customers at any price.

THE MORAL: Customers deserve better. Companies that become too self-absorbed sometimes confuse the consumer with the competition.

BE WHAT YOU ARE, NOT WHAT YOU AREN'T

A company that has built a particular reputation for the quality and character of its products and services has an established consumer base. The market already has certain expectations about the company's products and services, and to some extent the company's innovation will be accepted. But as General Motors was to find out, a complete face-lift is not always the wisest course of action. Having set the standard for American luxury automobiles, General Motors' attempt to forgo the features that made its Cadillac sedan great and replace them with European styling was not what their faithful fans wanted. Nor was the quick remake a hit in Europe because the cars were still too American, albeit with a friendly mask.

To General Motor's credit, the company took the withering criticism of its Seville car to heart. It also slowly began making it more internationally driver-friendly. The company premiered its first right-hand-drive Seville model at the 1997 Tokyo Motor Show.

Although built at GM's Detroit-Hamtramck, Michigan, assembly plant alongside the US version, the new car was specially tailored for the Japanese market. It was a full five inches shorter than its US counterpart. Interestingly, it was equipped with outside rear view mirrors that folded into the body of the car by remote control for maneuvering through narrow streets, and it had brake and gas pedals designed for shorter-stature Japanese.

The new Seville basic *SLS* model was priced at about $43,000 and the higher-horsepowered *STS* model was priced at about $50,000. Both prices were lower than that of the rival Toyota *Lexus* vehicle (sold as the *Celsior* sedan in Japan), which was at the time more than $62,000.

In response to reporters at the auto show, GM chairman and chief executive Jack Smith said, "It took us a long time to re-establish ourselves in Japan...but we're back and we're here to stay." Quoted by the Associated Press, US-based auto industry analyst James Hall said, "This is the first time the modern Cadillac is trying to retail cars in Japan. They're starting from zero. This is not a three month thing....You have to have commitment and for commitment, you have to have time."

THE MORAL: If it's not broken, don't fix it. If it is broken, don't tear it down and start over, but instead make innovations that build on and enhance the best of the past.

CHAPTER 4

Distribution Blunders

GETTING IT THERE IN ONE PIECE—BUT THEN WHAT?

SEVERAL YEARS AGO, I happened to interview a senior executive of a manufacturer based in the US Midwest. Just a few months before, his company had a major international deal—one of its first—fall through because a container-load of its high-value machine parts was smashed to a pulp while being off-loaded from a ship in a Southeast Asian port.

Getting the container to the Port of Oakland for transshipment to its final destination was easy: the company's logistics management provider had made sure the documentation was in order and had planned that the container would arrive in the San Francisco Bay area with a minimum amount of lag time before it would be loaded aboard the ship. Transportation time of 12 days would get the container to its transit port. There it would be off-loaded and moved via a smaller, feeder-type cargo ship to its destination port. A truck would then shift the container to a warehouse to await final disposition by the buyer—a manufacturer of plastic consumer goods.

But, alas, it wasn't meant to be. Some of the container-handling equipment in use at the transit port was in a serious disrepair, and poorly trained workers (filling in for striking regulars) had to make do with improvised chain slings to unload the boxes off the ship. The improperly positioned sling slipped—dropping the container and its $1.1 million cargo 60 feet onto the dock. "I was told the sound it made when it hit the dock was really something," the president of the US company said wistfully. "What was salvageable could have fit into a suitcase."

Sure, he said, most of the loss was covered by the insurance the freight forwarder had insisted his company purchase. But the deal was squelched: the customer, in desperate need of equipment to meet his own production schedules, went to a European company for the machine tools.

Fortunately, the incident didn't turn the company off to expanding globally. Nevertheless, the affair teaches some serious lessons. "Getting the goods to market is just as important an element of success as the design of your product or its suitability for the global market you want to penetrate," the executive told me. "You can design the best, most attractive product in the world, but if you don't get it where it needs to be, when it needs to be there, you're dead. If we'd paid a little more attention to the process, we could have done it differently."

The Devil Is in the Details

Distribution, simply defined, is the management of inventory to achieve consumer satisfaction. From that perspective, distribution can be seen as the pursuit of any company's ultimate goal in any country and in every market, rich or poor. From the supply chain that forms the logistics part of the equation to the distributor, agent, or overseas partner that deals directly with the foreign retailer—who then sells to the consumer—distribution is key to any successful global business deal.

The "golden thread" that links the entire process is the logistics that provides the actual arterial system through which the goods flow—the trucks, trains, ships, aircraft, and documentation. But, as with anything developed by fallible humans, problems arise—trucks break down, trains are delayed, an endless number of snags might occur. Mismanagement of, or inattention to, the process can lead to kinks in the distribution channel. Those very kinks can disaffect overseas partners and pave the path toward eager competition for customers who rank availability as a key issue.

A ROLL IN THE HAY

While distribution systems everywhere bear general similarities, the assumption that the method of getting goods to market in, say, Japan is the same as it is Norway is false and leads to no end of grief.

Several sources tell of a Taiwanese company that sent a shipment of drinking glasses to a buyer in the Middle East via ship. The glasses were packed in wooden crates with hay used as dunnage to prevent breakage. Despite the company's precautions, the glasses arrived in shards. Why? The moisture content of the hay dropped significantly when the crates moved into the warmer, less humid climate of the Middle East. The hay shriveled to the point that it offered virtually no protection at all against breakage.

MISSING THE BOAT

Attention to detail—or a lack thereof—was also the issue with a manufacturer I once spoke with at a reception. After the usual formalities, our conversation—as conversations at parties usually do—drifted off into the "What line of work are you in?" direction. The gentleman was in his second decade of handling the international sales, marketing, and distribution operations for a midsize manufacturer. He was keeping all this going with a single assistant and a secretary—I was impressed. Usually each of those three areas of responsibility would be broad enough to keep their own respective multiple-member teams up to their knees in work.

"How do you handle the load? Don't things sometimes fall in the cracks?" I asked.

"Well," he replied, "sometimes, but nothing really that big." He told me how his load was eased by the fact that he relied "heavily" on a freight forwarder to process his export shipments, which were valued at several million dollars annually.

"Do you work with the forwarder to find ways of cutting costs and developing volume discounts for your container shipments?" I asked.

"They handle it all," he said, smiling a little nervously. "I usually don't have to worry about a thing...really." He told me of his latest sale, a multiple container shipment to a buyer in Eastern Europe, which he hoped was only the first of many to come with that particular customer.

"What carrier are you using?" I asked innocently.

He answered. (Later, another guest at the party told me that when I heard the answer I looked like someone who had a bucketful of snow crabs dumped on his feet.) I stood there speechless, as a vision of the Flying Dutchman flashed before my eyes. Apparently my new friend didn't know that the steamship line he had been told was handling his shipment had gone out of business the preceding year.

HELD UP AT THE BORDER

Stories abound of shipments delayed in ports, airports, and cross-border rail and highway points. Shipments have been frustratingly delayed because paperwork was rubber-stamped instead of embossed, or the wrong color ink was used by an inspector to sign off on a customs declaration.

A rather well-documented story tells about an entire intermodal train that was carrying hundreds of loaded containers from manufacturing centers across the US as it moved south through El Paso, Texas, to distribution points in Mexico. There, the containers holding consumer goods were forwarded on by truck to retail distribution centers and retail stores throughout the country. Meanwhile, the large number of 20- and 40-foot containers stuffed with industrial goods, such as machine parts and electronics components, were moved on to factories to be assembled into everything from wiring harnesses for the US automotive industry to hair dryers and stereo systems.

The problem came at the border. Despite the advances made in computerizing shipping documentation, a huge amount of paperwork is necessary to get goods across foreign borders—particularly for a shipment made up of multiple products for multiple consignees. Each container requires its own documentation for what's inside, which could be anything from corrosive chemicals or computer peripherals to fresh-cut flowers or raw animal skins. And, while most of the business of moving goods from "Point A to Point C via Point B" is fairly routine, the fact remains that the documentation must be in order—otherwise, quite simply, the goods may not be allowed entry into the destination country.

After studying the voluminous paperwork for this particular intermodal train, a Mexican Customs officer noticed that a certain piece of documentation for a single container—that's for one among hundreds—lacked a required signature. The officer held the train until every container was unloaded and opened to verify that the contents matched what was entered on the accompanying manifest. The exercise took the better part of two days. Obviously, this delayed the train and threw to the breeze the delivery schedules of hundreds—perhaps thousands—of shippers in the US as well as manufacturers and retailers in Mexico. All for want of a single signature.

A BRIDGE TOO FAR

In many ways, physical distribution of a product is impacted by politics. Duties and tariffs, documentation, transportation infrastructures, free-trade zones, and the regulations regarding air, ocean, rail, and truck transportation all impact not only where, but also how efficiently and expeditiously, a cargo is moved.

In Eastern Europe, particularly, the demise of a rigidly centralized Communist system has given way to an evolutionary new economy based on privatization and free enterprise. This shift has brought a number of issues into clear focus. One of the most obvious is the true nature of the region's physical distribution system. According to transportation writer Hugh Quigley, "A planned economy leads to very big companies which must now be split up into smaller pieces. This disaggregation profoundly affects all aspects of logistics and distribution."

According to Quigley, who in the early 1990s authored an analysis of the region's distribution system, Eastern Europe "has three systems—one each for foreign, Eastern European, and domestic markets. Their relative quality directly reflects their importance to governments in short supply of hard currency." Each system, he says, "supports a particular industry or sector. The wholesale distributor supports the retail sector, while a distributor supporting the chemicals industry has no common ground with another in metals."

But the situation is changing: wholesale companies have begun to sell to all types of operations. A vibrant entrepreneur class of trader/merchants has emerged; in many cases they are actually forming the most stable and resilient component of the region's economies.

Shippers in the early 1990s could only struggle with an outdated surface transportation infrastructure that had creaked and wheezed along under Communism and was totally inadequate to meet the needs of Eastern Europe's new economies. They quickly turned to the barges and small feeder ships that ply the Danube—stacked high with brightly colored containers—as their link to both suppliers and buyers in other parts of Europe and beyond.

The Danube is the longest international river in Europe. It runs southward for almost 1,800 miles from the German Black Forest—bisecting both Vienna and Budapest—and on through Romania to the Black Sea. Connected by a channel to the Main River near its source, the Danube is the largest artery of a waterway that links the bustling port of Rotterdam—one of the busiest ports in the world—with the Romanian port of Costanza.

From 1992 until the conflict in the Balkans flared in late 1998, the 10 countries that depend on the Danube for water transport (including landlocked Austria, Hungary, and the Czech Republic) were increasing their trade significantly. But then battles interfered. During the most recent period in the ongoing conflict that has torn the Balkans apart, when North Atlantic Treaty Organization (NATO) aircraft tried to prevent the movement of forces into an already inflamed area, they bombed and destroyed most of the bridges spanning the river. The hardest hit were those at Novi Sad, Serbia.

The Danube Shipping Convention—the pact that regulates barge and container traffic on the river—didn't help much, according to an article in the July 2000 edition of *World Trade* magazine. Under the pact, ships can only trade between their own country and another one on the river. Because of this, Ukranian-Danube Shipping, for example (the largest container carrier serving the region), couldn't use 70 of its 700 barges; they were prevented from moving down river by the downed bridge spans. Hungary's state shipping company had 20 barges idled in the Lower Danube for the same reason, while almost three-quarters of Bulgaria's Danube River shipping fleet was put out of service by the blockage. As a result of the blockage, much of Hungary's grain harvest was moved to markets in the Mediterranean region by rail. The cost was 70 percent higher than it would have been had it moved by barge.

Estimates of the cost to clear the river ran as high as $23 million—the European Union pledged to pick up most of the bill. Quoting the head of Hungary's Department of Shipping, the article claimed that the greatest hurdle was neither technical nor financial, but political. This contention was demonstrated by the attitude of the Federal Republic of Yugoslavia, which refused to cooperate with the European Union's proposed river clearance efforts—at least until one of its own non-Danube bridges would be replaced first.

ROLL, YOU MIGHTY RIVER, ROLL

Author and international business educator David Ricks has written of a US-based food processor that located a cannery at a river delta in Mexico, on a site that was downstream from a large pineapple plantation. The plan, Ricks says, called for the company to barge the ripe fruit downstream for canning, load the cans directly onto oceangoing ships, and send them directly to the company's various markets around the world.

When the pineapples were ripe, however, the company found itself in trouble: the time of crop maturity coincided with the flood stage of the river. In flood season, the river's current was too strong for back hauling empty barges upstream. So the plan to use barges to transport the fruit had to be abandoned.

With no alternative, the company was forced to close the operation. Its new equipment was sold for 5 percent of its original cost to a Mexican group that immediately relocated the cannery. "A seemingly simple, harmless oversight of weather and navigation conditions became a significant cost, and, in fact, the primary cause of major losses to the company."

The "Single Center" Concept (Becton Dickinson)

One company that originally blundered while trying to distribute products in the European Union was Becton Dickinson, a manufacturer of medical diagnostic equipment headquartered in Sparks, Maryland. Having built up a network of national distribution centers throughout Europe in the early 1990s, the company found its business there expanding beyond its own projections.

The system initially worked, but the company soon discovered that it was riddled with inefficiencies. Inventory costs were high, and stock had to be written off because the shelf life of products expired before shipping. The company also began suffering from poor stock availability and skyrocketing distribution costs.

A British consultant who was brought in to study the situation recommended that the company close its national centers in Sweden, France, Germany, and Belgium, and shift all of its European regional distribution operations to a single site in Temse, Belgium. In less than a year, over-stock levels were down 45 percent, write-offs were reduced by 65 percent, and incidents of stock unavailability were cut by three-quarters.

Although Becton Dickinson had stumbled, it recovered by learning a lesson taught by the late James Cooper, former director of the Centre for Logistics and Transportation at the Cranfield School of Management in Bedfordshire, England, before the formation of the European Union. Cooper, quoted in the June 1997 issue of *Management Today,* said that companies facing the prospect of a single market like Europe "should reorganize themselves as regional entities, approaching their customers wearing a European rather than a national hat, and cutting out layers of cost by centralizing functions" like transportation and distribution. Distribution systems designed "for the old Europe," the article said, "were ill-suited to the new one, particularly if a company's manufacturing, marketing, and sales strategies were to be Europeanized." Organizing, distributing, and warehousing "on a country-by-country basis," Cooper continued, "breaks a cardinal rule—the rule that says storage should be located according to the patterns of demand, and patterns of demand don't necessarily relate very closely to where, by an accident of history, a country's borders are."

Making the Connection

The logistics involved in getting a product to market on time and on target aren't the only crucial components of an effective distribution system. They're only part of the equation. International distribution is actually the synergy of the logistics function and the on-site, regional, or in-country distributor, agent, joint venture partner, or offshore office representative.

To operate a fully functioning distribution chain, an international company needs to look at the challenge of getting its products into the hands of the customer with what's been called a "whole channel view." Serious problems await any company that thinks its work is done the moment the product leaves its hands and heads out the door for parts, in effect, unknown.

In their book *The Principles of Marketing,* Philip Kotler and Gary Armstrong say that distribution channels vary greatly from country to country and region to region. First, they write, there's a wide range in the numbers and types of middlemen that serve various foreign markets. For example, a US company marketing in China must operate through "a frustrating maze of state-controlled wholesalers and retailers. Chinese distributors often carry competitors' products and frequently refuse to share even basic sales and marketing information with their suppliers."

"Hustling for sales," they say, "is a foreign concept to Chinese distributors, who are used to selling all they can obtain. Working or getting around this system sometimes requires substantial time and investment. When Coca-Cola and Pepsi first entered China, for example, customers bicycled up to bottling plants to get their soft drinks. Now, both companies have set up direct-distribution channels, investing heavily in trucks and refrigeration units for retailers."

Another important difference, Kotler and Armstrong say, lies in the actual size and character of retail units abroad. In the US, large-scale retail chains are dominant, while most foreign-sourced retailing operations are carried out by small, independent retailers. For example, they state, hundreds of thousands of retailers in India conduct their businesses out of tiny shops or in open-air markets. Supermarkets could offer lower prices, "but supermarkets are difficult to build and open because of many economic and cultural barriers." Low incomes compel people to shop daily for small purchases rather than weekly for larger quantities. Storage and refrigeration is virtually non-existent, and packaging isn't sophisticated because it would only add to production costs. All these factors, they conclude, "have kept large-scale retailing from spreading rapidly" in India and the world's other lesser-developed countries.

A company's success at effectively delivering its product into the customer's hands is directly proportional to who is on-site in the target market to ensure that the "whole channel view" isn't distorted or clouded over by circumstances, trends, or other factors. Without such vigilance, even the most finely crafted international business strategy can be brought to a screaming halt.

The International Alter-Ego

Any successful international marketing plan pivots on the correct selection of the kind of distributor to best suit a company's needs.

Conversely, the failure to select the appropriate overseas distribution partner has caused myriad companies, both large and small, as much grief as any smashed container-load of expensive machine tools or mindless reliance on a misanthropic freight forwarder. Insurance can alleviate some of the grief from lost or mishandled cargo, and there are thousands of logistics service providers to choose from—but lost customers can almost never be recovered. As the old saying goes, "You can't un-ring a bell."

The sheer complexity of creating the correct channel of distribution lends itself to serious mistakes. The nature of adequately managing a smoothly functioning distribution system hinges on the seller's capability to control two separate systems: one in the home country, the other in the target market.

In the home country, the company must ensure the timely flow of raw materials, component parts, and assemblies to production facilities that might be located in separate geographic locations.

In the target market, the company must monitor and control as well as possible the distribution system that gets the finished product into the hands of the consumer. That role calls for a true partnership perspective between the at-home supplier and the distributor in the target market. This relationship, based on mutual respect and trust, is absolutely crucial because the distributor becomes, in effect, an arm of your company. If the distributor fails, you fail. If you fail, the distributor does the same. It's simple.

Protecting the Flanks (Raytheon)

In October 1959, *Forbes* magazine ran a brief story on recent developments at Raytheon, a Lexington, Massachusetts-based electronics manufacturer.

"Protecting its flanks, Raytheon never had much luck in the civilian market," the story read. "But military uncertainties being what they are, [Raytheon] president Charles Adams is set to try again. In May, Raytheon took over Machlett Laboratories, maker of X-ray tubes and high-power electron tubes. Two months later, the company absorbed Sorenson & Company, a producer of power supply equipment. Should even partial disarmament ultimately take place, Adams wants to have some thriving commercial sidelines to protect Raytheon from too severe a contraction in its business."

In the early 1960s, Raytheon and Machlett Laboratories together owned Elettronica Sicula SpA (ELSI), a manufacturing subsidiary in Palermo, Sicily, built to manufacture electronic components, such as semiconductor rectifiers, surge arrests, and vacuum tubes for televisions. Raytheon found itself out on a limb when the Italian joint venture fell through because of declining profits, mismanagement, and, as events later showed, a distinct lack of commitment from Raytheon headquarters.

From 1964 to 1966, ELSI squeaked through by producing enough of a profit to remain in the black, but not enough to offset its debt expenses or operating losses. Then in February 1967, Raytheon and Machlett began to talk with the Italian government about finding a partner to buy out the operation, but any hopes of selling off the facility were dashed when a number of potential partners came, took a look, and walked away shaking their heads. It had become obvious that Raytheon was unwilling to spend the money needed to modernize ELSI's production facilities. And Raytheon hadn't expended any energy to develop export markets in the areas of Europe, Africa or the Middle East that still held some potential for vacuum tubes.

DIM...DIM... AND DIMMER

One now-retired Raytheon executive said that the company "didn't have any interest in establishing the kind of distribution system that would have been necessary to grow the company in Europe or elsewhere. Management saw overseas market development as a distraction and turned its back on trying to find non-military markets for its products. The Department of Defense had become the company's most flush [with cash] suitor and the pressure was on to keep it that way."

With no buyer standing near, in March 1968 Raytheon decided to close the facility in Palermo—despite admonitions from the Italian authorities not to close the plant and thus lay off its 900 Sicilian employees. Three days after the plant closure, the Mayor of Palermo issued an order requisitioning the factory and its assets for a period of six months. In Sicily, the mass firing of employees is unacceptable, particularly if the people who are let go don't receive sizeable sums of money as a token of good faith. Shortly after, ELSI declared bankruptcy saying that the requisition of the plant removed "effective control of the facility from the company," and as a result, "ELSI could not avail itself of an immediate source of liquid funds."

Months and months of legal wrangling ensued involving local Italian courts and intervention between the US and Italian governments. Months of dispute dragged into years. Finally, in 1986—18 years after the original bankruptcy filing—the US Department of State issued a bulletin innocuously stating that "the two governments have come to the conclusion that they are unable to resolve the diplomatic claims of the United States on behalf of Raytheon and Machlett Laboratories through diplomatic negotiation or binding arbitration." The US took the dispute to the five-member International Court of Justice. Three years later, the court rejected Italian objections to the US filing, but also rejected reparation claims by Washington on behalf of Ratheon and Machlett. It was at best a Pyrrhic victory—one that cost Raytheon more than $25 million.

GOING...GOING...GONE

Raytheon's slide away from non domestic and nonmilitary operations continued through the 1990s. In 1994, the company raised a stir when it announced it would close a facility in Wales that produced Hawker business aircraft and move the operation to Wichita, Kansas. The British government rallied in an effort to change Raytheon's mind about the closure, intimating that if the operation were relocated, "the government may look dimly at Raytheon's future bids for business in Great Britain."

By the end of 1999, Raytheon's newly appointed chief executive officer, Daniel Burnham, found himself needing to tell the company's shareholders that, according to *Business Week* magazine, "Raytheon's supposedly firm financial footing was a mirage." Earlier, the company was forced to admit that its year 2000 projections would be only $715 million—less than half of what the company had forecasted earlier in the year. The company's overreliance on military contracts, and a management style that seemed based on military contracts, had come home to roost.

In 1998 Ratheon ranked as the third largest defense contractor in the country. During the previous several years, it had absorbed five smaller defense contractors specializing in such diverse fields as surveillance equipment, radar, and advanced electronic warfare systems. Industry analysts said at the time that the acquisitions were ill-advised, given government cuts in military spending and a general shift among defense contractors to take advantage of the so-called Peace Dividend. The Cold War was over—companies across the country were reassessing their core businesses and "beating their swords into plowshares."

Facing a widening array of difficulties, Raytheon—$10.1 billion in debt ($9 billion of that long-term)—put its Wichita, Kansas-based aircraft operation up for sale in June 2000. The sale was prompted by the company's need to raise capital and clarify its goal of becoming a purely defense and electronics company.

"The decision's been made to concentrate on our core competency and go after the kind of business that we have expertise in," said one Raytheon executive. "We've tried over the year to do other things, but it just hasn't paid off. You need a flexible management mentality to make that transition from a defense base to a 'civilian-style' operation. That [mentality] hasn't existed here and it shows. A lot of time and money's been wasted."

Getting the Goods on the Ginza

Literally scores of magazine articles have been written about the Japanese distribution system, and how many in the West claim that the system has been allowed to become a nontariff trade barrier designed solely to vex foreigners and protect domestic Japanese business from foreign competition.

In truth, there is no single Japanese distribution system. Rather, there are dozens and dozens of separate distribution systems—each with its own arterial network of inter-reliant components. For example, fish products go through an average of three intermediary distributors before they reach consumers; shoes, on the other hand, only go through one. Distribution in Japan is a highly complicated, multilevel system that must be patiently navigated like a maze to get the desired result—with the emphasis on the word "patiently."

WARNER-LAMBERT

Warner-Lambert jumped the gun in its efforts to market *Chiclets*, *Trident*, and several other brands of chewing gum to consumers in Japan. The company felt that its Japanese distributors weren't exerting enough effort to promote its products, leading to it bypassing its wholesale distributors. The move not only alienated the wholesalers, but created suspicions among retailers—who often consider suppliers unreliable if they change business tactics. To recover its market share, Warner-Lambert was compelled to direct its sales force to collect the retail sales orders for the wholesalers.

LAWSON-JAPAN

The November 14, 1988, the *Wall Street Journal* reported on a situation that underscores an extreme example of the complexity of getting goods to market and into the hands of consumers in Japan. It's only fair to say here that much has happened in Japan since that article was written: the devaluation of the yen, the deflation of Japan's bubble economy, and the Asian financial crisis of 1997, among other factors, have combined to force the Japanese to take a long, hard look at the entire structure of their economy.

In this particular situation, modern chain store owners in Shizuoka, Japan, the Wall Street Journal article read, "don't worry about armed robbers. They worry about the small shopkeepers down the street." The paper reported that irate shopkeepers beat up a worker who was helping to build one of Shizuoka's first Western-world-style convenience stores, a franchisee of Japan's Lawson chain. Later, gangs of enraged "mom and pop" shopkeepers wearing motorcycle helmets and samurai-style headbands repeatedly stormed the store at night—they screamed at employees and intimidated customers who patronized the "devil businesses."

In Japan, "a deep-rooted, even violent, resistance arises against the kind of distribution system that has long and efficiently provided Americans with cheap goods. The world's second-largest consumer market, …[Japan] is held captive by tiny stores." the paper reported. These papa-mama shops, as the Japanese call them, "have a stranglehold on store shelves that could display American products. While providing excellent service, the shops also keep prices high, limit selection, and, the US government argues, obstruct imports."

If American-style convenience stores, supermarkets, and mass-market merchandisers had free rein, "imports—including American products—would stand a much better chance in Japan, but the papa-mamas would lose their cozy, but grossly inefficient, control of 56% of Japan's total retail sales."

It seems the city of Shizuoka was trying its best to enforce the guidelines which had been crafted by the city's small merchants, which required national retailers to get the approval of every single small shopkeeper within a five-kilometer radius of a new store's location before government approval was granted for its construction. That's the reason, the *Wall Street Journal* said, that Shizuoka, "with a market the size of Atlanta," didn't have a single convenience store until Lawson, itself owned by Japanese retail giant Daiei Inc., challenged the regulations to do business there. At the time, some 60 percent of all Japanese metropolitan areas imposed constrictive regulations similar to those on the books in Shizuoka.

The papa-mamas proved so powerful that they pushed through a national law stipulating that no retailer could open a store larger than 5,382 square feet in size—that equates to about one-tenth the floor space of the smallest K-Mart in the US—without the express permission of the respective communities small retailers. The Ministry of Trade and Industry in Tokyo "administers the law in such a way that eight to ten years pass before a store gets approval...Only about three dozen large stores open each year in all of Japan, and usually at half the [physical] size requested," the paper said.

Any attack on Japan's retail labyrinth is perceived as an attack on its social welfare system. Labor-intensive and inefficient, the article said, Japan's "retail system is almost the flipside of Japan's factories," with cramped shops lined with dusty shelves "and the attendant layers of distributors that deliver a half-case of soy sauce or three boxes of disposable diapers at a time offering jobs to the marginally unemployable."

"Japan's shopkeepers are fiercely protective. And they keep Japan as the United States would be if frozen in time in the early 1960s, before the development of huge shopping centers, with the local TV shop still selling only Zeniths and RCAs, with Chevrolet and Ford dealers not even dreaming of handling a Japanese product," the piece concluded.

Technology to the Rescue? (Snap-On Tools Inc.)

An attempt to support its distribution chain and ease the ordering process for franchisees in the US and Europe led Snap-On Tools Inc. to cave in on itself in the summer of 1998: the company's new computerized distribution system failed due to chronic software problems. The software problems led to delays in order turnaround time, which prompted some frustrated dealers on both sides of the Atlantic to order tools from rival manufacturers instead of Snap-On, reported *Computerworld* magazine. The problem was so severe that the Kenosha, Wisconsin-based company lost more than $50 million in business during the first half of the year.

The "enterprise resource planning software" supplied by a software developer based in Northern California couldn't handle the high volume of domestic and overseas orders, which caused problems that "had a significant adverse effect on service levels, with a negative impact on sales, expenses, and productivity," said a company executive. The *Computerworld* article said that the software glitch, "combined with the impact of the Asian economic crisis, could drag the company's third-quarter earnings 10% below last year's figures." Up until the computer problem, Snap-On had experienced five consecutive years of earnings-per-share growth. At the time of the software meltdown, the company announced plans to close five manufacturing plants, five distribution warehouses and 40 small offices in North America and Europe "as part of a restructuring effort."

Facing a Faceless Product

Stephen Kaufman, chairman and chief executive officer of Arrow Electronics Inc., a Melville, New York, distributor of electronics components, wrote an opinion piece that succinctly sums up the risks involved in lacking a viable product distribution plan in a world economy that is becoming more and more globalized. The opinion appeared in the May 1999 issue of *Electronic News* magazine.

According to Kaufman, whose company does business in 65 countries, there are a number of distribution industry observers who question the efficacy of globalization in distribution. "Who really needs global distributors, they ask, when everyone knows that distribution is, at its heart, a local business." Face-to-face business is in, faceless global corporations are out, they say. Business tastes sweeter when it's served hot at the local diner, not cold over the Internet.

Still others, he said, form a Greek chorus to bemoan the global acquisitions, mergers, downsizings, joint ventures, and other tectonic shifts in the distribution industry over the past decade, and see the resultant declining revenues as proof positive that the ripples of Arrow's entrée into the European market in 1985 continue to haunt a logistics sector that would be healthier and more profitable had the company stayed in its own backyard. Kaufman called these sentiments "understandable," but way off the mark because they overlook the trends that have rewritten the basics of both macro and micro international economics, as well as the "significant changes" in customer and supplier relationships that "are leading us inexorably toward even greater globalization."

A "very embarrassing example of this reality," Kaufman said, happened when he received a pointed letter from a senior procurement executive of one of Arrow's largest Europe-based customers. Arrow had previously served the customer locally with distribution centers in several countries there.

"He informed me that he had requested a meeting with representatives of our company from four countries in Europe to negotiate prices, terms and conditions of a major bid that would cover the next 12 to 18 months," Kaufman said. "However, the customer wrote, because we had no one there to commit to prices and terms of the support of their factories in two American cities, we were likely to be disqualified as a bidder. His time, he said, had been wasted in traveling to and attending this meeting, and that unless we were able to clearly commit to a coordinated and complete bid for support in six locations in five countries, we could expect to lose the business we had enjoyed with them, which amounted to several millions dollars a year."

Arrow's customers were continuing to look to the global market to expand their businesses and add to their bottom line. To keep them competitive, Kaufman said, they need products that are "truly world class." The more internationally competitive they are, the less they'll look to government for protection and the more they'll work toward producing and distributing quality goods efficiently, and creating a quality service network that has the capability of reaching a customer no matter where he is on the globe. This will set him apart from the competition. The most successful companies, he said, have come to understand that the customers they serve have, at the same time, become world shoppers.

This particular development has compelled those customers to out-source large segments of their manufacturing activities and to rationalize their international operations that rely extensively on suppliers that can provide the same levels of service, product quality, responsiveness, and pricing in every corner of the world.

Given this reality, customers who don't have access to global product information, global product availability, and global parts pricing "will be operating at a severe disadvantage." And as for those companies that can successfully ("for now," he adds) operate in a local or regional niche and ignore these trends, "these niches are bound to become fewer and fewer." Those companies "may prefer to remain in the comfortable mode of dealing with their traditional local sources, but the competitiveness of their markets will soon force them to meet these global imperatives."

Lessons Learned

"If a consumer can't find the right product at the right time, the retailer and suppliers could lose the consumer, as well as the sale." So stated Robert E. Swift, former executive director of the apparel industry's Crafted with Pride in the USA Council, in a 1989 issue of *Express*. This quarterly publication distributed by the Federal Express Corporation focused on a "quick response" management concept developed by the Boston Consulting Group for the US apparel industry, but which has direct application to any industry virtually anywhere in the world. The concept? Simple: provide the most value at the lowest cost in the least amount of time. These words reflect the very heart and soul of international business.

It's important to note that Swift's three fulcrum points—maximum value, low cost, and availability—themselves balance on the tip of a blade edged on one side by distribution logistics and on the other by the correct approach toward an overseas distributor partnership. The criticality of both, as well as their interdependence, can't be overstated. The successful completion of this marketing mix relies on a company's clearheaded approach toward getting its product into the consumer's hands through channels that best suit its requirements. The appropriate channels vary greatly depending on market location, size, infrastructure, level of sophistication, and the competition.

CHART THE CHANNELS, STAY ALERT FOR THE SHOALS

The distribution channel system, then, must fit the special characteristics of the company itself and the unique requirements of the market in which it's going to do business. The company that forgets this runs the strong risk of losing its market share (if it gains any in the first place) due to its distribution channels' failure to reflect the changing needs of its markets.

When entering a new market, a review and analysis of existing distribution channels is essential, but it is also only the beginning. Like Becton Dickinson, companies that have established working distribution systems in one country sometimes employ the same methodology in other places, often with initial success. But continued vigilance is essential to keeping and building market share once it is established. At the sign of a slide, it may be time to reevaluate and adjust.

Companies must make the commitment to understand and control their distribution chain to account for the peculiarities of the market if they are going to stay. Thus, Becton Dickinson revamped its European distribution system on a regional instead of a national basis, while the cola giants Pepsi and Coca-Cola provided their own equipment to move their products into the Chinese market. On the other hand, failure to make this commitment shook up Raytheon's Italian operations and caused havoc to Warner-Lambert's share of the Japanese market.

In the late 1970s, a US-based company found itself going nose to nose in Latin America with competitors from The Netherlands, the UK, and Germany. Within 12 months, the firm lost 50 percent of its business in the region because two of its major competitors had simultaneously come up with an ironclad method of squeezing the US company out of the market. One, marketing a very broad line of products, forced regional distributors to drop the narrower US line if they wished to keep its business. The other purchased a controlling interest in several large distributors who happened to be carrying the US company's product lines. Within a year, the company not only lost half of its regional business, but also found that a full quarter of its global sales had evaporated.

THE MORAL: A farmer may have a cart piled high with produce, but without a horse to pull the cart out the gate, down the rutted road, over the stone bridges, and into the town square in time for market day, the farmer is going to have to eat his own eggs, tomatoes, carrots, and potatoes.

SMOOTH OUT THE KINKS IN THE CHAIN

In terms of logistics issues, Asia is a good example—companies that plan to do business there run into a myriad of unique challenges. The transportation infrastructure is overtaxed, chronically plagued by bottlenecks that can create lengthy delays in moving goods to inland points from coastal ports. Each country requires its own customized product distribution scheme, and the multi-tier distribution systems are generally inefficient. All this combines to make the universal goals of customer satisfaction and cost control difficult at best and disastrous at worst.

According to Steven Harbour, an international business attorney writing in the May-June 1997 issue of *Business Horizons,* "An inadequate, inflexible, or disadvantageous distribution system is like a slow cancer that attacks a company's competitive position." He writes that there is "no clear indication that the problem is the system. Sales margins may decline, so new products are introduced, costs are cut, or prices are slashed to deal with the symptoms in the short term, leaving the problem to fester."

A lot of patience, a head for details, and once again an unfailing commitment are needed to wend through maze of problems likely to arise in getting the goods to market. From climate, to customs forms, to efficient intermodal transfer, to alternative transport means, every exigency should be anticipated, considered, and covered to the extent possible. Contingency plans and clear chains of command can smooth out many of the bumps—such as lack of a single signature on a customs form, breakage from bad handling or packing, and even loss of one mode of transport.

Thinking through distribution issues "logically and systematically, focusing on value, obtaining as much flexibility and/or control as possible, managing distributors' economics, and making sure everyone has the same goals," Harbour says, "can allow the firm to prosper" in any mercurial international environment.

THE MORAL: A plan for the details is a plan for efficiency. Even a small hole below the waterline can eventually cause a ship to list and sink.

Advertising Blunders

IT'S ALL ABOUT IMAGE

FOR YEARS, AN APOCRYPHAL STORY has floated around business schools about how the Gerber Company wrecked any chances it might have had of selling its line of baby foods in sub-Saharan Africa. According to the yarn, Gerber spent hundreds of thousands of dollars to get the word out about its product. But the company was disappointed by an almost total lack of sales there.

The management team discovered that, because of the region's high rate of illiteracy, consumers had come to expect that whatever image appears on a container, box, or jar is a literal depiction of the contents inside. The illiteracy rate was particularly high among women—the very target consumer Gerber wanted to reach. The Gerber jar is adorned with its picture of a cute white baby. In other words, Gerber found itself, unwittingly, encouraging young mothers in Kenya and Botswana to feed their children white baby parts.

While fictitious, the story does have a lesson: Advertising is all about image, and image is everything. Just ask the Swiss...

Switzerland Sends in the Moo-rines

Many envision Switzerland as a composite of lush Alpine meadows inhabited by milk cows tended by hearty militia dairymen in lederhosen who yodel away the hours as they carve chocolate cuckoo clocks. They sit on a rock, whittling with high-quality *Swiss Army* pocket knives and their inebriated St. Bernard beside them. All the while, they maintain a stoic neutrality.

The somewhat inclusive, if not idiosyncratic, Swiss idyll took a heavy hit in the late 1990s when the harsh spotlight of history shone into some unexplored corners. The country's banking industry had been criticized in the past for actively squirreling away huge sums of money for the Nazis during World War II. The Swiss government had reportedly turned a blind eye to the reports and made a national sport of bureaucratically dragging its feet in returning the money of Holocaust victims to their families.

Switzerland had an image problem, particularly in the US, where many Holocaust survivors relocated after the war. What to do? The answer was obvious. As Switzerland doesn't have a Marine Corps, the answer was to send in the cows.

Fiberglass cows, that is. Fifty of them, shipped to New York City in the fall of 1999, where they would be the focus of a marketing and advertising campaign. Thus began an officially sanctioned "cow parade"—to reclaim Switzerland's international reputation as the laugh-a-minute, fun capital of Europe. The shrewd plan would deposit life-size and mass-produced cows at public schools throughout New York City, where crowds of schoolchildren could paint or decorate them as they wished.

FLAMING COWS AND INCENDIARY EGOS

The same somewhat creative, if a trifle bizarre, plan had seen some success elsewhere. The year before, 800 fiberglass Holstein cows were allowed to "graze" in Zurich, where local artists decorated them à la Andy Warhol. By 1998, a shoe salesman tourist had spread the word across the Atlantic. A Chicago cow parade ensued, where an estimated 40 million people saw 340 cows, some attired in NASA spacesuits and others dressed as cowboys. The response was overwhelming—about half of the cows were later auctioned off, with about $3.5 million going to charity.

The Chicago parade was eagerly seen as a bellwether. All went well in New York, too, until people discovered that the cows were made of a fiberglass that, if exposed to flame, exploded like napalm—"transforming the glossy figures into Roman candles," according to *The New York Times*.

The offending cows were discreetly deported back to Switzerland, and the Coordinating Commission for the Presence of Switzerland Abroad (CoCo) saw a filet cut of its $30 million budget go up in acrid smoke. The official Swiss government agency canceled the cow parade and nervously released a statement to the press proclaiming that both the Swiss government and CoCo wanted to make it clear that they "did not want to endanger the lives of schoolchildren." The cows, said Jacques Reverdin, the Swiss Consul General in New York, "will be used in other countries, but certainly not in schools."

The US co-sponsor, the Cow Parade Holdings Corp. (CPH), pulled out of the event, saying the Swiss cows were junk. According to a spokesman, the cows weren't even made in Switzerland—it seems they were produced in Bosnia. He said, "The resin was of poor quality, there were no metal supports. They [the cows, not the Bosnians] could fall over on people and when you flipped the reclining cow upside-down it was hollow. It looked like a bathtub. Someone could get trapped inside."

CoCo and Cow Parade Holdings are planning future parades with cows manufactured in Florida and California. However, problems continued to rain on the Swiss attempt to improve its image abroad.

COWS, FLAMINGOS, AND HOGS... OH, MY!

The story gets really strange at this point. Shortly after the cows returned to Switzerland with their proverbial tails between their legs, the Swiss filed a lawsuit against CPH (its former joint venture partner) and its president (Jerome Elbaum of Hartford, Connecticut) charging CPH and Elbaum with stealing the international copyright for the cow parade. Elbaum reacted with a countersuit charging that the Swiss were impossible to work with, owed him a substantial amount of money, and actually had planted a spy within CPH to report back to CoCo headquarters in Zurich.

The accused spy was fired by Elbaum and withdrew to Miami to work with city officials in developing a parade for that city based on either dolphins or flamingos. Enter Cincinnati, Ohio, which announced soon after that it plans within the next few years to host a "porker" [pig] parade.

"These forms, like flamingos or hogs," Elbaum told *The New York Times*, "will not produce significant or lasting art, because the shapes of the animals are wrong. Flamingos do not have a large surface. A flamingo does not lend itself to art. They [cows] immediately attract art. You speak to artists, serious artists, and they only want to paint cows. Cows are benign."

The recriminations flashed like broadsides across the Atlantic between Elbaum and CPH on one side and Switzerland's Cow Parade Worldwide Inc. on the other. "It is sad what happened. It is as if we had a baby and someone took it from us. We have no influence anymore," said Kurt Blickenstorfer, president of Cow Parade Worldwide. Elbaum continued to press his claim that he controls the global rights for all cow parades everywhere.

REJECTED COWS FIGHT BACK

Elbaum's dream came true. Five hundred fiberglass cows—"US-bred" in Florida and California—were herded together in Forest Park in Queens, New York, for Cow Parade 2000. They were decorated, at $7,500 per cow, by sponsors ranging from Yahoo and a couple of New York steak houses to church groups and community organizations.

Conscious of the cultural impact of the event, strict guidelines were set up for entries and several were rejected. These included the "Moo-ni-Cow Lewinsky" cow, the Hassidic Jewish cow, and a cow that was decorated by the Queens chapter of People for the Ethical Treatment of Animals (PETA) with butcher's marks and unbecoming graffiti critical of "meat eaters." (PETA took the rejection to court where a judge dismissed the activist group's claims that the decision was a denial of their right of free expression granted under the US Constitution. "A cow," the judge ruled, "is not a traditional public forum for the expression of free speech.") To placate PETA, Elbaum and the selection committee allowed the organization to put up another cow in Greenwich Village dressed in imitation leather boots, jacket, and pants provided by a London-based designer of fetish sex apparel.

The cows were placed in public areas around New York City. One upright bovine dressed in judicial robes stood outside the federal courthouse in Manhattan, while an extravagantly dressed cow posed for the paparazzi outside the Bloomingdale's store. All in all, Cow Parade 2000 was well received and none of the cows ignited.

But sometime after 11 a.m. on June 28, the unthinkable happened. One of the most popular cows, Moo-Stripa, disappeared. The cow had distinguishing marks of orange, white, green, and blue stripes liberally laid on by the kids of PS 43 in the Queens. The cow was last seen securely (it was thought) bolted to a 500-pound concrete base. Police immediately suspected foul play, and a $1,000 reward was posted by Elbaum for information leading to the arrest and conviction of the cow rustler.

THE SWISS MISS

From start to finish, the episode that led up to Cow Parade 2000 "is another illustration of the failure by the Swiss to understand the Americans, how they do business, and American culture," said Peter Hossli, a Swiss reporter who covered the incendiary cow story for the Swiss weekly business magazine *Cash*. "The Swiss do not grasp the shrewdness of the Americans and the drive they have to get things done. In Switzerland, business is based on customs and personal relationships. In New York, it's based on legalities. The Swiss lost out again," Hossli told *The New York Times*.

As of this writing, the whereabouts of Moo-Stripa and the status of Switzerland's image is just about anyone's guess.

Now, to speak of real cows, maybe the Swiss should have taken a lesson from the marketing fiasco generated by the US Dairy Association when the association attempted to generate more business in Mexico for American milk producers. The association attempted to transplant its highly successful "Got Milk?" US advertising campaign south of border only to discover that the literal translation of its catchphrase appearing on billboards throughout Mexico read "Are You Lactating?"

Out of the Fast Lane and Into the Ditch (General Motors)

In the early 1990s, a tidal wave of product liability lawsuits crested and crashed on the US legal system, with results that are still felt today. Companies of all sizes in the widest spectrum of industry sectors across the country found themselves under siege—some legitimately, others not. Various consumer advocacy groups, environmental organizations, and individuals were charging businesses with negligence and disregard in their quest for corporate profit.

The charges against some companies were justified. But others, like General Motors, found their corporate reputations tarnished by design.

GENERAL MOTORS GETS BLINDSIDED

In the fall of 1992, GM found itself drawn into a controversy: consumer activists charged the automaker with negligently putting on the market pickup trucks with improperly positioned gas tanks. The activists said this flaw was responsible for more than 300 accident fatalities when the vehicles burst into flames during side-impact collisions.

As damaging as the charges were, they were overshadowed by a 15-minute news segment on the National Broadcasting Company *Dateline NBC* program—the show took GM to task, accusing the company of gross negligence. Centering on two side-impact collisions involving a pair of 1977 GM pickup trucks, the segment (entitled "Waiting to Explode?") caused a scandal when NBC later admitted that the producer had rigged the trucks with remote-controlled incendiary devices; the apparatus would ignite fuel spewing from the trucks' overfilled gasoline tanks, which had been fitted with the wrong size cap. Further, it was determined that the piece featured interviews with dubious experts and people involved either directly or indirectly with making a living from filing product liability lawsuits against companies like General Motors.

The president of the network resigned over the incident and NBC was compelled to make an apology. The network was made to repay the $2 million that GM was forced to spend to repair the damage to its reputation.

Volvo Gets Squashed

Just a year before the *Dateline NBC*-GM scandal, several thousand miles away, another automaker found itself, like GM, having to repair some major damage to its reputation. But, unlike General Motors, this damage was self-inflicted.

By the late 1990s, Volvo of Sweden had spent considerable time and effort establishing itself as one of the most efficient, dependable, and customer-conscious manufacturing concerns in the world. The company prided itself on the quality of its cars. At the time, more than 80 percent of its total annual revenue came from international sales. In 1990, the US Highway Loss Data Institute conducted a series of road tests that rated the Volvo station wagon as the safest car sold in the US compared with other similar vehicles produced in Europe, Japan, and the US. In 1944, during the height of World War II, the company had developed its "safety cage" design to crush-proof the passenger compartments of all its cars with reinforced steel door pillars and extra-thick steel plating on the roof and rocker panels. The concept exceeded many countries' mandated safety standards—it was so well designed that it's become an industry standard for virtually all passenger cars made anywhere in the world since the late 1940s.

Always extremely aware of its image, the company has spent millions to underscore its corporate dedication to passenger safety. Advertising campaigns have stressed not only the safety of its cars, but also the dedication of the company to its relationship with its faithful customer base.

Volvo scored big with an ad campaign based around the minimal hurricane damage sustained in the late 1980s by 54 Volvos that were waiting to be unloaded from a ship at the Port of Mobile, Alabama. Company engineers in Sweden had just recently determined that the strengthened door pillars in any Volvo were strong enough to support the weight of six more cars stacked on top of it. The automaker and its ad agency created a campaign centered around a photo of the cars with the tag line, "We sincerely hope you never find yourself in a predicament like this. But if you do, we sincerely hope you're in a Volvo." In early 1990, the company approved a magazine ad showing five photos of small children with the headline, "Are they as safe around town as they are around the house?"

That June, riding the wave of customer goodwill and confident of its position, Volvo decided to take the safety issue to the next level. The company tasked its advertising agency—New York-based Scali, McCabe, Sloves Inc.—with the job of developing a new campaign to drive the issue of safety home even further. The agency soon unveiled a new television ad. It was filmed in Austin, Texas, in front of a paid audience; the ad showed a supercharged so-called monster truck running over a line of parked cars, crushing every one to a pulp—every one, that is, except the lone Volvo. The response to the ad traversed the spectrum: *USA Today* called the TV ad the "best of the best" television promotions for 1991, while a columnist for *Adweek* said the monster truck approach "has all the obnoxious, annoying energy and quasi-phony spectacle of a wrestling match."

But the kudos would soon fall flat. Just a few months after the start of the ad blitz, reports began to circulate that the "crush" test had been rigged. The Volvo that survived the crush by the monster truck (dubbed "Bear Foot") had been artificially reinforced with steel and lumber braces, and the structural steel pillars in the other cars had been cut or removed. Texas Attorney General James Maddox filed charges against Volvo for fraud, stating in court documents that "the car-crushing competition was a hoax and a sham."

TELL US IT'S NOT SO, VOLVO!

Volvo immediately responded by organizing a joint press conference with Maddox, joined by William Hoover, senior vice president of Volvo Cars of North America. At the event, Hoover admitted that modifications had been made to the Volvo "for the purpose of filming" and to "insure the filming crew's safety, and also to "allow the Volvo to withstand the repeated runs by the monster truck."

It was "unfortunate," said Hoover, "that we didn't label the ad as a dramatization." In admitting its culpability, Volvo agreed to voluntarily withdraw the ad, reimburse the state attorney general's office for the costs incurred in its investigation, and publish a corrective statement. The latter—in the form of an open letter from John Nicolato, president of Volvo Cars of North America—eventually appeared in 19 Texas daily newspapers, *The Wall Street Journal,* and *USA Today.*

In August 1991, the Federal Trade Commission issued a consent decree that ordered Volvo and the ad agency to each pay a fine of $150,000 to settle federal charges that the ad campaign was misleading. An internal investigation of the affair was ordered by Pehr Gyllenhammer, president of Volvo in Sweden. As a result, Scali, McCabe, Sloves resigned the Volvo advertisement account, valued at $40 million, after a 23-year relationship.

With a new ad agency on board, Volvo went right back to trying to reestablish its credibility with the auto-buying public.

While some analysts felt that the heaviest hit resulting from the ill-starred ad campaign was taken by the advertising industry, some felt that the timing of the blunder couldn't have been worse. In the late 1980s, Volvo—like Mercedes, Volkswagen, and its Swedish counterpart and rival, Saab—was facing stiff competition from the Japanese, who had just begun their initial foray into the US luxury car market. Unable to compete with the Japanese in terms of price or performance, Volvo stood apart from the competition with its long-standing, unchallenged reputation for safety—at least before its reputation was almost flattened by, of all things, an oversized, fire-breathing "muscle" truck.

Playing the Numbers Game (Avis and Hertz; Pepsi and Coca-Cola)

AND THE WINNING NUMBER IS...

Sometimes good things can come from being "number two." In the 1960s, Avis, the second-ranking car-rental agency in the US created a highly successful advertising campaign aimed at appealing to the American penchant to root for the underdog. Avis took the wraps off its "We Try Harder" slogan. In doing so, Avis effectively defined its competition with mega-market dominator and arch-rival Hertz as a David-and-Goliath-like battle for the hearts and minds of customers. The company recognized that, bottom line, the customers have the make-or-break power to choose the company that will get their business. Avis's message: we may be smaller, but we go the extra mile for you because we want your business.

The car rental agency spun off a major promotional distribution of campaign buttons carrying the "We Try Harder" slogan. They were produced in more than 30 languages, including Finnish, Chinese, Arabic, Japanese, Korean, and Russian—to appeal to foreign travelers visiting the US. The buttons found their way onto the uniforms of Olympic team members; they showed up particularly on those from smaller, supposedly less-competitive countries, who wanted to show the world that they were at the Olympics to compete, not to roll over and play dead.

Perhaps if a few buttons had made their way to Eastern Airlines, that company would have had a longer life, but being in the number two position doesn't always mean that a company tries harder. Several years ago, the US Department of Transportation conducted a historical review of the on-time performance of all major US domestic air carriers. The review covered a 25-year period and determined which ten airlines could boast the best on-time performance records. Number two on the list was Eastern Airlines, with an astounding 88.1 percent ranking. Punctual as the airline may have been, it hadn't had a plane in the air since 1991, when the sputtering air carrier was micro-managed into the ground—never to fly again.

Avis was successful because it did, in fact, try harder.

PEPSI-COLA "SPINS" THE WRONG NUMBER

A similar approach backfired with dire consequences, though, when Pepsi-Cola was a little too creative in its attempt to snatch market share from The Coca-Cola Company in the Philippines.

To say that Pepsi-Cola sodas were number two in the Philippine soft-drink market in late 1991 would have been a model of understatement. The New York based company had actually seen its share of the country's cola and non-cola beverage market shrink to an anemic 17 percent, while Coca-Cola dominated the scene with 75 percent. This was a complete turnaround of fortune from the early 1980s, when Pepsi was "King Cola" in the island nation. To make matters worse, another competitor had emerged, the homegrown Cosmos Bottling Company, which was holding a steady 8 percent cut of the business.

Something had to be done. Company management in Purchase, New York, wanted to light a fire under the company's international business and "burn" rival Coca-Cola to the core with $2 billion in global sales by 1992 and $5 billion just three years later.

In December 1991, Pepsi-Cola headquarters dispatched Pedro Vergara, a Latin American marketing expert, to the Philippines to help create an effective advertising and promotions program to jump-start operations there. After several weeks of burning the midnight oil, Vergara decided on a scheme that had proven moderately effective in boosting Pepsi-Cola's market share in ten Latin American companies in the past. Called "Numbers Fever," the plan combined the universal attraction of instant wealth with the Philippine fondness for gambling in all its forms.

The plan was simple: the underside of the bottle caps of three of Pepsi-Cola's best-selling drinks—7-Up, *Mountain Dew*, and *Miranda Orange*—would contain three imprinted markings—a three-digit number from 001 to 999; a cash prize amount ranging from 1000 pesos (about $40) to 1 million pesos (about $40,000); and a seven-digit alphanumeric code to ensure security, prevent tampering, and authenticate the numbers imprinted on the caps.

The cash prize payout amounted to 10 prizes of 1 million pesos; 40 of 100,000 pesos; 80 of 50,000 pesos; 500 of 10,000 pesos; and 5,000 of 1,000 pesos. Pepsi-Cola would announce a winning three-digit number every day from Monday through Friday. And the winning number for the following day would be announced each evening on national television, 29 radio stations across the country, and in the morning editions of four major metropolitan daily newspapers.

The promotion period was scheduled to run from February 17 to May 8, 1992. Although all caps were imprinted with cash prize amounts, buyers wouldn't know if they'd won until the three-digit number was announced.

This is where things started to get a little dicey.

WELCOME TO THE PROMOTION PIT

Pepsi-Cola in New York had contracted with a highly recommended Mexican consulting firm to oversee the management of the promotion. The Mexican company, D.G. Consultores, would use a computer to randomly preselect a list of 60 winning numbers and their security codes—that is, 60 winning numbers seeded among 5,630 bottle caps out of the 288 million bottles produced during the prize period. The odds were strong—some would say outrageously so—in Pepsi's favor: with only ten 1-million-peso prizes, laying out the figures showed that a Pepsi-Cola customer would have a 1-in-28.8-million chance of winning 1 million pesos. That made the chances of hitting the Pepsi jackpot the same as standing still in one spot and, over the course of an average lifetime, being hit by lightning three times.

Within a month, Pepsi's market share in the Philippines soared, with total sales exceeding the costs associated in crafting the Numbers Fever campaign. By the end of March, Pepsi's Manila plant was humming 20 hours a day, with the company claiming a 24.9 percent cut of the market. Meanwhile, Coca-Cola and Cosmos saw their share cut to 68.8 percent and 4.2 percent, respectively.

The campaign took rival Coca-Cola completely by surprise, occurring just two weeks before it planned to launch its own $3-million-prize bottle-top promotion. "We were really concerned," said one Coca-Cola executive in Manila. "The rise in Pepsi sales was really dramatic."

According to one observer, more than half the population of the country (about 63 million at the time) participated in the promotion at one point or another, and its success prompted Pepsi to extend the promotion for 5 more weeks, from May 10 to June 12. Finding itself caught up in its own heady success, Pepsi-Cola told a frenzied public that it would "sweeten the pot" by offering a total of 1,635 more prizes that would total more than 10 million pesos during the extension period. The enhanced promotion would include eight 1-million-peso winners, and a new 1,000-peso category with one thousand winners.

Pepsi was riding high. But on May 25, exactly halfway through the extension period, it all came crashing down. The company was assured by its Mexican consulting company that a non-winning number in the pre-extension promotional period would not be picked as a 1-million-peso winner by its computer. Oops. The consultant was wrong. Pepsi selected number 349 as the winner. It was a nonwinning number in the first phase of the promotion—however, as many as 800,000 bottle tops had been imprinted with that number before May 10.

The reaction was immediate, as the company's offices were flooded with calls from winners demanding their prize money. An emergency meeting of Pepsi Cola Products Philippines Inc. (PCPPI) lasted into the early morning hours of May 26. Angry crowds assembled around the company's two largest bottling plants near Manila, as well as at other company offices and facilities around the country. But what struck cold terror into the hearts of PCPPI management was the fact that as many as 400,000 of the 349-imprinted bottle caps were 1-million-peso winners.

The potential cost of the blunder was astronomically staggering. Paying off the 400,000 people who had 1-million-peso winning bottle caps would cost the company US$16 billion. That would be, according to one analyst, more than the $15 billion market capitalization of all 273 issues listed on the Philippine stock exchange in June 1992.

Pepsi attempted to placate an angry public—and an even angrier government in Manila—with an across-the-board 500-peso payoff to all 349 bottle-top holders. The outlay drained the company of US$10 million. However, the larger toll for the fiasco made truly somber reading: two people were killed and scores injured in several riots; 38 Pepsi trucks and vehicles were destroyed or damaged; facilities were vandalized; and more than 10,000 civil lawsuits were filed against Pepsi in the Philippine's notoriously Byzantine court system. The suits still occupy much of the company's legal staff's time.

In the years immediately following the now-infamous "349 Incident," Pepsi-Cola saw its share of the Philippine market drop to an all-time low of 7.6 percent. Six-thousand five-hundred of the lawsuits against the company were dismissed as then-Philippine President Fidel Ramos steadfastly refused to intervene, allowing the legal actions against Pepsi to run their course.

In 1994, as the issue seemed to be winding down somewhat, the 349 case hit the headlines again, when proceedings against Pepsi were suspended after Pepsi claimed that a fair trial wasn't possible, because a significant number of the people still pursuing legal redress against the company had failed to fill out the questionnaires sent them to verify their claims that they were indigent. An appeals court upheld the suspension, but in late 1998 the Philippine Supreme Court ordered that the original trial be resumed.

In January of that year, a Manila City court ordered the company to pay the 349 winners a total of 10.8 million pesos in damages. The court concluded that the company "must have known of the injurious effect that its reckless public announcement and subsequent turnabout would have upon its customers."

It's important to note that Pepsi Cola Products Philippines Inc. neither created nor oversaw the 349 promotion. The idea was devised by a marketing staffer from the company headquarters in Purchase, New York, and launched based on its success in other markets. PCPPI input in planning or implementing the promotional campaign was minimal—but, in the eyes of the Philippine consumer, the local subsidiary company (not so much the multinational in far-off Purchase, New York) was to blame.

SAME SONG, DIFFERENT VERSE

Pepsi would have done well if it had learned a lesson from the difficulties it encountered during a similar bottle-cap advertising/promotion campaign in Chile. In the spring of 1992, one of Pepsi's largest bottlers in the country—Embotelladora Chile—refused to pay off the holders of the original winning number announced during its own *Numbers Fever* promotion. The bottler claimed that the incorrect number (688) was made public because of the misreading of a smudged facsimile transmission, what it called a "human and involuntary error."

The correct number, the company said, was 588. Despite a huge public outcry, the government found that neither Pepsi nor Embotelladora Chile were at fault, a decision that was made after the direct intervention of Chilean president General Augusto Pinochet.

Hoover Gets Sucked Into Its Own Vortex

Although not as staggering as Pepsi's 349 fiasco, Hoover Europe Ltd. (HEL) had a similar experience. The London-based subsidiary of the venerable Maytag Corp. of Newton, Iowa, exhibited an almost fatal lack of common sense in a total misread of the company's customer base.

Hoover Europe suffered a major blow in 1992 when it tried to recapture its share of the household appliance market in the United Kingdom. The company's marketing crew came up with the idea of offering customers in both the UK and Ireland free airline tickets with certain appliance and floor-care purchases. The plan called for a very high profile—they advertised in major newspapers and magazines, as well as television commercials and radio spots. The half-baked nature of the plan became glaringly evident when more than 200,000 customers qualified for the tickets—a figure more than three times greater than the company had originally intended.

Telephone calls from qualifying customers were disconnected and letters were ignored. Those disgruntled buyers who wanted to find out firsthand what had happened showed up at the company's imposing headquarters, only to be turned away with shrugged shoulders and no answers.

The overcooked promotion eventually cost HEL almost $49 million (pretax) more than it had originally budgeted with Maytag. This forced Maytag to take a $30 million after-tax write-off the first quarter of the following year to compensate for the loss.

Sadly, Hoover Europe's reputation took an even heavier hit because the company refused to fulfill the promises it had made to customers who legitimately qualified for the free flights. This precipitated a marketing blunder that turned into a customer relations catastrophe. The media reported on how the company was expending its energy to duck responsibility and affix blame everywhere other than where it really belonged, and the public's reservoir of good will ran dry.

In the end, Hoover Europe's president was joined in the unemployment line by the company's vice president of UK marketing and its director of European marketing services. But the greatest loss and lesson to learn was the unmasking of Hoover Europe as a company that really wasn't interested in taking care of its customers after all.

My Product Can Beat Up Your Product

Like all companies, Volvo, Pepsi, and Maytag in their own way thrive on competition. They must or they wouldn't be successful.

In the US, firms of all sizes can take full advantage of comparatively liberal federal laws that allow (with some reservations) so-called comparative advertising. During the early 1970s, a series of landmark rulings by the Federal Trade Commission in Washington, DC, cleared the way for the use of comparison advertising. Such advertising allows a company to position its product with a similar product made by a competitor based on a comparison— bigger, better, faster, and more stylish, for example. A 1998 study by the American Academy of Advertising shows that almost 40 percent of all advertising in the US is comparative in nature.

Many countries around the world place a taboo on comparative advertising, for a myriad of legal and cultural reasons. A primary reason is that comparative advertising is seen as ruthless and amoral. At one extreme is US political advertising, about which it is said that truth has no standing and anything goes in the quest for votes. At the other end of the spectrum, the Japanese are distinctly nonconfrontational in both their business and personal lives. Indeed, some Americans may relish a "get in your face" approach, but in Japan such a tack inevitably results in long-term damage to any relationship.

PEPSI CHALLENGE BACKFIRES IN JAPAN, SCORES IN INDIA

Thus, when Pepsi-Cola decided to take its "Pepsi Challenge" to Japan in 1994, the Japanese didn't respond as planned. The company wanted to transplant its successful US television ad campaign to Japan, but did not consider the cultural nuances involved. The ad starred rap music icon M.C. Hammer and was staged as a comparison taste test of the Pepsi and Coca-Cola cola drinks. It didn't take a genius to figure out who the winner would be, and the obvious contrived nature of the advertisements caused all five major television stations in Tokyo to refuse to air the campaign.

Just a year earlier, Pepsi ran into the same hurdle in Argentina. That country's legal system does not specifically prohibit comparative advertising, but since 1971 it has had a law on the books making the use of a competitor's trademark without its consent in an advertising campaign an act of "unfair competition."

Pepsi found a smoother ride in India, where comparative advertising is marginally legal, even though the strategy it took might have been illegal in other countries. In India, Pepsi battled with Coca-Cola from a rare position of strength. Pepsi has been selling its products in India since the government opened the market to foreign competition in 1991, and it has held a firm grip on a substantial share of the country's $1 billion soft-drink market. India is one country where icon Coca-Cola sodas actually come in third, after Pepsi and the locally made competitor soft drink, *Thums Up*. In fact, Coca-Cola left the country in 1977 and didn't return to compete in the Indian market until 1993.

Both Pepsi and Coca-Cola have pumped millions of dollars into advertising and marketing in India, aimed specifically at attracting the under-18 consumer, which in early 2000 comprised nearly one-third of the country's total population. A 1997 industry study (quoted in an article in the June 2000 issue of *Asiaweek* magazine) forecasts that the Indian soft drink market will expand in value to around $2.4 billion by 2005. This growth will be driven, in large part, by the changes in drinking and eating habits of the country's youth. Per capita soft drink consumption, it said, is 6 bottles a year, compared with 15 in Pakistan, 22 in China, and more than 600 in Mexico.

"Drinking a cola is not an everyday habit," said one Indian beverage executive in the piece. "It is reserved for special occasions—religious festivals, family outings, and sporting events." This is what both Pepsi and Coca-Cola set out to change. The potential was staggering: just increase consumption by one soft drink a day—no, just one a week—and the faces of the High and Mighty Ones in far-off Purchase, New York, and Atlanta, Georgia would smile.

Envisioning millions of hyperactive, hip, culture-conscious Indian teenagers searching for "The Real Thing," Coca-Cola took the first shot in what's come to be known as "The Great Cola War." The company beat out Pepsi by putting enough money on the table to sign India's then teenage heartthrob, Hrithik Roshan, as its pitchman and as star of a 60-second TV commercial *cum* music video promotion. The ad was choreographed and shot in record time.

The Coca-Cola campaign was derailed, though, when Pepsi countered with its own television advertisement. Produced from the outset as a slam at Hrithik, the Pepsi commercial featured a Hrithik look-alike, wearing glasses and braces on his teeth. He is spurned by a lovely young woman, who, in turn, kisses Shah

Rukh Khan—another famous Indian movie star who had already been Pepsi's commercial spokesman for several years.

Stung by the humiliation, Hrithik wrote an "open letter" to Pepsi's Indian management, while newspapers in Bombay (known as "Bollywood," the capital of the Indian movie industry) and New Delhi were bombarded by thousands of letters from loyal fans. Hrithik's admirers also organized a huge anti-Pepsi demonstration in Calcutta. Pepsi, tongue in cheek, denied that the young man in its commercial was meant to be a spoof of Hrithik. In the words of a company spokesman, said with a straight face: "There's only a passing resemblance."

Just four years earlier, Pepsi had taken another swipe at Coca-Cola when it produced a TV commercial that poked fun at Coca-Cola's $4 million bid to be named the "official sponsor" of the 1996 Cricket World Cup. Pepsi's satiric commercial took several shots at its arch-rival by capitalizing on the disdain most Indian youth have for anything "official." The dueling commercials had the effect of positioning Coca-Cola sodas as the more sophisticated drink with a more mature pedigree, while Pepsi scored a few points by creating an image as the beverage of choice for younger, more independent, free-thinkers.

Many people actually saw the whole fracas as entertaining. According to a consultant with McKinsey & Company in Bombay, "The more the competition, the more the noise, the better. It'll help the soft-drink market to take off." As Vibha Rishi, Pepsi's marketing manager for India, said at the time, "It was barrels of fun."

LOCAL RULES... GLOBAL HEADACHES

Comparative advertising elsewhere, though, can lead to a company having to deal with barrels filled with something other than fun. While some countries straightforwardly exert rigid controls over advertising of all kinds—Myanmar and China immediately come to mind—others exercise exasperating selectiveness; the Australian government, for example, requires that advertising of any kind be locally produced.

In Brazil, advertising industry regulations are so strict "that no advertiser...has been able to create a comparative advertising spot that hasn't been challenged and subsequently stopped," wrote Rik Turner in a September 1991 edition of *Advertising Age* magazine. He wrote: "The code, which dates back to 1978, specifies comparative advertising can be used only when there is an objective statistical basis, when the advertising seeks to clarify positioning, and when the products compete in the same product segment."

EUROPE LEVELS THE PLAYING FIELD... SORT OF

Utilizing comparative advertising in Europe has always been a challenge—even after formation of the European Union (EU). Every new member nation has its own rules and standards. But all that changed in the spring of 2000. That was when the European Commission in Brussels approved a directive compelling each member of the EU to implement bloc-wide regulations on the approved usage of comparative advertising. The new directive was hammered out in 1997 after more than six years of sometimes heated debate. It effectively neutralized the disparity of regulations that made comparative advertising in the EU a nightmare for companies wanting to tout their products there.

While allowing each member country to continue, at least for now, to maintain some control on other forms of advertising, the directive permits comparative advertising throughout the 18-member (and ever-growing) EU if it follows prescribed guidelines: the advertisement must not be misleading. It must take into account "objectively comparable" goods and services. In addition, the advertiser must ensure that the piece "does not give rise to confusion" in the marketplace. And it can not "discredit or denigrate" a competitor. Nor can it address goods or services that are reproductions or imitations of protected names and trademarks.

Anecdotes about companies caught up in the web of regulations before the directive went into effect are legion. Prior to the directive, Belgium, Luxembourg, and Germany had all banned comparative advertising. In 1997 a German judge in Frankfurt ruled that a local company providing a link to an American Internet web site that featured comparative advertising was liable for the site's "unfair commercial practices." The relationship between the German firm and the US-based web site was a breach of Germany's national competition law. The German company was ordered to sever its link to the US Internet site and pay the damages that the court said the relationship had caused the plaintiff.

Prior to the EU directive, it was assumed in France that any Internet web site in the French language was automatically targeting French customers. Therefore, it was subject to all the French regulations regarding advertising and sponsorship. For example, the maze of French laws that applied to advertising prevented not only overtly comparative advertising, but any ads that "evoke sympathy." Thus, before the implementation of the new EU directive, the French media banned all commercials for groups that solicited money for starving or orphaned children in Africa or Bosnia.

Procter & Gamble (P&G)—which, incidentally, spends more money on advertising than any other company in the world—found itself on the threshold of things to come in Sweden in 1994. P&G was fined $30,000 by a local court for "falsely advertising" its *Ariel* line of household detergents. An expensive advertising campaign for *Ariel Ultra* and *Ariel Color* had claimed that they were better than the competition—without even specifically alluding to or naming the other competing brands.

In England, Burger King lost in court when its campaign to compare the qualities of its signature *Whopper* hamburger with those sold by rival McDonald's backfired. In the late 1990s, the company had launched a series of television commercials and newspapers with the tag line, "It's not just big, Mac." The ads centered on the perceived positives of the Burger King product— 100 percent pure beef that was flame-broiled, never fried, and a choice of toppings. Alluding in this way to the "mass produced" fare served at McDonald's led to a suit in British court.

US-based McDonald's charged Burger King—which has a huge US presence though owned by a British parent—with "passing off," or misrepresenting a competitor, in British legal parlance. The company also charged that Burger King's claims were "maliciously false"; McDonald's alleged that the claims were not only inaccurate, but were "maliciously intended" to harm their reputation. McDonald's won the suit, but the action compelled the presiding judge to comment that "it's all very sad and all very silly."

HOW DO YOU INSULT TWO ISLANDS? (McDONALD'S)

On another occasion, McDonald's found itself having to pump out an oil slick to calm the waters of a minor storm it created for itself when it tried to parlay a local bias into a positive marketing message. The company produced a television advertisement in The Netherlands ridiculing the chances of the Maltese football (European football, that is) team to win the Euro 2000 championship scheduled for that summer. The commercial showed a line of actors wearing Maltese team uniforms, standing in line to buy tickets for the upcoming championship event. The implication was that this was the only way the team would ever get into the finals. In April 2000, the company found itself having to issue an official apology to the tiny island nation of Malta.

"It is never our intention to offend anyone and we have apologized in a letter to the Maltese Football Association," said a spokesman for McDonald's Netherlands. The ad also showed actors portraying the Icelandic football team waiting in line, "but no complaint has yet been received from Iceland."

Incidentally, neither country qualified for Euro 2000. No one has looked into the possibility that the commercial impacted their performance.

Sometimes the Pegs Fit, Sometimes They Don't

Every year, companies all over the world spend billions of dollars trying to create, improve, maintain, or adapt the image they want to present to potential customers. In 1998, *Ad Age International* magazine published results of a survey of the top multinational advertisers. Procter & Gamble topped the list spending $5.7 billion, General Motors ranked second with $4 billion in global ad expenditures, Unilever followed with $3.4 billion, then Philip Morris with $2.9 billion, Toyota Motor Corp. spent $2.1 billion, Ford $2.1 billion, and Nestle SA $1.8 billion. Rounding out the Top 10 list were Coca-Cola ($1.7 billion), McDonald's ($1.6 billion), and Sony ($1.5 billion). In fact, the galactically lucrative business of creating global images has placed several international advertising agencies, such as Dentsu, McCann-Erickson, J. Walter Thompson, and BBDO Worldwide, on the list of the top revenue-generating companies in the world.

An international advertising campaign, like the product it's touting, is most effective if it is crafted in a way that best suits the idiosyncrasies and tastes of the target market. Some companies' best results come from nuances in the ads that are so subtle to most viewers or readers that the message almost seamlessly transcends any cultural differences existing between the company and the intended customers. Other companies, however, link their product and the buyer or end user in a manner so vague or amorphous that to an outsider it seems as if the ad has no connection whatsoever with the product.

TONY THE TIGER GETS IT RIGHT

A good example of the former is the global campaign for Kellogg's *Frosted Flakes* cereal, a product that has market share in virtually every developed country in the world. The company produces essentially the same television advertisements anywhere you go, but with very minor changes that help them effectively penetrate their respective targeted markets. Potential buyers don't have to make a great leap of cultural faith when purchasing the product.

In the European edition of the textbook *The Principles of Marketing*, the authors cite the effectiveness of one of Kellog's most successful international advertising campaigns. Based on a common tennis theme, Kellogg's "generic" international TV ad campaign featured teenagers who looked neither too European nor too Latin American. The teenagers were completing a match with Kellogg's character "Tony the Tiger." In the English version, he growls the familiar, "They're Gr-r-r-eat!," while in German, it's "Gr-r-rossartig!" In the US ad, the animated Tony leaps over the net in celebration after winning the match against his human opponent. In the European version, he "high-fives" his opponent. Europeans wouldn't leap over the net after besting an opponent in a tennis game—to do so would be considered rude and obnoxious.

Incidentally, though, the company did miss the mark when it advertised one of its most popular products in Sweden. The company thought it was using a translation for "Bran Buds," but instead it was telling customers that they were buying boxes filled with "Burnt Farmer."

TIMELESSNESS AND TIME

On the other side of the spectrum was a television ad that ran in Japan a few years ago for a readily identifiable manufacturer of high-quality wrist watches. The ad's quality was superb and the professionalism of the production itself—from the costuming and the scenery to the photography—underscored the value of the timepieces it was designed to promote.

Everything in the ad dated the scene at around 1905, the time of the Russo-Japanese War: a steam engine hissed in the background to the foreground of troops in uniforms and accoutrements rushing to board the train. A young couple, the man in an army uniform and a beautiful girl dressed in kimono, stood on a train platform looking longingly into each other's eyes. The scenario was obvious—the brave young soldier was off to war, and his beloved would wait for him. He boards the train and it chugs off with an army band playing an appropriately muted martial air in the background. No words are spoken as the young couple, their eyes still locked on one another, wordlessly communicate their love as others cheer the send-off. The train whistle sounds farewell.

Only at the end of the visually stunning piece (a sort of Kurosawa meets *Masterpiece Theatre* effect) did viewers learn what company—that's company, not product—was being touted. The name of the internationally known company that created the ad was flashed discreetly in the lower right-hand corner of the TV screen.

Anyone, anywhere would be drawn into the ad. The identification was immediate. With virtually no dialogue, the ad drew the viewer back in time and into an emotionally touching universal human condition that transcends both time and culture—war forcing the separation of two young people who are deeply in love. But overshadowing it all was her unspoken promise that, yes, she would wait for him and count the minutes until his safe return...on her *Seiko* watch.

TRYING TO WRITE IN THE RIGHT STYLE

Most international advertising campaigns, however, fall into the middle ground between the two opposite approaches taken by Kellog and Seiko. Most standardize their message from country to country, attempting to appeal to perceived values and positive images. This challenge to keep many balls in the air at the same time sometimes results in amusing faux pas—spectacular for their seeming innocence and blissful ignorance of how images are best crafted to potential foreign customers. Just about everybody stumbles at one time or another.

Parker Pen, for example. The Wisconsin-based manufacturer of fine pens has traditionally based its international advertising campaign on market themes that stress positive images like style and high quality. In the US, its ads emphasize status and image, while in Germany, the company's most successful magazine advertisement simply showed a hand holding a Parker pen with the headline, "This is how you write with precision." In England, where the company has been the longtime market leader, the ad stressed the time invested in the process of making the pens.

In Mexico, however, the company's efforts to emphasize the inherent quality of its pens fell flat. Wanting to position itself ahead of the producers of generic ballpoint pens, Parker zeroed in on one of the most annoying tendencies of inexpensive, poorly made writing instruments—their nasty habit of leaking and causing an embarrassing stain. The company contracted for advertising space in several of the country's classier magazines. Business professionals were the target audience. The ad was supposed to read, "Parker. It won't leak in your pocket and embarrass you." Incorrectly assuming that the Spanish word "enbarazar" means "embarrass," the company produced an ad telling Mexican business men that "It won't leak in your pocket and make you pregnant."

Lessons Learned

Tales of combustible fiberglass cows, rigged television commercials, promotional campaigns centered around decidedly wrong numbers, and the unintentional claim that a leaky pen might lead to pregnancy—these all could be grist for the Friday night lineup at the local comedy club. Nonetheless they provide concrete examples of what can happen when an intentional advertising strategy has been given insufficient thought.

ANTICIPATE MARKET REACTION

As shown in example after example, when companies pump money indiscriminately into an advertising campaign without giving serious thought to the ad's cultural and social implications, the money has, simply, been thrown away. The most crucial element of any international advertising or promotional campaign is a thorough knowledge of the likes and dislikes, nuances and peccadilloes of the consumers in the target market. The range of considerations is probably more comprehensive than any other component of a well-crafted international marketing plan—including everything from color and sexual predilections to gestures and the viability of discount promotions.

Companies that have had marked success globally are those that have carefully read their target markets, and even more importantly have shunned sensitive issues. A good example is the innocuous tennis match concocted by Kellog's and only slightly altered from country to country to avoid bad press from an overly exuberant winning tiger. On the other hand, playing on local bias may seem funny at the time, but it ignores sensitivities among the insulted market segment and can cause whiplash, as McDonald's learned in its Netherlands poke at the Maltese football team. Humor across country borders is tough but important to understand, also, as the Swiss learned when their gift to America intended for the burgeoning artists of New York City's boroughs became a canvas for the tongue-in-cheek American sense of humor.

Comparative advertising is an especially tempting scenario in the marketing world, but this ploy must fit the market—both in terms of legality and cultural tastes—to succeed. Thus, Pepsi fell flat in Japan when it introduced aggressive comparative advertising without recognizing the Japanese penchant for more subtle, nonconfrontational messages. On the other hand, rival Coca-Cola's campaign for the India market forgot that by appealing to loyal fans of one popular star, it opened the door for a Pepsi retort.

THE MORAL: Remember that advertising must deliver a message to a target audience in a language they can understand; and if they laugh, it's best to make sure they're laughing with you, not at you. Just ask Parker Pen.

HOLD THE REINS

Most company managers will agree that allowing any program or project to run unchecked is likely to have disastrous effects. Checks and balances—which work so well in government—are also essential in the operation of a business. In the advertising and marketing department, ideas may be allowed to flow freely, but someone must still be holding the reins.

If this is a widely recognized principle, why then do some promotions simply spin out of control? Often, the answer lies in short-circuiting the necessary research and homework on the targeted market, which is considered less important than getting the word out immediately at minimal cost. Thus, Hoover presents such an alluring package that it is overwhelmed with the unanticipated response and cannot deliver on its promises, causing its reputation to crash instead of fly. The Swiss try to build a relationship of trust and good will with America, but fail to realize that cow art—and for that matter cows—does not elicit great reverence on the other side of the Atlantic, particularly when the cows are incendiary. Nor is it wise to bring a promotion to fever pitch without careful control, as Pepsi came to know in its Philippine and Chile fiascoes.

THE MORAL: A success in one market does not automatically translate into success in another. Every promotion requires consideration of market reaction and thorough planning of the logistics, plus an emergency plan to reassure the public and keep the promises made.

OFFER WHAT THE COMPETITION CAN'T

The best marketing strategy is not always the most obvious. Going nose to nose with the competition in a direct or indirect comparative advertising campaign is like going into court without a witness—it's your word against the other party's word. Why should the public believe you, or for that matter, either of you? On the other hand, your company's unique characteristics can make it great, provided that you in fact back up your claims.

To rise out of the competition requires a considered analysis of the needs of different segments of the market. This analysis is aimed at finding a market niche of consumers that are not satisfied. So if you are second in market share, perhaps you should try harder and mean it, like Avis did, to attract customers who appreciate the diligent service of the underdog. The leading competitor in market share certainly won't claim to be number two.

THE MORAL: Give the market what it wants, particularly when your competition can't and therefore won't be able to attack you.

GET THE FACTS STRAIGHT

It's a fact that lies and cover-ups just don't work very well. False and misleading advertising will quickly and sometimes permanently disillusion consumers, let alone that it is prohibited and sanctioned in most countries. Politicians are commonly lambasted for not telling it straight, but for some reason this lesson is hard to learn and easy to forget.

Outright dishonesty is not a recommended advertising strategy, but worse is a company's attempt to justify what seems to be a public lie with what seems to be a lame excuse. Such justification tends to lower a company's credibility even more. The great monster truck crush test devised by Volvo's advertising team was a fun spectacle, but turned into a debacle with the news that the car had been reinforced, if only for filming that required reshoot after reshoot.

Professed public abhorrence for falsehoods—never mind that everyone privately tells at least a little lie once a day—creates vulnerability. Whether ugly rumors begin with a competitor or an overzealous consumer watch group, they can cause havoc to a company that is otherwise well-known for its quality and honesty in the marketplace. General Motors has paid the price for unverified and even false news reporting, as have many other companies. But imagine what the price would have been if the news reports had been true.

THE MORAL: Never say "I do" when you don't.

A Ladder to Advertising Success

The purpose of any advertising plan is to get potential customers to buy a particular product or service. To achieve that goal, a series of questions need to be addressed. In fashioning your advertising plan, be sure to answer all the following:

1. What is the true purpose of your advertising campaign? Is it intended to create an image for your company? Is it intended to create such an impression that consumers will remember your brand and seek it out among the competitors? Or are you trying to develop a sense of identification between the consumer and the product or service?

2. Do you go nose to nose with the competition in terms of positioning your product or service in the marketplace? How do you set yourself apart from your competitors given the restrictions that might exist on comparative advertising in your target market?

3. Which medium—radio, magazines, newspapers, television, the Internet—is best suited to your purpose?

4. How do you use the media to your best advantage?

5. How do you find the right advertising agency to handle your business? What qualities are you looking for in an agency? Is there an agency whose work you admire? Does that agency have experienced in promoting a product or service like yours? Think carefully before selecting an agency that is inexperienced with regard to promotions in your industry.

6. Are you expecting too much from your advertising campaign? Does your product or service live up the advertised claims? Don't expect a finely crafted image to compensate for a poorly produced product or service or an inability to provide support and follow-up services to customers.

CHAPTER 6

Japan: A World Unto Itself

A MOST MISUNDERSTOOD MARKET

FEW COUNTRIES "have been more copiously described than Japan, and perhaps few have been less thoroughly understood." So stated Edwin Reischauer, the noted academic, historian, and former US ambassador to Japan, in writing many years ago about the relationship between Japan and the rest of the world.

The United States and Japan have each subconsciously cultivated a sophisticated form of protectionism. Each has, in its own way, fended off the other even though—despite their checkered histories—they rely heavily on one another politically and economically.

Japan is much maligned in the United States as a totally closed export market where it's virtually impossible for any US-based company to succeed. This perspective persists despite the fact that Japan is currently the third largest market in the world for American-made products and has historically run a trade surplus with virtually ever country it does business with, not just the US.

On the other side of the coin, Japanese insularity and cultural arrogance has many subtle, and exasperating, forms. For traders, perhaps the most obvious are the country's convoluted distribution system and continuation of an almost feudal concept of society that unnecessarily complicates the internal processes involved in facilitating foreign commerce. While blame abounds on both sides of the Pacific, Japan remains a mystery to many Americans, as does America to many Japanese. In a sense, our mutual pasts tend to cloud our future excessively. The results, in their turn, are often outrageously amusing and profoundly vexing.

While attending business school in Japan, I can remember seeing a cartoon in a weekly business newspaper that profoundly underscored the love-hate symbiosis that has overshadowed economic relations between the US and Japan. Two men, one Japanese and the other American, sit quietly on a bench in one of the small parks that dot metro Tokyo. The Japanese speaks: "Johnson-san, I understand your company is sending you back to your home office in New York. I want you to know how much I've valued our friendship." The American responds: "Thank you, Sato-san. We have grown close over the past 20 years. I will miss you." A long pause. "That's just like you Americans," Sato-san concludes, "Here today and gone tomorrow."

Otter Pelts and Culture Clash

It was, after all, pure business.

Through the second half of the 18th century, the trading posts along the northwest coasts of the North American Pacific had supplied the Hong merchants of China with beaver pelts. The Chinese held a firm grip on the trade, leaving little opportunity outside their far-ranging sphere of influence. However, they maintained their grip on the lucrative trade through artificial controls that, at any given time, could sharply undercut the profit a shipment might bring.

The situation was fairly straightforward. After a transpacific journey of several weeks, Captain John Kendrick, a hard-nosed New England Yankee with a reputation as both a keen navigator and a shrewd businessman, sailed his little brig, the 170-ton *Lady Washington* of Boston, into the south China port of Lark's Bay. On arrival, he found that fur prices in China had hit bottom and he would hardly recoup the cost of the voyage if he unloaded his cargo there. So, in mid-March 1791, the *Lady Washington*—her hold crammed with pungent bales of Northwest sea otter pelts, copper, iron, and firearms—sailed out of port. She was accompanied by another, smaller American-flag sloop, the Grace of New York. They were seeking untapped markets and, of course, a tidy profit.

In early April, driven north by the so-called Black Current, the *Lady Washington* and the *Grace*, under the command of Captain William Douglas, made landfall dropping anchor in the protected bay adjacent to the small Japanese town of Kushimoto, at the southernmost tip of the main Japanese island of Honshu. Quite by accident they had become the very first American ships to visit the "Land of the Rising Sun." The time that both ships spent anchored in the bay provided what could be seen as a template for an overall analysis of US-Japan trade relations.

For the 150 years preceding the visit of the *Lady Washington*, Japan had hidden itself from the world behind a tightly-woven curtain of self-imposed isolation and draconian protectionism. The empire had severely limited its exposure to outside influences and rigidly controlled its foreign commerce to the little business it did with the Dutch. Japan saw itself as a nation—if not a world apart—entirely self-sufficient and unwilling to risk the social corrosion that exposure to "barbarian" ways would have on its highly structured, homogeneous society.

BARBARIANS, DISGRACE, AND AN UNFRIENDLY DOG

One of the few surviving contemporary Japanese documents produced during the *Lady Washington's* visit refers to it as a "disgrace" to Japan. The document alludes to the embarrassment of the Kushimoto authorities at being unable to prevent the "barbarian" foreign sailors from setting foot on Japanese soil and foraging for water and firewood.

That last issue underscores the others. Kendrick had on board three Chinese who he had hired as shipwrights and carpenters. Their usefulness as interpreters was limited and they could communicate only the most basic information on the name of the ship, her captain, nationality, and the cargo. The local Japanese authorities—thinking that all foreigners spoke Dutch—prevailed on a learned doctor from a nearby town to assist. Approaching the *Lady Washington* by boat, the good doctor was warned off by the sailors, who later permitted another villager to climb aboard. What would have been in itself a historic event was cut short when the ship's dog chased the man back over the side into his boat.

Eventually, the Japanese delivered a message in Chinese stating that the ships would be permitted in Japanese waters for no more than five days. As the five days stretched into 11, the locals became increasingly agitated by what they perceived as the foreigners' arrogance and unwillingness to acquiesce to Japanese authority. Always the businessman, Kendrick had actually hoped the extra time could possibly be used to find local buyers for his cargo. The Massachusetts native had cut his teeth plying the trade route between the Pacific Northwest and China. He had gained a reputation that traveled all the way back to New England because he created the lucrative trade in sandalwood— much in demand in China—after discovering it growing wild on the island of Kauai.

Japan, however, proved to be another matter. So, the *Lady Washington* and Captain John Kendrick sailed away from Kushimoto into history and each to a sad and violent end a long way from Boston and home. Kendrick was killed in the Sandwich Islands in 1794 when a saluting gun exploded; the *Lady Washington* was wrecked in the South China Sea in 1800.

Kendrick's visit was marked by several key insights. He wanted to do business if the opportunity arose. But the Japanese have a historic aversion to dealing with foreigners. Kendrick ultimately realized that, according to historian Samuel Eliot Morison, "the natives [the Japanese] knew not the use of fur." And perhaps the most important awareness is that they all lacked the tools that could have aided them in their attempts to establish useful lines of communication and understand each other's genuine intentions.

And so it was that the very first contact between Japanese and Americans was a botched business opportunity punctuated by cultural misunderstandings. These were underscored by tense communications attempted in ways entirely unfamiliar to both sides. It would seem that as much as things change, they tend to remain the same.

Driving Blind On the Wrong Side (Ford Motor Company)

It was not in a vacuum that one of the largest corporations in the world failed to penetrate effectively what is, arguably, the most sophisticated consumer market on the planet. That failure, as well as the company's continuing difficulties there, was borne out of a collision of two legacies: (1) the company's perceived birthright to claiming credit as the "petri dish" for the American ideal of entrepreneurship and innovation, and (2) the genesis of a country, and a nascent industry, hungry for recognition on the world stage and eager to prove itself in the very living room of its biggest competitor.

Ford's experience (and indeed that of many other US-based companies) in Japan has been inexorably driven by the same attitudes and presumptions that mirror the trade policies of the US government toward Japan. These policies have in many ways often reduced US-Japan business relations to the level of playground bullying and finger-pointing.

WHERE QUALITY WAS JOB ONE

Ford ranked as the second largest car maker in the world in 1999, behind arch-rival General Motors. Headquartered in Dearborn, Michigan, Ford racked up $162.6 billion in 1999 sales earning it spot number four on the year's *Fortune 500* list.

Brainchild of the legendary Henry Ford, who revolutionized world industry by adapting Ransom Olds's assembly-line concept of mass production, Ford Motor Company opened its first assembly operation in Japan in 1927. Ford planned to expand the facility in the port city of Yokohama as a jumping-off point for the rest of the Asia market. But just a decade later Ford was forced to scrap its plans as all the makings of a trans-Pacific war began to surface on the horizon.

War came and went, but it wasn't until 1974 that the company reentered the Japanese market—a critical lapse of almost three decades since the end of World War II. During that lapse, the Japanese economy had grown into one of the world's most powerful, the economic relationship between the US and Japan had become increasingly complicated, and the tastes of the Japanese consumer had been honed to a high state of sophistication.

For the next decade, Ford struggled to find the right combination to unlock what was perceived as the inscrutably closed, but not-totally-impossible-to-penetrate, Japanese auto market. The most notable example was unveiled in 1983 when Ford rolled out a new sales center system aimed at bundling car sales—particularly the company's *Mustang*, *Thunderbird*, and *Mercury Marquis* models—with an impressive array of other so-called soft services. These services ranged from financing, insurance, and self-service repair bays to on-site displays of designer clothes, camping gear, toys, home-security and stereo systems, and *Yamaha* motorcycles. Dubbed the "Autorama" by marketing experts in Dearborn, the sales concept was designed to attract young, upscale Japanese consumers with a lot of disposable income but not a lot of time to kill.

Announcing the new plan, John T. Eby, then president of Ford Motor Co. (Japan) Ltd., appraised the total potential of the Japanese auto market and told *Ward's Auto World* that "to sell cars successfully in Japan, you need Japanese dealers, Japanese techniques, and the general Japanese approach to doing business." Several months later in the same publication he said, "To get customers to come to dealerships, we need a broad range of merchandise. Smart dealers in the US have been doing this for years."

Ah… "Smart dealers in the US." So that's the secret.

CARS THAT CAN REALLY CORNER

The early story of the Japanese auto industry, compared with that of the United States, could almost be written on the back of a business card. According to auto writer Philip Powell, the first cars in Japan arrived as late as 1904; they were imported from France by the Mitsui family. In 1912, Japan had 22,403 rickshaws, but a mere 82 automobiles. It was, Powell says, "hardly an auspicious beginning."

Full-scale auto production in Japan only began after World War I, and then it was nearly four more decades until cars produced there made any impact on the world's most sophisticated auto market—that is, the United States. Beginning in the early 1960s, Japanese automakers carefully studied American tastes, styles, and driving habits, over time developing their original basic subcompacts into midsize, midrange, midprice, more traditional "American-style" coupes.

The real effort began in 1973 when, spurred by a nationwide gas crisis in the US, Japan pounced on the opportunity to market a panoramic selection of fuel-efficient, affordable, and well-made cars to US consumers. In 1979 and 1980, history repeated itself with a second gas shortage. Within three years, Japan automakers had cornered more than 20 percent of the entire US car market. This compared to 1976 when Japanese cars accounted for only 8 percent of the market.

In 1981, for a variety of reasons, the US auto industry was unable to meet the Japanese competition head-on. The US industry went hand-in-hand with the politically connected United Autoworkers Union to lean on Washington. They requested the government to pressure the Japanese government and compel Tokyo to agree to voluntary limits on its auto exports to the US. Washington did, and the self-imposed restraints had two results: first, the US "Big Three"—General Motors, Ford, and Chrysler—reaped windfall profits. They drew in some $25.2 billion between 1984 and 1988, none of which was invested in increasing productivity. The vast bulk of that money was used to expand market share in Europe through acquisitions and joint ventures. Second, the restraints only suppressed the supply of popular Japanese-designed cars in the US. It did not lessen their demand among US consumers—for whom fuel efficiency and quality designs had become key issues.

MR. BUSHIDO, MEET MR. DIXIE

Perhaps the most effective tactic the Japanese automakers employed was the campaign to move huge chunks of their assembly and component manufacturing operations to sites in the US. Within a few years, seven Japanese automakers—led by Honda—had built manufacturing facilities in the US; Toyota alone had invested more than $1 billion in a plant near Georgetown, Kentucky.

By 1990, Japanese auto companies were firmly established in the US and were building some 1.2 million cars and trucks annually. In response, even with competition tight and a recession on the horizon, the Big Three put themselves on life support by maintaining production to avoid a strike by the United Autoworkers, increasing wholesale deliveries to fleet customers, and drastically reducing retail prices. Despite these measures, over the next two years, Big Three car sales fell from 9.3 million to 8.2 million units—the worst performance since 1982. Ford lost $2.2 billion in North American business alone.

By 1993, it was obvious that the auto import sanctions—originally intended to give US producers some breathing room to get their act together—were having the opposite effect. Something had to be done. So again, the Big Three, with Ford in the lead, cranked up the heat on Capitol Hill. Twenty months of heated negotiations in Geneva followed. A major trade war was averted only after Japan knuckled under to a threat by Washington to slap 100-percent tariffs valued initially at about $6 billion on 13 types of Japanese imported cars; Japan promised to ease the regulations restricting the importation of US-made auto parts. One of the key provisions of the July 1995 agreement was Japan's pledge to increase the number of dealerships that sold US cars in Japan and compel its auto industry to buy more American-made auto parts.

Once more, Ford had been handed the strategic high ground. For the second time in 10 years, a golden opportunity fell out of the sky and rolled down the Capitol steps into the company's corporate lap. But, even then, the magic didn't happen. In 1996—the same year that Ford began offering its high-priced, luxury *Taurus* model on the Japanese market—the strengthening dollar and continuing customer dissatisfaction conspired to restrict Ford sales in Japan. Ford sales amounted to only 45,592 cars of all makes and models, less than half the number of Mustang cars it sold in the US during the same period.

FORD SEES THE LIGHT... WELL, MAYBE A GLIMMER

Around this time, the company experienced an epiphany of sorts. While not the major reason it had started and sputtered time after time in Japan, Ford realized they had a glaring design defect. Actually, this flaw was so obvious to many both in and outside the industry that it had almost become a symbol of Ford's lack of understanding of the real needs of the Japanese auto-buying public.

The issue was not dual air bags, steel side panels, or even fuel economy; it didn't even have to do with price or availability. Ford had taken nearly 70 years to realize—or admit—that it was about time they seriously study the placement of the steering wheels on the cars they tried to sell in Japan.

Traffic in Japan, like that in the United Kingdom, Australia, and a handful of other countries, flows on the left-hand side of the road. While cars with their steering wheels on the "wrong" side have a certain romantic, "foreign" cachet (like the appeal of British sports cars in the US, for example), mass market appeal equates to providing what the mass market really wants. In this case, the market wanted US style, safety, design, and appeal...without the nuisance (and potential danger) of misjudging oncoming traffic and having to reach all the way across the front seat to pay highway tolls. But still, obsessed with the "how" of doing business in Japan, Ford continued to disregard the "what."

OH, FOR A PLACE OF ONE'S OWN

In early 1998, Ford announced that it would "soon" start building its own vehicles in Japan in cooperation with Mazda at a refurbished and fully automated manufacturing facility in Hiroshima. One-and-a-half years later, the company announced for the second time its plans to start making sport utility vehicles (SUVs) in Japan exclusively for the Japanese market. This time the company elaborated with a deadline—the end of 2000 or early 2001—and the pledge to design and build the cars with "Japan taste."

In the spring of 1999, Ford pulled its Taurus model from the market in Japan. Despite considerable pressure from the management in Dearborn, dealers were able to sell fewer than 500 Taurus cars during the preceding year—far fewer than the original sales goal of 18,000. Some analysts viewed the withdrawal of the Taurus car as a harbinger of Ford's ultimate retreat from Japan as well as the company's focus on the domestic US market, and the restructuring of its operations in both Europe and Latin America.

But, no. At the same time as Ford announced the withdrawal of the Taurus, the company trumpeted that it would seek a replacement auto to market to the Japanese. The company had actually been looking for the right car to market in Japan for a couple of years. Ford finally settled on the *Ka* subcompact, which it had developed in Europe and was assembling at production facilities in Spain and Brazil. They projected that the Ka would fit the bill: the right size for Japan's unique driving environment, fuel-efficient, manufactured by a US company where "Quality is Job One," and yes, with right hand-drive.

But, again, no. As of this writing, auto analysts have proclaimed the Ka car— ironically the Japanese word for "mosquito"—dead on arrival. It seems that the Ka was designed with a stick shift, even though repeated studies concluded that more than 90 percent of Japanese prefer to drive cars with automatic transmissions.

When Oatmeal Takes the Place of Brains (Snapple)

The Snapple Beverage Company has taken its fair share of hits during the course of its remarkable success. Some of them were the kind normally endured during the process of a small company growing into a market-dominating giant. But some of them were self-inflicted, as the firm's odyssey through the 1990s will attest.

In 1972, three buddies from Brooklyn (Arnold Greenberg, Hyman Golden, and Leonard Marsh) started a small company to bottle and sell pure fruit juice. Within a few years, Unadulterated Food Products Inc. acquired the Snapple trademark from a Texas entrepreneur for $500 and overcame a series of initial product development setbacks to become the first US company to produce a food product line based entirely on "all-natural ingredients."

The company's success was staggering. By 1988, the company's net revenues reached $13.3 million. By the end of the third quarter of 1992, the figure hit $177.4 million, up almost 1,300% in less than five years. With 52 beverage products on the market—sodas, teas, juices, sports drinks, and seltzers— *Snapple* was widely regarded as one of the fastest growing and best managed companies in the country.

BLINDED BY AMBITION

Despite this phenomenal and consistent triple-digit growth, the company found its reach exceeding its grasp. In 1994, the company's management decided that to reach its marketing goals it would have to link up with a larger, more established food company. The word went forth that the company was ripe for acquisition. It didn't take long, and by Christmas 1994 Snapple had been purchased by Chicago-based Quaker Oats Company for $1.7 billion.

But, to everyone's surprise, what filled out Santa's gift sack didn't stay secret for long. Quaker Oats's chairman and CEO, William Smithburg, was quoted as saying that the Snapple acquisition was "part of an evolving realignment of Quaker's portfolio." Another part of that realignment receiving scant attention in the trade press was Quaker Oats's plans to sell off both its European pet food business and its chocolate manufacturing facilities in Mexico. In fact, Quaker Oats was seriously looking at reducing its overseas operations, not expanding them.

Almost immediately, on the home front, entrepreneurial Snapple found itself steamrolled like roadkill on America's rigid mainstream capitalist highway. Under the new regime, Quaker Oats cut Snapple's staff from 270 to 24 and ended the company's long-standing relations with its 330 nationwide distributors in favor of a plan to link Snapple with Quaker-owned *Gatorade* to gain shelf space in retail stores. The company also shot itself in the foot by arbitrarily pulling all Snapple radio advertising from the two most popular and politically divergent radio talk shows in the country. Not stopping there, it pulled the plug on Snapple's highly effective "Ask Wendy" promotional campaign.

The shadow quickly lengthened. The year before the acquisition, Snapple had led the country in iced-tea sales—holding almost 30 percent of the total US market. Snapple's market share shrank to 24 percent the year after the sale. Meanwhile, its major competitor, Lipton, saw its cut of the market climb to a dominating 38.4 percent.

But, at least in the beginning, there was one ray of hope. Snapple had laid out extensive plans to expand market share by devoting considerable time and expense in international sales. During the windup to the eventual sale of the company, in May 1994 Snapple's management contracted with Calpis Food Industry Ltd. of Tokyo to distribute the company's beverages throughout Japan.

Some beverage industry analysts feel that the initial success of Snapple beverages in Japan—2.4 million bottles sold per month—was at least in part due to its American mystique and, of all things, the shape of the bottle. But whatever the reason, a lack of commitment on the part of Quaker Oats to do what was necessary to gain and hold long-term marketshare in Japan was largely to blame for what came next.

THE RAY OF HOPE FADES

Within a year, sales of Snapple beverages in Japan fell to only 120,000 bottles a month. One industry publication said this was evidence "of Quaker Oats failure to eliminate traits in the drinks that Japanese consumers disliked such as the murkiness of the teas and sweet fruit juice flavorings," while another criticized the company's paltry investment of only $2 million to promote Snapple products in Japan. Simple market research would have told them that sediment in a drink tells an American that the drink is natural, while the same sediment would tell a Japanese that the drink is, in a manner of speaking, dirty. The same holds true for sweet flavorings that may do the trick in quenching thirst in a dry climate like Texas or California, but are sticky and throat-gumming in the humid environment of Japan and most of Asia.

Quaker Oats's ambivalence to expanding its Snapple brand elsewhere in Asia was also becoming more and more apparent. This stance was amazing considering the outcome of a well-researched contemporary study conducted by Japanese market researcher Dentsu International. The study (published in the US by *Advertising Age* magazine and several other publications) showed that the Asian food, beverage, and tobacco market (the fastest growing consumer sector in the region at the time) was valued at a staggering $7.2 billion in 1995. Ironically, that was the same year Snapple's Asian regional sales went into the tank.

To add insult to injury, the year following the acquisition, Quaker Oats reduced its efforts entirely to maintain the hard-won market share for Snapple beverages in South Korea, Hong Kong, Australia, and 12 other countries. It even degenerated to the point of restricting Snapple's efforts to market in Singapore to ads plastered on the front of vending machines.

In 1997, "reading the writing on the wall," (Braille writing, said one wag at the time), Quaker Oats sold Snapple to Triarc Companies Inc. for $300 million. Fewer than three years after it had promised to take the company "to a new level," instead, Quaker Oats was recording a loss of $1.4 billion on the sale. "The decision to sell Snapple," said Quaker Oats chairman and CEO William Smithburg, "was reached after an extensive review of various shareholder value-building options…. We decided it was in the shareholders' interest to remove the financial burdens and risks Snapple brought to the portfolio and better focus on our value-driving businesses."

The Great Cake Mix Case (General Mills)

In the military, there's an expression for a bullet that, when fired, doesn't make it all the way to the target. During production, the brass casing of the bullet isn't filled with the proper amount of propellant, so when the weapon is fired at the right trajectory, the bullet drops far short of what it was intended to hit. Such a bullet is called a "short round."

AN AMERICAN-STYLE CAKE FALLS FLAT

Sometimes the same thing happens to businesses planning to insert a product into a new environment. It seems like everything that should be done has been done, but, in the end, the plan didn't go quite far enough in exposing potential market problems and pitfalls.

In his 1983 book, *Bonsai to Levis,* George Fields cites an example of just how the short-round scenario impacted the efforts of a large, well-respected American company to get one of its core products onto Japanese dining tables. What's come to be called "The Great Cake Mix Case" was of particular interest to Fields because he watched the developments first-hand as a member of the project's Tokyo advertising team.

Propelled by the shrewd use of radio and television advertising, by the late 1960s *Betty Crocker* had taken her proper place in the pantheon of American iconography. Along with Mickey Mouse, Roy Rogers, the *Reader's Digest,* and Notre Dame football, the Betty Crocker name (and face) was firmly established as the epitome of wholesome American domesticity. For generations, it was mom and Betty Crocker recipes in the kitchen who made it worth getting up every morning and facing the horrors that only elementary school could inflict on fresh-faced American kids. Many of us who came of age in post-war America can remember the days when the aroma of a Betty Crocker chocolate cake in the oven would take the edge off almost anything. As Fields put it, Betty Crocker was perceived as a "real person who baked cakes; she was not a manufacturing process."

That's what General Mills wanted to export to Japan, and so it took the first, sensible, step by joining together with Morinaga Ltd., one of Japan's largest confectionery companies. They went to work on a plan to market Betty Crocker brand cake mixes in Japan.

Primary market research had uncovered several factors pointing out the obvious potential of General Mills's newest target market: (1) the standard of living in Japan was on the rise; (2) consumers there, particularly women, were beginning to show a marked preference for quality foreign-sourced products; and (3) it seemed that Japanese eating habits and tastes in food were becoming increasingly Westernized. Further digging, however, also determined that Japanese families only consumed store-bought cakes. Also, few—if any— housewives in the country produced their own cakes because cake making was seen as a specialty occupation, and few Japanese homes at the time had an oven.

AMERICAN LOGIC FALLS FLAT

Fields outlines the (American, not Japanese) line of logic that drove the effort: "The poor Japanese housewife," he wrote, "was being denied the opportunity of making her own cakes; she was being forced into buying expensive shop cakes and hence restricting her level of consumption because she lacked an oven in her own kitchen.... If she could be given the means, she would not only buy fewer shop cakes, but she could also increase her family's consumption by making inexpensive cakes at home." The benefits were obvious, he wrote, as "the emotional satisfaction would enhance the economic benefits," and the solution was "nothing short of brilliant."

Somewhere in the mile-high pile of research studied by the company was a report showing that, despite the inroads of other types of food at the time, 90 percent of the main meal in the average Japanese household centered around rice. (The country's menu census repeatedly confirmed this.) Every meal, then, included rice prepared in the ubiquitous rice cooker.

The answer became increasingly obvious: Develop a quality cake mix that could be prepared in a rice cooker. Under the name *Cakeron* (a name General Mills felt Japanese housewives could better identify with than *Betty Crocker*), the new product performed well in its initial tests among Japanese consumers. A professional advertising campaign followed. At first, the results seemed to justify every penny spent to develop, advertise, and market the new product.

But within a few months, sales began to slacken. The company had focus group sessions set up to find the answer. Was the cake too dry? Too moist? Don't the Japanese like vanilla? Too much chocolate? Not enough? The color? The aroma? All the "right" questions were asked, but they didn't evoke the answers—that is, until a group of Japanese housewives participating in one of the focus groups obliquely hinted at the reason Cakeron wasn't something they'd go out of their way to serve their families.

Fields recounts how one of the housewives asks, "But doesn't it have vanilla in it?"

"Yes, and chocolate, too," responds the second.

"Don't you think it will remain in the cooker?" says the first.

The third replies, "I suppose you could wash it off, but...those things have a scent."

"Wouldn't it come off on the rice?" another asks.

"If you really scrubbed the cooker, it would be okay," adds the first. "Well, I don't know about you, but I cook more than I need for dinner and leave some rice for breakfast, and perhaps my lunch. Then I have to go out shopping in the afternoon. Then it's time to cook the rice for dinner."

In other words, the women were concerned that the cake mix might taint the flavor of the rice. And, more important, rice cookers are in almost constant use, leaving no time to use it for some other purpose—let alone to bake a cake. Few, if any, frugal Japanese housewives were willing to buy an additional rice cooker to prepare something seen almost as an alien extravagance.

According to Fields, the major stumbling block for General Mills was built on a basic misunderstanding of the needs of the primary consumer of the product. The marketing gurus at the company's headquarters in Minneapolis assumed that housewives in Tokyo are like their counterparts in Toledo. In a sense they were right: both target consumer groups want to create a positive dining experience for their families and themselves. But General Mills missed the boat when it failed to research the differences in the ways those housewives achieve the same goal. Culture nuance and the practicalities of a unique segment of the Japanese consumer market didn't play the role they should have in the company's decision-making process.

Disposable Diapers...Disposable Market Share (Proctor & Gamble)

Procter & Gamble (P&G) could see the writing on the wall by the time 1986 had rolled around. The company—with almost 150 years of business expertise under its belt—had lost an estimated $250 million over the preceding 13 years in Japan trying to sell its laundry detergents, bath soaps, and disposable diapers.

The company's Japan venture started out well. By 1979, its *Cheer* and *Bonus* brand laundry detergents were holding their own with a respectable 15 percent share of the Japanese laundry soap market, and one out of every ten boxes of detergent sold in the country was Cheer. Procter & Gamble introduced disposable diapers into Japan in 1978; its *Pampers* brand almost immediately dominated the product niche, holding an astounding 90 percent share. *Camay* soap, in the late 1970s, held a respectable 3.5 percent share in Japan's crowded personal care sector.

Just 7 years later, though, P&G found itself in a downward spiral with its share of the country's detergent market at 12 percent and falling. Camay soap—

one of its hallmark products—had dropped to only 2.5 percent of the $500 million in bath soaps then sold annually in Japan. And the Pampers brand took the heaviest hit of all: its commanding lead in the disposable diaper market, valued at more than $625 million had shriveled to only 15 percent.

THERE IS NONE SO DEAF AS HE WHO WILL NOT LISTEN

What happened? "They just didn't listen to anybody," said an ex-P&G employee (a Japanese who had worked at the company's Tokyo headquarters) in a December 1986 issue of *Forbes* magazine. The "they" he referred to was the company's management team back in Cincinnati. Thousands of miles away from the front lines of the highly charged war for the hearts and minds of the Japanese consumer, "they" hadn't done their homework—and it showed.

According to writer Andrew Tanzer, "When the Japanese study a US market, they study it carefully. They don't assume that what goes in Japan will go in the US." P&G, he continues, "lacked this necessary humility."

The sales of Cheer detergent, long a household mainstay in laundry rooms and cupboards across America, sailed off the charts in the beginning because it was cheaper to buy. But this alienated a critical component of P&G's future success in the Japanese market—the wholesalers. They felt that the efforts to undercut the competition on price was cutting deeply into their profit margins.

This disaffection of the wholesalers also worked to undercut the company's reputation as a manufacturer of quality goods—the very cornerstone of its most basic marketing plan. According to one consultant with many years' experience working in Japan, "Once you cut the price on a product in Japan, it's almost impossible to raise it again. That's one of the things that makes Japan different from the US or Europe. You become a captive to your own attempt to increase market share 'on the cheap,' and, at the same time, throw a shadow over the perception of the quality of what it is you're trying to sell."

Several other flaws in P&G's initial marketing plan conspired to create migraine moments back home in far-off Ohio. In researching the Japanese market, Procter & Gamble completely overlooked the fact that many Japanese housewives, unlike their counterparts in the US, do not have a family car in which to carry their groceries. This limits their shopping to the smaller "Mom & Pop" neighborhood stores. In fact, the smaller stores account for fully one-third of the household product sales in Japan every year. With limited shelf space and a keen eye on the needs of their regular clientele, these stores are reticent to carry discounted or sale items, because—like their wholesale suppliers—to do so would cut into their own narrow margins.

OF RED TIDES AND PORCELAIN DOLLS

In addition, it seemed as though nature itself was conspiring against the company. In the late 1970s a major chemical spill caused a much publicized "red tide" incident at Lake Biwa, a popular and historic tourist spot in central Japan's Shiga prefecture. According to Tanzer, the incident turned public opinion against the detergent manufacturing industry. While Japanese manufacturers responded immediately by developing and successfully marketing phosphate-free soap, P&G dragged its feet for almost two years—

despite the fact that it already had a successful phosphate-free product available in the US.

Then there were advertising issues with Camay bath soap. The problem centered on the offensive depiction of a Japanese woman "with the skin of a porcelain doll." The objectors' outcries took their toll on the company's image. "We told them that Japanese women would be put off by the campaign, but they [P&G management] just wouldn't listen," said one Japanese ad executive working on the Procter & Gamble account at the time.

What happened to the company's share of Japan's disposable diaper market proves, in many ways, that the first one out of the gate isn't necessarily the first one to the finish line. In the three years since the first container filled with Pampers diapers was unloaded at the Port of Yokohama, P&G outmaneuvered US-based arch-rival Kimberly Clark to dominate the Japanese disposable diaper market. Virtually overnight, 9 out of every 10 boxes of "use and lose" diapers sold in Japan was produced by Procter & Gamble. The company scored big points by investing heavily in educating young Japanese mothers on how much easier their life would be if they would only "switch to Pampers."

In 1981, success crashed, however, when Unicharm, a small Japanese manufacturer of feminine napkins attempted the impossible and went nose to nose with the giant P&G. Producing a better-designed product, Unicharm sales went through the roof, and, by 1985, Pampers's share of the market had plummeted to only 5 percent.

According to one company insider interviewed by Tanzer for *Forbes* magazine, "P&G underestimated the technical capabilities of the Japanese competition." Fighting back hard, Procter & Gamble tripled their market share back to 15 percent—acceptable growth, but a sorry fraction of its once overwhelming market dominance.

Topping it all off, during this period, the company blindly held to its corporate policy in Japan of advertising its brands, not the company itself. This proved to be a serious blunder in a consumer culture that thrives on relationships—not with products, but with the companies that manufacture those products. In Japan, television commercials very often end with a company logo flashing on the screen. This goes a long way to combine the concept of quality and service not only with a specific product, but with the company that makes it, and, by association, all of the other products and services that company might provide.

LESSONS THE LONG WAY AROUND

On the positive side, and despite the major blunders, when Proctor & Gamble decided to tackle the Japanese market, it made the commitment for the long haul. The company learned from its mistakes. It took the first step on the road to recovery in 1986 when it introduced a new laundry detergent called *Ariel* to the Japanese market. The new soap was specially formulated for typical Japanese laundry habits and practical needs—namely, shorter washing cycles in smaller washing machines and use in cold water.

Since then P&G has pumped significant capital into plant expansion, product development, and the construction of a technical research center. The company, with its country headquarters in Kobe, is currently a major player in Japan. It has four manufacturing facilities and a dozen offices overseeing the distribution of a wide variety of products—from fabric softener and cold remedies to shampoos and, yes, Pampers diapers.

Edwin Artzt, then vice chairman of the P&G board of directors, was quoted saying, "We learned a lesson here about tailoring your products and marketing to the market." Their manufacturing facilities and technical research center have proven to be an example to Japanese consumers of the company's commitment to the marketplace and to providing function by studying and modifying their product to meet the unique needs of the Japanese market.

The lessons have paid off. Currently Procter & Gamble's international sales account for about half of its annual sales, which in 1999 alone amounted to more than $38.1 billion.

Conventional Wisdom—Not Always So Wise (General Electric)

The Japanese penchant for foreign-made products is insatiable. Does this mean that any product can be sold in Japan? Yes and no, says Patrick Bray, president of IBT Ventures, a consultancy specializing in the development of marketing strategies for US companies that want to do business in Japan. Bray, who works out of offices in Menlo Park, California, and Tokyo, spent several years as director of business development for the Japanese External Trade Organization (JETRO) in San Francisco.

"Flexibility and adaptability are very important in Japan because sometimes what we call 'conventional wisdom' here in the US gets tossed on its head in Japan," he says, alluding to the oft-cited example of General Electric's experience in trying to sell refrigerators in Japan.

Conventional Wisdom (or "CW"), Bray says, dictated that only very small refrigerators manufactured to fit in tiny, undersized kitchens would be the type of unit that could sell in crowded Japanese cities. "GE took this as gospel and wanted to confine the sale of their large, US-style refrigerators to the very narrow niche market comprised of the wealthy Japanese who have large country homes." Partnering with Toshiba, GE limited its vision and balked at the idea of selling its refrigerators to a broader market. That is, until a Japanese distributor approached the company and offered to sell GE refrigerators as a "high quality, big ticket" product.

"In Japan, price is a determinant of quality," says Bray. "The Japanese distributor promoted the refrigerators as a type of urban status symbol. The popularity of the refrigerators was based on their cachet, their price, and their perceived value. Available space became less a determinant as the Japanese just made room for them."

It paid off well, Bray says. Within a few months, the distributor sold more than 80,000 units. The CW about Japan, in this particular case, got turned on its head.

On the other hand, there's the case (no pun intended) of Johnnie Walker Black Label whiskey, long a standard staple in the Japanese culture of corporate gift-giving. For the longest time, Black Label had been held up as the penultimate business gift. When the Japanese importer or distributor, under pressure from the distiller, dropped the price—hoping to boost sales—sales nose-dived. The perception among the whiskey's loyal clientele was that Black Label had a quality problem and the company was trying to unload it in the market "on the cheap."

Hard Lessons—Firm Mattresses

Betty Jane Punnett and David A. Ricks, in their textbook *International Business,* cite the example of a company that blindly entered the Japanese market only to have a series of misjudgments compound to virtually force it out of the market. The Simmons Company, a marketer of quality beds and mattresses, had several international successes under its belt by the mid-1960s and planned to both manufacture and distribute its products in Japan. The company understood that it would face a number of unique problems—a complicated distribution system, a virtual choke-hold on the small mattress market by a few domestic manufacturers, and most significant, the fact that most Japanese sleep on futons.

The company formed a subsidiary in Tokyo and planned to enter the market with a splash to coincide with the opening of the Tokyo Olympic Games. Here was a crucial window of opportunity when the company brass felt the demand for mattresses would take off sharply over a relatively brief period of time. Production issues and pricing problems were compounded by the fact that the company's Japanese sales force had trouble identifying with the product—most of them had, in fact, never slept on a bed. Simmons made a final fatal error when it chose to advertise exclusively in print media. This effectively confined the company's message to the Tokyo area; television is generally seen as the most effective way to reach potential customers throughout the entire country.

Mitsubishi Comes Out of the Closet

In the early morning hours of Sunday August 27, 2000, investigators from the Tokyo Metropolitan Police, acting under orders from the Ministry of Transportation, raided the offices of the Mitsubishi Motors Company (MMC). They left a few hours later carrying boxes of documents, files, computer disks, and reports—evidence of what turned out to be one of the most incredible corporate cover-ups in the history of postwar Japan.

Just a few days before the raid, the country's largest mass-circulation daily newspaper, the *Yomiuri Shimbun,* published a front-page story on Mitsubishi. The article asserted that Mitsubishi, Japan's fourth largest automaker, had circumvented the law by concealing from the government more than 64,000 customer complaints about its defective cars for more than 20 years.

In 1969, a law had been passed requiring auto companies to report customer complaints to the government, which would then determine whether a general recall would be necessary. Instead of adhering to the law, the company handled each complaint on a case-by-case basis, thus undermining any possible method of compiling the data necessary for a model-wide defect recall.

The paper told that the complaints covered more than a dozen defects—including everything from failed brake systems and leaking fuel tanks to malfunctioning clutches and accessories that simply fell off. Incredibly, not only were these never reported, but they were sealed in boxes that were then shut away in a locked room at the company's Tokyo headquarters. Each box was marked with the letter "H," for "himitsu," the Japanese word for secret, and the employees who handled them were told not to talk about the boxes, their contents, or where they were stored.

A COMPLICATED "SIMPLE" PREMISE

For two decades, the company had carried on a charade, an effective deception based on a simple premise: if the company concealed the complaints from the government, it couldn't be compelled to order recalls for its cars. No complaints, and thus no costly and embarrassing recalls, would equal increased revenues and happy shareholders.

In July 2000, the Transport Ministry in Tokyo received an anonymous tip that led to the discovery of a handful of "H" files secreted away in a manager's locker room in the company's headquarters. Moving to squash the story before it would get out of control, Mitsubishi immediately ordered the recall of more than 500,000 cars that were produced in Japan and sold to Japanese customers, plus some 45,000 sold in the US, and an unspecified number sold elsewhere in the world. The recall, the company said, would cost almost $45 million.

But immediately after the predawn August raid, the company acknowledged the 20-year deception in the press and expanded the original recall. It upped the recall to 692,000 cars and trucks in Japan plus more than 200,000 that were produced in the country and sold around the world.

The cost of the expanded recall jumped to almost $70 million—a heavy hit for a company that had lost more than $213 million during the fiscal year ending in March 2000. The company was slightly in the black at the end of fiscal 1998, but it had a loss of $940 million the year before. Frighteningly, Mitsubishi analysts were forecasting that its losses could top more than $600 million in the fiscal year ending in March 2001, mainly due to the need to cover liabilities for government-mandated retirement benefits.

The day after the raid, Mitsubishi president Katsuhiko Kawasoe promised "a thorough house cleaning," reported the Associated Press. According to Kawasoe, who had joined the company in 1997, "Together with my management team, I will devise a set of measures to rectify the situation and prevent any recurrence, as well as take strict disciplinary action within the company."

NO ONE AT THE HELM

Three days later, Kawasoe was gone. He had resigned in disgrace after initially offering to take a self-imposed pay cut.

The initial suggestion as a replacement—a Mitsubishi vice president—was rejected by the very dour Mitsubishi Group, the giant "keiretsu" monolith that included MMC as a member. Rudderless, and with no one at the helm, Mitsubishi requested to a grim DaimlerChrysler AG—the German automaker that the previous March had acquired a 34 percent stake in Mitsubishi—that they send a replacement for Kawasoe.

Another blow came when Mitsubishi Heavy Industries Ltd., the carmaker's majority shareholder, refused to send a top executive to take over the senior-level post.

Soon thereafter, officials from the National Highway Traffic Safety Administration (NHTSA) in Washington, DC, demanded that Mitsubishi Motor Sales of America, the North American subsidiary of the Japanese parent, vouch for the quality of the cars it sold in the US. The agency, overseeing auto safety recalls in the US, admitted that it had no evidence that Mitsubishi had failed to report defects with its cars to US authorities. Nevertheless it stated: "We are asking Mitsubishi, for the record, to tell us if there is any obligation to report problems with its cars to US authorities...we want assurances no such lapses have taken place."

Forty-five thousand Mitsubishi-made cars exported to the US were affected by the recall, the NHTSA said. They included *Montero* SUVs with brakes that could fail because of leaking brake-fluid lines; *Galant* model sedans with defective fuel-tank weld joints; and *Mirage* midsize sedans that would have to be inspected for improperly installed drive shafts that could cause the car to stall.

A SCANDALOUS HISTORY

The company, quick to respond only after the recall scandal was made public, was no stranger to scandal.

Kawasoe had been known throughout the Japanese auto industry as "Mr. Clean." Just three years before the scandal broke, he had been brought into the company to clean up Mitsubishi's image: his predecessor had been forced to resign over allegations of racketeering. The situation was compounded by a major scandal in the US following charges of sexual harassment at the company's production facility at Normal, Illinois.

The company had struggled for years with giants Toyota, Nissan, and Honda for market share both at home and abroad. But unable to control costs and increase market share, the company backed itself into a corner by artificially bolstering its image—trying to create the illusion that Mitsubishi's management had everything under control. The illusion didn't work and that was when Mitsubishi tried to recover by partnering with DaimlerChrysler.

Just before he resigned, MMC president Kawasoe told a packed news conference at Mitsubishi's Tokyo headquarters, "I have no option but to admit [an internal report in the scandal] reflects a truly regrettable state of affairs [which is] the result of a lack of respect for rules and regulations on the part of the company officers and employees involved."

A LACK OF CONSCIENCE

But, in truth, it reflected much more than that. The long-term Mitsubishi scandal was cultivated by two major factors: first, the cultural environment evoked a fear of the humiliation and embarrassment that product recalls would cause. Kawasoe said there was "a lack of conscience among our employees…and an impression that recalls meant we were making shoddy cars." Second, however, the company had a more pragmatic understanding that if caught, it would not bear any great punishment—either from its customers or the government.

According to a Japanese auto industry analyst, "Hiding claims for a long period is bad, but the problem looks to be a past story. I believe Mitsubishi has the ability to change itself." In fact, a detailed account of the entire affair by the Associated Press indicated that after the scandal became public, consumer reaction was "muted and sales have not taken a hit." Mitsubishi car sales in Japan—a country where products are rare and boycotts are even rarer—actually totaled about 12,000 units in the month following the disclosure, up from the 10,800 the same month in 1999.

History, too, proved to be on Mitsubishi's side. Before the Mitsubishi scandal, only one other company, Fuji Heavy Industries Ltd. [FHI], had ever been sanctioned for failing to file properly consumer complaints with the government and issue orders for a product recall. FHI manufactures Subaru autos. In 1997, the company was slapped with a fine of only $12,900 and an "administrative reprimand" for secretly trying to repair problems with more than 1.5 million defective cars.

Commenting on the government's efforts to have criminal charges brought against Mitsubishi, Transport Minister Hajime Morita said that the government would file a complaint against Mitsubishi with a fine of $9,000 per recall case. But, he added, the ministry would only include three or four violations verified since April 1998 and would ask for a separate, one-time fine of $1,800 for filing false reports.

Amazingly, under that scenario, the most Mitsubishi would pay is $37,800 in fines and penalties. "The Transport Ministry needs to do a much better job penalizing automakers," Fumio Matsuda, president of the Japan Automobile Consumers Union, told the Associated Press.

Lessons Learned: Getting It Right in Japan

ENTER INTENTIONALLY FOR THE LONG HAUL

"The basic rule of thumb on doing business in Japan," says Los Angeles-based Japan business consultant Mike Moretti, "rests on three basic things—patience, perseverance, and commitment." Without those three qualities, he says, "any attempt to get into the Japanese market is doomed to fail. A marketing plan can appear to cover all the bases, but unless the Japanese see that these attitudes underline the relationship, whatever you plan just won't work there."

For a business to develop over the long term in Japan, it needs patience in dealing in an unfamiliar business setting, perseverance in cultivating strong relationships with both business partners and customers, and the commitment of resources (time, money, and people). These precepts, if adhered to, might lead to success. To ignore these tenets will surely break any deal in the highly competitive Japanese market.

Ford, it seems, is in a class by itself when it comes to Japan. Oceans of ink have been expended and piles of aspirin have been consumed in efforts to analyze how and why a big-league player like Ford could simply fall on its face in Japan over and over again, tripping over the same issues like an Arctic explorer lost in a blizzard. But at the core of that failure is the mentality engendered by the tension between pleasing the shareholders and the willingness to accept the risks inherent with developing a business in a foreign environment.

The absolutely necessary component is what older generations of Japanese called *gambate*. In the West, we'd call it "stick-to-it-tiveness"—the willingness to commit for the long term. This is one thing that Proctor & Gamble turned to its advantage, even after almost blundering itself out of the market. Lack of it spelled the end of any hope Quaker Oats/Snapple might have ever entertained about long-term market share in Japan.

THE MORAL: If you want to climb Mount Everest, be prepared to expend the time, money, and labor to reach the peak. Once you've made base camp, it's still a long way up.

COMPETE ON THE COUNTRY'S TERMS

Success in Japan—as well as any other new market—requires an in-depth understanding of such issues as how that market is structured, its consumer preferences, the state of the domestic and foreign competition, and the country's regulatory requirements. It is also essential to recognize and accept the risks of being the new kid on the block. To fit into the new neighborhood, it may be necessary to make some changes, alter some features, consider a new style. Back home, the attitude might have been one of comfortable confidence, even cockiness, at being able to stand up with the tallest in the crowd. A move into a foreign market may mean that you have to start over again to gain acceptance, but if you work hard to compete on the country's terms, you will have found a new home.

Snapple's failure in Japan and the rest of Asia was a direct result of the almost fatal blending of two divergent philosophies. Snapple climbed into the corporate sack with a rigidly structured larger company completely unwilling to commit to investing in success in Japan. This massive error of judgment turned toxic when it was combined with a total misunderstanding of the basic tastes of the Japanese market. A quote in a news brief in the May 1994 issue of *Beverage World* magazine succinctly summed up half the problem: "Snapple chairman Leonard Marsh believes the Japanese market is similar to the US."

The die was cast. The company had lost sight of its core competency and surrendered the sum total of its experience to an uncaring parent with different goals and expectations. Quite simply, Snapple wanted to expand further into the global market; Quaker Oats—which loftily held both the reins of power and the purse strings—didn't.

Under its new owner, the Triarc Companies Inc., Snapple was able to recoup lost ground, and over the past 4 years has revitalized its international operations. The company currently sells its products in 40 countries, but Snapple still suffers from the damage done to its reputation. The Quaker Oats-Snapple affair was a classic case of a big corporation trying to heavy-handedly fix a company that wasn't broken, almost destroying it in the process.

General Mills found itself with a daunting challenge—selling to Japanese housewives, arguably the most discerning consumers in one of the most defying markets in the world, the idea of buying a product with absolutely no history in their country. In the end, creating a taste, as well as carving out a niche, proved to be just beyond the company's abilities. The marketing research team tasked with crafting an entry strategy for the company had fallen into the most common trap of all—fully aware of General Mills's success in marketing the Betty Crocker name in the US and elsewhere, they assumed that the product would be a perfect fit for Japanese consumers. They were wrong.

Other examples abound:

■ FRITO-LAY Texas-based Frito-Lay's corn chips and the company's *Ruffles* brand name potato chips and *Cheetos* cheese snacks are found in millions of American households. But the company quit their attempts to sell their three premier products in Japan almost as soon as they began when the company quickly discovered that they don't suit the market's taste. Both *Fritos* corn chips and Ruffles potato chips are too salty for the Japanese palate. And the Japanese don't like the greasy orange glaze that coats your fingers after you eat Cheetos cheese snacks.

■ EL POLLO LOCO El Pollo Loco, the Southern California-based fast-food franchiser, took a shot at the Japanese market in the early 1990s, but the company quickly decided to call it quits after determining that its barbecued chicken—with its signature spicy yellow skin—made health-conscious Japanese customers think the chicken was, at best, spoiled, or at worst, diseased.

■ Then, of course, there's the story of the US-based manufacturer of ladies' underwear that tried to sell its American-size brassieres in Japan without checking out the somewhat obvious fact that most Japanese women are not exactly anatomically structured to the same dimensions as Western women.

THE MORAL: You will always be just visiting until you consciously act to make a place your home.

USE THE COUNTRY'S MARKETING STRUCTURE TO YOUR ADVANTAGE

Presumably, you are not in the business of reforming marketing structures. Every country—and Japan is certainly a prime example—has idiosyncratic marketing methodologies. Success in the marketplace usually requires acceptance not only by consumers, but also on the various levels of influence that tend to control, directly and indirectly, the market. You will need to recognize and employ the "right" media, the "right" distribution channels, the "right" retail outlets, the "right" promotional schemes, and the "right" government contacts.

Proctor & Gamble's explosive entry into Japan's diaper, detergent, and soap business fizzled because US management misread the market. They forgot to watch the local competition and were caught by surprise when a domestic company—thoroughly familiar with the best way to market in Japan—grabbed substantial market share. They attempted to impose US marketing philosophies on a well-entrenched distribution system, and they failed to recognize the significance and importance of Mom & Pop retailers.

Sleepless nights were the result when Simmons tried to enter the Japanese market without a well-considered plan, focusing instead on the need for speed to take advantage of what was considered a single golden opportunity when the Olympic Games came into town. Facing tight domestic competition and lack of consumer awareness of the product, they failed to effectively use the market structure offered by the country. The company neglected its own Japanese sales representatives, who may have had significant insights to offer if they had been allowed to "sleep on it." In addition, it selected the wrong media for its promotion.

An essential ingredient in every marketing plan is the consideration of government regulations, as Mitsubishi can tell having climbed out of the bath. Consumer laws, unfair competition rules, advertising restrictions, and many other regulatory issues can wreak havoc with a new market entry. At the same time, with advance planning, comprehension, and acceptance of the restrictions, living within the rules can be extremely advantageous. It shows a respect for the country's practices and authority, engenders good will among those with influential power, and brings favorable hype in the media—all of which can ease and smooth the inevitable bumps and bruises of getting to know a new market.

THE MORAL: Reinventing the wheel is not always the best use of your resources. The tire could well go flat. It's better to use what is already around and slowly work with the inventor to introduce innovations to your benefit.

IF YOU CAN DO IT HERE, YOU CAN DO IT ANYWHERE

Some final thoughts. If there's any global market where you can learn much from the mistakes of others, it's Japan. Over and over, people say it is the most unique—and unforgiving—market in the world. Practically speaking, companies that want to do business there should be prepared to give the highest possible level of support to their customers. Learn every detail, however insignificant it might seem (remember "The Great Cake Mix Case") and design for the market (remember Ford). Expect small orders at first that will test your commitment. Emphasize quality (remember Snapple) and be reliable. Most important, accept, but don't waste time trying to completely understand, the Japanese sense of structure.

According to Michael Perry, former head of Nippon Lever in Tokyo, Japan "is quite the most competitively challenging market, so you have to take very much the long view." Quoted in Philip Oppenheim's 1992 book, *Japan Without*

Blinders, Perry says, "In many ways, it's really no different from anywhere else. Having strong brands is obviously vital and there's no alternative to doing your homework, researching the market properly, and putting in a long-term investment of time and money."

He concludes, "You immediately face the question, as a newcomer, of what to offer the customer that's better than their current supplier.... But if you can crack the Japanese market, it's going to benefit your operations all over the world, because if you can succeed in Japan, you can sell anywhere."

THE MORAL: Take a lesson from the Japanese when they look toward American markets and successfully integrate their products to become major players over time.

CHAPTER 7

Internal "International" Blunders

REMEMBERING THE FOLKS BACK HOME

DIVERSITY WITHIN DOMESTIC MARKETS can lead to market blunders that are equally as significant in terms of cost and reputation as those that arise when products or services cross country borders. Companies that confine marketing efforts by country borders and assume that all people within are of a single mind have forgotten about the German-speaking population that lives in France, the substantial Indian immigration to England, the English, Dutch and French influences in Africa and Southeast Asia, and the Italian settlements in Argentina, to name only a few. Such assumptions often create unpleasant surprises. Many of the most famous incidents of domestic cross-cultural blunders have been reported in the United States, in part because of its high influx of immigrants and also its freedom of the investigative press. But past histories of colonization and migration, combined with the ever-increasing world travel industry of today, have resulted in checkered populations in nearly every corner of the globe.

When Cultures Clash (General Mills)

Sometime in late 1995, General Mills announced that it would celebrate its 75th anniversary with an ethnic makeover of Betty Crocker—by far the company's most readily identifiable product icon. The company said it would transform the facial features of 75 ethnically diverse women into a single, new composite "Betty" in an attempt to increase the appeal of the company's brands "to a broader range of housewives representing the country's shifting ethnic diversity."

Since the "birth" of Betty Crocker in 1921, this was the eighth time General Mills transformed the fictional character with an appearance felt to be more in tune with the makeup of its traditional customer base. "She will be less white bread and more whole meat," opined Russell Adams, then chairman of the African American studies department at Howard University in Washington, DC, in an interview in the October 1995 issue of *Jet* magazine. He predicted that the new character would "have a light tan hue, a hint of a slant to her eyes, and perhaps, a bit of width in the nose." General Mills, he said, "will be shrewd enough not to let her looks be offensive to anybody."

America: Melting Pot, Stew, or Chef's Salad?

Call it an "Old World" and "New World" thing if you want. A line from the popular comedy film of the 1970s, *Stripes,* sums up the irreversible, consuming fact—said by a reluctant volunteer soldier in the US Army, trying to lift his fellow recruits' spirits by reminding them about the country they've volunteered to serve. "Our ancestors," he tells them proudly, "were kicked out of some of the finest countries in Europe."

They were kicked out or left on their own—in times of war and peace, prosperity and famine. They came, and continue to do so, not only from Europe, but from Asia, Latin America, and virtually every region and country on the face of the planet. This ongoing global diaspora has changed the face of America, how it sees itself, and how it does business.

Between 1970 and 1997 (the latest year for which complete figures are available), the US became home to almost 19 million legal immigrants from virtually every country in the world. Factoring in the number of undocumented, or illegal, immigrants entering the country boosts that figure by another 1.5 to 2 million, says the US Immigration & Naturalization Service (INS). The agency reports that the largest groups of new immigrants now calling the US home come from Mexico, the Philippines, Vietnam, the Dominican Republic, China, India, Cuba, Ukraine, Jamaica, and South Korea.

HOME AWAY FROM HOME

When first arriving, many immigrants settle into communities inhabited by people from their native land, where the common background of language, culture, and values eases the process of assimilating into their new home of choice. Providence, Rhode Island, has its Federal Hill (Italian) section; San Francisco, New York, and Washington, DC, have their Chinatowns; Orange County, California, has its Little Saigon; Brighton Beach, Brooklyn, is known as Little Odessa by the Sea because of the number of Russian immigrants there. Also, countless communities in Minnesota and Wisconsin were (and some still are) scaled-down versions of villages in Sweden, Norway, and Denmark. Chicago is home to the largest ethnic Polish community outside of Poland. And Los Angeles takes the red ribbon as the second-largest Spanish-speaking city in the world after Mexico City.

According to extensive research, the immigrants who assimilate the fastest are the ones that have had some American culture or some positive exposure to American culture in their home country. Background could be anything from a discussion with an American tourist to an "addiction" to American-made TV shows. Although the changes that come with assimilation begin to make their mark, some things remain the same—such as tastes in food, reading materials, music, leisure time activities, and movies.

With some ethnic groups, assimilation takes only a generation or two. My own mother's parents, for example, emigrated from Italy in 1911, but my mother can neither speak, read, nor write Italian. On the other hand, other immigrants find comfort in so-called "ethnoburbs"—communities populated predominantly by a particular ethnic group—to minimize what they perceive as the negative impacts of America's influence on their own unique, delicate, cultural fabric. This latter phenomenon has generated much debate among demographers. Some feel this "self-ghettoization" is caused by the fear of bias and discrimination, while others attribute it to the perception of America as a way station, or temporary haven, where one can gain an education, make money, or escape persecution until conditions "at home" improve enough for them to return.

But whatever the outward manifestations, some intangible link always remains that binds the immigrant—and his descendants—to the "old country." This link can both charm and vex us, sometimes at once: for example, this phenomenon is what drives the great-great-grandson of an escapee from the Irish Potato Famine to quaff a memorial Guinness in a Seattle theme pub on St. Patrick's Day (despite the fact that, in reality, he's never stepped foot in Ireland). And it is this link that compels blond high-school girls in Minnesota to rise early on St. Lucia Day, don red-sashed white gowns, light the candles festooning the wreathes in their hair, and hand out sticky buns and coffee to total strangers.

Not that many years ago, American ethnic stereotypes reflected the social fact of massive immigration to the United States primarily from Europe and Asia, said M. Mark Stolarik, director of the Balch Institute for Ethnic Studies in Philadelphia in an article published in the March 1989 issue of *American Demographics*. The attitude reflected in the stereotypes was "usually crude and condescending, and appealed to largely Anglo-American audiences who found it difficult to reconcile their visions of beauty, order, and behavior with those of non-Anglo-Americans."

LEGAL OR ILLEGAL...CONSUMERS ALL

But America isn't alone. In the 1980s and 1990s, the "Old World" (Europe) began to experience—in unprecedented fashion—what the US had been experiencing to a greater or lesser degree for almost a century. Europe has had an influx of huge numbers of immigrants, both legal and illegal, seeking jobs and some degree of stability.

The examples are many: the turnover of Hong Kong to Beijing in 1997 caused thousands of ethnic Chinese British citizens to apply for admittance to the UK. (Interestingly, London is home to 150,000 Chinese, the largest Chinese community in the European Union.) The economic turmoil caused by the meltdown of the Soviet Union in the late 1980s compelled many Eastern Europeans to head west in search of work. Chronic Balkan strife has sent thousands of refugees west to Italy and south to Greece. And the huge numbers of East Germans settling in West Germany after the country was reunified have exacerbated the existing and sometimes violent tensions between neo-Nazis and Turkish emigrants who settled in Munich and Dusseldorf.

And the issues continue to mount. An average of 500,000 people have illegally tried to enter the European Union each of the past several years, according to the European Commission in Brussels, Belgium. Currently, three million to 5 million "illegals" reside in the EU. This compares with the seven million who lived in the US in 1999, according to the INS.

In the UK alone, the number of people trying to illegally enter the country climbed from 616 in 1996 to more than 16,000 in 1999. At the port of Pas de Calais, France, immigration officials detained 8,500 illegal immigrants in 1999, up more than 500 percent from the previous year.

Whether legal or not, when all is said and done, these "New Europeans" (like their transatlantic counterparts in the US) are consumers. And as they assimilate and take root, they provide "domestic international marketers" with a host of challenges similar to those they face when trying to penetrate an overseas market thousands of miles away—that is, product suitability, quality, reliability, and value, to name a few.

Sometimes the greatest opportunities for tremendous successes, and equally staggering failures, lie right under our noses. A variety of influences—from movies and the media to the accidental bumping of shopping carts in the local supermarket—influence how Americans, Europeans, Asians, and Hispanics, whether assimilated or not, perceive other races and ethnicities. The impressions we carry from these influences strongly tint how we then carry out social intercourse—particularly business.

Since the end of the 19th century, motion pictures have transcended culture for the better (stories are common of immigrants to the US learning English by spending their Saturday afternoons at double-feature matinees), and as the following examples show, movies have also triumphed over culture for the worse. So grab your popcorn and your air sickness bag and let's go to the movies...

Arabian Nights and Terrorist Days

"When an Arab sees a woman he wants, he takes her!" That famous line, uttered by Rudolf Valentino in the 1921 silent film epic *The Sheik,* was said to have caused some women sitting in darkened movie theatres from Rochester to Sacramento to swoon and faint as they projected themselves into the role of the proud, haughty Lady Diana Mayo, humbled and seduced by Ahmed Ben Hassan, the powerful, darkly romantic Son of the Desert. (Even though it was later revealed he was really the Earl of Glencarryl, an overly tanned Scottish nobleman who had been abandoned in the Sahara as a baby and raised by Arab Bedouin tribesmen.)

"Shriek! For the Sheik Will Seek You Too!" screamed the movie posters as the cash poured in and the ladies continued to swoon. Meanwhile, their men folk felt oddly outclassed by the sheik (or the earl, as the case may be), who in reality was a corset-wearing Italian immigrant agricultural student turned actor.

Anyway, the die was cast and soon other desert dramas were packing women viewers in droves—*Arabian Love* with heartthrob John Gilbert (a native of mysterious, far-off Orem, Utah) in the leading role, and *Arab,* starring Ramon Navarro (a dark and swarthy Mexican character actor). Down the years, legend built on myth and legend became reality. Theatres were crammed with adoring fans watching Gary Cooper and company repel an army of screaming, scimitar-wielding Arabs in *Beau Geste*. The Three Stooges and Laurel and Hardy bungled their way through tours of duty with the *Foreign Legion*. Hope, Crosby, and Lamour laugh it up on the *Road to Morocco*. Sean Connery portrays the noble Lord of the Berbers in the laughable, historically inaccurate farce, *Wind and the Lion*. And Warren Beatty and Dustin Hoffman almost ruined their careers in the eminently forgettable *Ishtar*.

The entertainment industry's portrayal of stereotypical Arabs continued through the 1970s and 1980s. By that time, wrote pollster and demographer John Zogby, the US "witnessed a uniquely negative atmosphere for Americans of Arab descent, due to the stereotyping, harassment, defamation, and exclusion of Arab-Americans brought on by the widespread perception of Arabs as immigrants from hostile, enemy lands," particularly Libya, Iraq, and Iran.

I've known a number of Iranian businesspeople in the US who hesitate to tell others that they are from Iran. Instead, they respond to the question, "Where are you from?" by answering "Persia." In doing so they hope to neutralize or downplay any possible identification with the anti-American Islamic government that overthrew the government of the Shah in the late 1970s.

The period was a vexing one. World events took a major role in negatively shaping attitudes toward Arab-Americans even further, which role Hollywood, again, did its best to exploit.

Rambo and the Nomad (COLECO)

Enter John Rambo—the fictional archetypal take-action hero of the 1980s. Portrayed by a sweaty, shirtless Sylvester Stallone, *Rambo* was a cinematic personification of all the frustrations felt by a disenchanted post-Vietnam America that saw itself, rightly or wrongly, on the downslide from a pinnacle of greatness. It was perceived that the attitude of many parts of the world toward America in effect had become, "We don't like your culture but we want your money." Americans were often rankled, thinking, "We're good enough to pay your bills and fight your wars, but you won't let us date your sister." This set the backdrop for Rambo.

A brooding, alienated Vietnam veteran, Rambo was a one-man army blasting his way through a trio of immensely popular films that took him from the US Pacific Northwest, where he wrought havoc on a bullying police chief, back to Vietnam to cleanse his soul (and the country's) by rescuing a campful of US POWs. Finally, he makes it to Afghanistan where he sneeringly annihilated the occupying Russians—one helicopter gunship and one tank at a time.

The trio of films spawned an avalanche of promotional products from sweatbands and toy weapon sets to combination wristwatch/compasses and a simulated Rambo foam-rubber "muscle suit." Millions were made and, as with all crazes, time was short to cash in.

So, in 1986, toy maker Coleco made its move by releasing its own line of Rambo action figures. The 54-year-old, family-owned company spent millions to develop, produce, and market the toy line in a move that was motivated less by a desire to gain market share than by a desperate last-ditch attempt to stave off bankruptcy.

Desperation has strange bedfellows. The Rambo action figures sold as well as any fad-generated product could be expected to. Such products have a certain shelf life—usually until the next craze comes along. Then they become collectibles or the topics of questions for nostalgia trivia games.

What landed on Coleco, however, wasn't the issue of shelf life. It was the issue of ethnic stereotyping engendered in the *Nomad*, one of Rambo's most ruthless enemies—a burnoose-wearing, obviously Arab figure described in its package insert as "dangerous, cold, unstable, and treacherous" with "an intimate knowledge of sabotage." In short, the Nomad action figure embodied everything people thought they knew about real Arabs.

The outrage was deafening, with Arab-American community activist groups and others demanding the toy be removed from store shelves. And newspapers across the country reported on planned boycotts and anti-Coleco media campaigns.

By the time the controversy reached a peak, however, financial reality had fired another torpedo at Coleco that left the company "dead in the water." The fiasco over Nomad became just one of a series of issues that eventually led to the company's total evaporation.

The company had actually slashed and burned a swath of self-destruction that would have made Rambo himself proud. After a painful belly flop into the competitive video game pool in 1984, Coleco found itself recording losses totaling almost $80 million. Not to be deterred, two years later the company torched some $111 million by allowing inept management to fritter away the initial success of its hugely successful *Cabbage Patch* doll line. The following year, the company threw another $105 million onto the already roaring fire; and, in 1987, the company filed for Chapter 11 bankruptcy.

An attempt to regroup failed. In June 1989 Coleco's assets were sold to a group of creditors headed by giant arch-rival Hasbro Inc. Thus, Coleco—once the King of Toys and global marketer of *Scrabble* and *Parchesi* board games—faded into oblivion.

Mickey of the Desert (Walt Disney Company)

It seems almost unbelievable that a huge international company, with an overseas presence that the competition would kill for, would be so remiss that it would get taken to task three times in just two years for perceived negative stereotyping of an ethnic group. But, yes, that's what happened to the Walt Disney Company when it took multiple broadsides from both the US and overseas for its depiction of Arabs.

In early 1996, Touchstone Pictures, Walt Disney's movie production subsidiary, released the comedy *Father of the Bride, Part II,* a comedy that the American-Arab Anti-Discrimination Committee (ADC) claimed portrayed Arabs as "unscrupulous, cruel, and shrewd." In his first four minutes on the screen, "Mr. Habib [the character in question] speaks with a thick Arabic accent and uses mock Arabic language"; he "manages to verbally abuse his wife, litter the garden, and extort $100,000" from the movie's main character, played by comedian Steve Martin," read the ADC letter sent to Joe Roth, chairman of Walt Disney Pictures.

According to a story in the *Arab-American News* of January 19, 1996, the ADC "reminded Mr. Roth of its prior agreement with Walt Disney, which grew out of negotiations regarding what the group felt were the objectionable aspects of Disney's animated film, *Aladdin*." Those talks, the ADC claimed, led to a promise by Disney to consult with Arab-Americans before releasing projects that involve Arab characters—a so-called Disney Principle. Despite Disney's promise, the newspaper, said, "It seems that *Father of the Bride, Part II* has fallen between the corporate cracks and has caused the kind of damage that the application of the 'Disney Principle' was meant to prevent."

A year later, Disney took another hit when it released *Operation Condor,* a film shot in 1990 starring Hong Kong martial arts master Jackie Chan. The movie was blasted by Jack Sheehan, author of the book, *The TV Arab,* and a consultant to CBS News on Middle East affairs. Writing in the *Las Vegas Review-Journal,* Sheehan charged that the movie "vilifies Arabs."

The movie's two Arab characters, he said, "surface as hopelessly stupid caricatures. One regularly calls his cohort 'idiot.' When trying to commit suicide, they blunder. In an attempt to subdue the blond heroine, they stumble and then fall off a balcony. Next, they actually trip down a sand dune. Both mock Islam by spouting such lines as, 'We will never give up the struggle for the holy battle,' and, 'praise Allah for delivering you [Chan] to us again.'" And, he adds, "when a generic thug threatens Chan, an Arab innkeeper exclaims, 'Pay me! No money, no shoot.'"

Disney's revitalization and mass marketing of *Operation Condor,* Sheehan said, "is shameful." He asserts that Disney president Michael Eisner "contends that his company professes integrity, ethical behavior, and civility, but when it comes to Arab Muslims, Disney's 1990s films demonstrate the opposite." Sheehan was alluding to what he strongly felt were Disney caricatures of Arabs in the films *In the Army Now* (1994), *Aladdin* (1992), *The Return of Jafar* (1994), and *Kazaam* (1996).

The following month, the Arab League—the Cairo-headquartered political and economic organization of 21 Arab and African countries—announced its intention to "take severe measures" against the Walt Disney company "because of the anti-Arab movies it produces." The move was prompted by an ADC report charging that Disney films "give a distorted image of Arabs and Moslems." The League charged Disney with "undermining their religion and Arab civilization." These movies, it added, "didn't stop accusing Arabs of being brutal and archaic, although warned by anti-defamation committees."

The ADC singled out *GI Jane,* which it said "contains a gratuitous end sequence with star Demi Moore and her Navy SEAL chums on a rampage killing Arabs. This is apparently how Moore can show she is truly worthy of being a SEAL. Once again, scores of faceless Arabs bite the dust and the world is better off with their extermination."

Disney denied the accusations of the ADC and the Arab League. The company issued a tersely worded statement that its films are not anti-Arab and do not wrongfully portray Arabs or Islam.

"I wonder how long it will be before people in the industry begin to cease denigrating people because of their religion, ancestry, or country of origin," concluded Jack Sheehan. "If Disney animators want to do another film about characters with huge noses, perhaps they should consider a sequel to Dumbo."

A Stitch Here, A Stitch There

In July 2000, Reuters filed a very brief wire story chronicling an incident that underscores how far businesses at all levels need to go in recognizing the diversity of cultures in the US.

A specialty clothing boutique in a mall near Detroit, Michigan, agreed to stop selling tight-fitting women's jeans emblazoned with verses from the Koran after vocal complaints from the local Moslem community called the apparel blasphemous. The pants were inscribed with the Arabic spelling for "Allah" and the phrase, "In the name of God, most gracious, and most merciful." To make matters worse, other verses from the Koran ran around the waist and cuffs of the jeans.

More than a dozen Muslim groups from the Detroit area threatened to boycott not only the store itself, but the entire mall, if the pants weren't immediately removed from the store's shelves. The owner of the store agreed to discontinue sale of the offending garments with the management of the mall buying the remaining inventory of about 20 pairs. "The pants have all been removed. Hopefully we'll stop getting all these telephone calls," said a spokesman for the shopping center where the store is located.

The incident seems outrageous when one realizes that in 1999 Detroit was home to 275,000 Arab-Americans—the largest concentration of Arab-Americans in the entire US. What's more, Detroit had more than 15,000 businesses run by Arab-Americans, which made it the largest, and one of the newest, concentrations of that particular ethnic group in the entire US. An incidental irony: the pants were manufactured overseas by a company called "Unity USA."

¿Viva Mexico...Viva El Salvador? Diversity and Unity

By the middle of 1999, the size of the Hispanic population in the US had exceeded the size of the entire population of Canada. Now more than 30 million people, the Hispanic segment of the US population is expected to balloon to 41 million by the year 2010—many being the first or second generation from their family to emigrate to the US. By 2050, according to the US Census Bureau, the Hispanic population will account for a full 25 percent of the total population of the US, up from the current 11 percent.

According to the US Immigration and Naturalization Service, six Spanish-speaking countries were among the top 25 nations supplying legal immigrants to the US in 1997—Mexico, Cuba, the Dominican Republic, El Salvador, Colombia, and Peru. Combined they accounted for almost 250,000 people, almost one-third of all processed by the INS that year.

More than 20 Spanish-speaking nationalities are represented in the United States, says Paul Herbig in his book *The Handbook of Cross-Cultural Marketing*. This translates into a significant umbrella issue that often crops up for companies wanting to reach the Hispanic market in the US—namely they fail to consider that each of those micro-niches has its own unique tastes and cultural habits, traditions, standards, and nuances.

At the same time, these Hispanic nationalities stem from varied and yet common roots in their Spanish heritage. "One of the major advantages of a 30-year growth period in media for Hispanic-Americans has been greater communication and stronger inter-relationships forged across all Hispanic cultures," comments Gustavo Godoy, publisher of *Vista Magazine* in an article in the May 1999 issue of *Adweek*.

Charles Fruit, vice president and director of media and marketing assets for Coca-Cola underscored Godoy's comments, saying: "I find it inconceivable that a marketer in one of the top urban markets today can succeed and not pay particular attention to the Hispanic market. Darwin's law will work out here and those who are not cognizant of the Hispanic market will ultimately become extinct over time."

Marketing, then, to this most diverse ethnic community can be fraught with pitfalls, some adding humor, and others actually fueling a sometimes heated social discourse.

Hola, Frito Bandito (Frito-Lay Inc.)

In 1932, a San Antonio, Texas, business promoter named Elmer Doolin paid a borrowed $100 for the recipe to a corn chip that he'd sampled in a small Mexican cantina. Setting up a production line of sorts in his mother's kitchen, what he was able to make he sold from the back of his *Model-T Ford*. A moderate local success, he moved to Dallas and settled in. By the end of World War II, he had firmly established himself as the snack-food king of the US Southwest. By the time of Doolin's death in 1959, says a profile in *Texas Monthly* magazine, "the Frito was an institution, one of the cornerstones of the snack food industry" It was the true-story successful venture of a "typical second-generation Texan of Mexican origins."

In 1961, the Frito Company merged with the Lay Company (makers of Lay's potato chips) to form Frito-Lay Inc. Four years later, the company merged with Pepsi-Cola to become PepsiCo.

Over the next few years, a trio of scandals stung the company: It suffered accusations of overcharging smaller customers; several top executives were indicted for extorting money from contractors; and, one of the company's commodity buyers was investigated for trying to corner the peanut oil market. The company found itself trying to reestablish its reputation by zeroing in on promoting one of its signature products—the classic Frito corn chip.

So, in 1967, Texas-based Frito-Lay Inc. launched a national promotion and advertising campaign featuring an animated character, the Frito Bandito. He was a lovable Mexican rogue who, unable to tame his passion for Frito chips, roamed the countryside à la Joaquin Murrieta relieving his victims of their irresistibly delicious Frito corn chips—at gunpoint.

The story, from this point, is chronicled by Chon A. Noriega, a professor of film and television at the University of California, Los Angeles, who authored a piece on the development of the Frito Bandito character. Noriega's article appears in the San Diego Latino Film Festival Current Trends web site.

Originally run to target the pre-teen snack-food niche, the animated Bandito commercials were shown during after-school and Saturday morning programs on both network and local television stations. The company even started a "Frito Bandito Club." As a member (a "Little Bandito"), you would be guaranteed membership in the very gang that included the promo-sidekicks of Frito Bandito: W.C. Fritos (a south-of-the-border "cousin" of comedian W.C. Fields), Muncha Buncha, and Cheetos Mouse. A letter to the Frito Bandito Club would reap an "official" certificate, a welcome letter signed by the Frito Bandito himself, a sticker, an official ring, a membership button, a song sheet, and best of all, a cardboard mustache that you could hook onto your nostrils.

With his huge, bullet-riddled sombrero, his drooping mustache, his bandolier, and his brace of pistols, the Frito Bandito proved to be such an "unqualified success" (said a company press release at the time) that Frito-Lay decided to use the character in all its print and television advertising.

"Caution!" said the tag line to one of the commercials. "He loves croonchy Frito corn chips so much he'll stop at nothing to get yours. What's more, he's cunning, clever…and sneaky!"

Developed by the New York advertising agency Foote, Come & Belding, the Frito Bandito was only one of several similar characters, both animated and live, used by a number of companies to promote their products. Granny Goose (potato chips) and Elgin (wrist watches) use Bandito-like characters. One of the most curious commercials was created by Liggett & Myers. The company touted its cigarettes with a character called "Paco" who never "feenishes" anything, not even the revolution. Bristol-Myers developed an outlandish television ad that showed the leader of a gang of outlaws on horseback stopping an "attack" long enough for him to spray on the company's *Mum* underarm deodorant. The commercial's tag line was, "If it works for him, it will work for you."

A growing number of Latino activist groups vocally protested what they felt were the negative stereotypes the characters in the ads represented. Paco and his friends gradually disappeared from their respective companies' advertising campaigns as pressure bore down.

WATCH YOUR MANNERS, FRITO BANDITO

By 1971, only Frito-Lay was sticking to its "pistoles," disputing any negative connotations to the character—but, at the same time, sanitizing the Frito Bandito to make him more acceptable. The creative team at Foote, Cone & Belding headquarters went into a mode of frenzied creativity borne of the possibility of losing the multi-million-dollar account. They found a solution: effective immediately, the Frito Bandito would not grimace as much as he had in the past; he'd appear clean-shaven; his gold tooth would be replaced with a "real" one; and, he'd have an overall friendlier face and a voice with "less leer" and "more guile."

To bolster its position that the Bandito was harmless, Frito-Lay decided to go directly to the public. The company commissioned its ad agency to survey a sampling of Mexican-Americans around the country to see whether they found the Frito Bandito character stereotypically offensive.

At least on the surface, the survey results seemed to support the company's contention—85 percent of those surveyed liked the Frito Bandito, 8 percent were offended, and the remaining 8 percent had no opinion. The problem, though, was that Frito-Lay used the empirical evidence to define Mexican-Americans as a demographic group, not as consumers. "Our opinion," said a company press release, "is that the facts we have indicate we are not offending a large group. We will continue to survey, and any time we find we're offending a substantial group of Mexican-Americans, we'll be the first to take the Frito Bandito off the air."

ADIOS FRITO BANDITO

The response to Frito-Lay's survey claims was not what the company had hoped for. Rather than stilling the critics, the way the survey had been conducted and its use by Frito-Lay merely exacerbated the situation. Noriega quotes a piece in a December 1969 issue of *Newsweek*, charging that the company did not object "to offending a small group" because there was a profit to be made. The article ends with a scathing quote from a Frito-Lay executive: "We don't need the flak if the Bandito wasn't selling Fritos."

An immediate response arrived from two of the company's most vocal critics—the San Antonio, Texas-based Involvement of Mexican-Americans in Gainful Endeavors (IMAGE) and the National Mexican-American Anti-Defamation Committee (NMAADC). The activist groups, angered by Frito-Lay's lack of a direct response to their complaints, acted quickly. It was a time, Noriega says, when consumer groups were demanding free air time from TV and radio broadcasters to respond to commercials "that dealt with controversial issues of public importance" under the terms of the recently enacted "Fairness Doctrine."

Two major market television stations—KNBC-TV in Los Angeles, and KRON-TV and KPIX-TV in San Francisco—decided to negotiate rather than fight the issue out in court. Gritting their teeth over the idea of losing millions in advertising revenue, they nevertheless agreed in November 1969 to no longer accept any Frito Bandito advertising. The following month, the two activist groups announced their intention to file a joint complaint with the Federal Communications Commission (FCC) within 90 days; they were giving Frito-Lay time to respond and themselves enough time to negotiate with both the company and more broadcasters.

Just two months later, Frito-Lay announced that the Frito Bandito had reached the end of the trail and would be permanently retired.... but the story doesn't end here.

A year later, the commercials were still on the air. Frustrated with the failure of the FCC to hold the three stations to their agreement, NMAADC and IMAGE announced in January 1971 their intention to file a $610 million lawsuit in federal court "for the malicious defamation of the character of the 6.1 million Mexican-Americans in the United States." According to Noriega, the suit would seek damages of $100 for each Mexican-American "based on earlier arguments about the psychological damage of negative stereotypes." The action was being framed in the most extreme rhetoric to date: a statement from an article in the activist newspaper *La Raza* said that "Chicanos have become the media's new nigger."

This time, Frito-Lay had no option. The company met criticism from all quarters—even *Advertising Age* magazine slammed the company for "its lack of corporate good faith."

The Frito Bandito lifted his last load of corn chips, for real, in January 1971, but his legend lives on. At this writing, at least a half-dozen toy collectors' Internet web sites do a brisk business in Bandito memorabilia with "complete genuine" Frito Bandito Club Kits for sale. All innocuous now to be sure, these tokens nonetheless reflect a time not that many years ago when two immutable forces—a desire for profit and a desire for identity—collided, setting shockwaves in all directions that are felt to this day.

Viva Speedy Gonzales...Viva La Revolución

The January 23, 2000, edition of *The Independent* carried a story showing how, curiously, one man's stereotype can become another's revolutionary icon.

"Hispanic pressure groups," the story reads, "have insisted for years that corporate America axe all the Latino cliches that they consider demeaning. But 20 years after Warner Brothers stopped making cartoons featuring Speedy Gonzalez (an animated, rather chunky rodent who races from Point A to Point B in a blur), Zapatista guerillas in Chiapas [Mexico] have adopted the Mexican mouse as an emblem for their revolutionary movement."

Speedy, the piece continues, "masked with a balaclava and smoking a pipe" just like the poetry-spouting Zapatista leader, Subcomandante Marcos, appears as the host of the National Zapatista Liberation Army (EZLN) Internet web site.

The Zapatistas clearly approve of how the character—which Warner Brothers touted as the "Fastest Mouse in Mexico"—outwits the opposition with his cleverness and, of course, speed. Village children in war-torn Chapas reportedly sell handmade Speedy Gonzalez key chains and bandanas to raise money for the Marxist EZLN, while a *GameBoy* video game is reportedly a best-seller in both Mexico and the US.

"Squeaking out 'Arriba! Arriba!,' the rodent with the greasy accent has long been reviled by Latino activists as the worst kind of Hollywood stereotype," the story continued. But according to a representative of the US-based National La Raza Council, "He was created when it was not politically correct to defend Mexicans, but Warner Brothers did so through Speedy. They allowed a Mexican mouse to triumph over an American cat [Sylvester the Cat, Speedy's bumbling, lisping cartoon adversary]. I think that was pretty subversive in the '50s."

Delving Into The New America (AT&T)

The essence of cross-cultural marketing, particularly to new immigrants, means "delving into the audience's collective psyche...to find out what's important to them and playing to their interests," wrote Shelly Reese in the May 1998 issue of *Marketing Tools*. "It requires a full acceptance of the fact that quintessentially American icons, holidays, and heroes are often meaningless to consumers from other cultures—even if doing so means tweaking a general market campaign or revamping it entirely."

THE RING OF "PRAVDA"

Such was the case, she wrote, when AT&T attempted to reach the growing number of Russian immigrants in the US.

The company used singer-actress Whitney Houston in a few "True Voice" television commercials touting the clarity of its long-distance telephone connections. While the ads were popular in the general market, they would have been meaningless to Russian immigrants, wrote Reese. "Not only did Houston lack cachet with this particular group, but the idea of fiber-optic clarity was irrelevant to people accustomed to unreliable, static-filled phone connections."

Even more damning, she added, was the tag line—"Your True Voice"—which, loosely and unfortunately, translated into "The Voice of Pravda." *Pravda,* of course, is the name of the Moscow-based newspaper that was the Soviet-era sock-puppet for the ruling Communist Party.

With the help of an advertising agency with some Russian experience, AT&T pulled back and successfully restructured its message. In the new ad, AT&T used a well-known expatriate Russian comedian as a spokesman.

KIM CHEE OR SUSHI...THERE IS A DIFFERENCE

Another AT&T mistake illustrates how poorly strategized domestic international marketing efforts can generate unintentional results. For her article, Shelly Reese interviewed Eliot Kang of the New York-based advertising agency Kang & Lee, who described how a commercial targeted for the general market missed the mark by a wide margin. The ad emphasized how a competitor's claims could mislead. According to Reese, "the spot, as originally conceived, featured an elderly Korean woman who was upset about being deceived by a competitor's claims. Because the woman spoke with a heavy accent, the ad seemed to imply that she was gullible and ignorant about doing business in the United States."

The ad, said Kang, "showed [the woman] as being weak and foolish. We suggested reworking the ad to show her as smart and aggressive. The new commercial used the Korean idiom 'To see which is longer, put them side by side'— and showed a very smart bilingual Korean-American woman. The final ad showed that AT&T represents value, which is important to the consumer."

While AT&T has learned to successfully market to this expanding community of "New Americans," other companies still struggle.

MIND YOUR SYMBOLS!

About the same time, a competitor of AT&T tried to reach the Korean-American community. The effort nearly failed due to a major error in a direct mail piece, which fortunately was discovered before it went into the mail. With raised eyebrows, someone happened to notice that the piece carried a prominent Japanese Buddhist symbol. The problem? First of all, Koreans are not Japanese. In fact, most if not all Koreans deeply resent being mistaken for Japanese; this very emotional feeling stems from Japan's brutal occupation of Korea from 1905 to 1945. Second—an ancillary point, but important nonetheless—most South Koreans are actually either Confucian or Christian, not Buddhist.

In a November 1998 edition of *Incentive* magazine, Jeanie Casison wrote about another example. The article discusses what occurred when comedian Margaret Cho became the first Korean-American to star in her own television comedy series in 1995. The show disappeared almost as quickly as it appeared. "The original premise of the program was to explore the tension between immigrant Korean parents and their assimilated children. The point was to show that such families are American despite their ethnicity." But that theme, she said, was lost by the time the show made it to the air. "There was definitely an East-West division," said Cho in the article. "The show's producers made the differences so extreme, the audience must have thought the characters were from another planet."

The program, Casison adds, was also a victim of bad advertising; the promos for the show had caricatures of Cho, a native of San Francisco, as a Chinese doll figure doing karate kicks across the screen. "The idea was I was kicking away old tradition by putting on a denim jacket and carrying an electric guitar. It was just so bad. Very stereotypical," Cho said. "But by paying so much attention to the fact that we were different faces, in the end they completely lost the point of what they were trying to do."

Procter & Gamble's Reverse Marketing Strategy

In light of all the other issues that Procter & Gamble was facing in the early 1990s, the company displayed keen insight when it decided to reverse its product flow and begin to market within the US Hispanic community brands that it had originally developed for sales overseas.

Over the years, the company's US customers had grown used to *Camay* and *Zest* brand hand soaps, but had never seen the company's most successful products, wrote Dan Koeppel in the June 24, 1991, issue of *Adweek*. "Ariel [a laundry detergent]," he said, "was born overseas, and conventional wisdom says that US consumers don't buy foreign household products. Even Ariel's brand name sounds odd. Most US detergents—Tide, Cheer, Gain—use names that imply a kind of happy hygiene."

Ariel Ultra, "packaged as a high-tech super-concentrate, is aimed at a different kind of American. Hispanics are the country's fastest growing ethnic group...and on the West Coast, they exert immense cultural and consumer influence." Seen in a "new light," Koeppel said, "the bilingual packages of Ariel hitting the store shelves in Los Angeles this week are as All-American as Tide or Ivory." P&G's plan, he continued, "is the direct result of the demographic changes sweeping American communities.... American tastes are lining up more with global preferences."

A P&G executive interviewed for Koeppel's story said, "Hispanics knew this product and wanted it. We realized that we couldn't convince them to buy [our] other laundry detergents." In fact, she added that Ariel detergent was so popular with Mexican immigrants in Southern California that a small industry had grown up around importing gray-market versions of the detergent from Tijuana (just across the US-Mexico border near San Diego).

But the thinking driving the company's new marketing strategy could be seen in other ways, as well. "When you met with P&G's top managers years ago, you wouldn't have seen a single foreign face," said an investment manager familiar with P&G's history. "Today, P&G is relying more and more on foreign talent"— talent, she said, that "is working to change US consumers just as P&G marketers sent abroad changed the preferences of overseas consumers."

Lessons Learned

TAKE A GLOBAL VIEW OF EVERY COUNTRY

Within a country there is an entire world of diversity. A company can choose to compete with many other companies for a small part of what is considered the country's national population, or it can tap into uncharted waters within the same country. Of course, some changes may be needed to appeal to the various demographic groups within a country. These might include groups characterized by ethnic heritage, education, economics, age, sex, and so forth. Such adaptations may allow ready expansion into related foreign markets.

Although the idea occurred to Proctor & Gamble after they had already successfully marketed their Ariel detergent overseas, when they finally woke up to the possibilities within the United States, they found immediate acceptance. Moreover, they all but cleared up a small gray market problem that would otherwise have festered and caused some expensive grief if they had simply asserted their rights against the illegal imports. It is often a wise strategy to fight competitors—even illegal ones—with fair competition on the same turf.

THE MORAL: You don't always have to go overseas to find new markets; sometimes you can just walk down your own block.

RECOGNIZE STEREOTYPES FOR WHAT THEY ARE

The fact is: stereotypes are insulting. They also tend to shadow a company's otherwise pristine reputation. As contact among different populations increases and acceptance of diversity grows, so also must cultural awareness. In essence, stereotypes portray the extreme differences among world populations and unfairly emphasize certain traits as general to all members of a certain group, forgetting that the same human characteristics can in fact be found in all peoples.

The benefit of recognizing and eliminating stereotypic advertising, packaging, promotions, and the like can actually be far more advantageous. When AT&T wanted an ad that positively portrayed an Asian, it found immediate acceptance not only among the non-Asian targeted audience, but also within the US Asian community. Thus, its domestic markets expanded merely by flipping the coin from weak and foolish to strong and smart.

On the other hand, companies like Coleco, Disney, Frito-Lay, Bristol-Meyers, and Ligget & Meyers have chosen promotions and products that are wrapped up in stereotypes thought to be funny to the "American" public. While some significant success can be claimed among segments of the US population that are perhaps less culturally aware, these companies have also taken significant hits from media and ethnic populations in the US and abroad. For the most part, they have also not penetrated into the US populations that are more culturally sympathetic, until moving away from stereotypic promotion.

THE MORAL: He who lives in a glass house should not cast stones on his neighbors.

GET YOUR OWN HOUSE IN ORDER

Time is of the essence when getting products into the market. Companies are constantly striving to beat the competition, to be the first, or at least the second, to come up with a startling innovation and turn it into an overnight success. Cultural awareness at home delays the immediacy of this process, and besides, if a company doesn't already know its home markets, who does?

Demographic studies, census and immigration reports, and similar resources are available for many countries. They show both pockets of immigrants living in concentrated groups and the population of assimilated immigrants who generally have kept their historical and cultural roots. Whether companies target these specific markets within their home country or the population-at-large, it is essential to do a cultural check. AT&T was fortunate to find and remove Japanese icons from promotional materials aimed at Korean consumers. How much better it would be to have a systematic cultural check in place for the domestic market so that nothing is left merely to accidental discovery a few days before the presses roll or the trucks are loaded.

THE MORAL: Because of changing demographics, domestic markets need just as much understanding and attention to detail as overseas markets.

USE IT OR LOSE IT

Technology has revolutionized the way the world does business. It has given businesses—particularly small and medium-size enterprises—the wherewithal to research potential markets and promote their products in ways unheard of just a decade or two ago. What before was beyond reach can now be touched more effectively and at less cost.

The tools are there, but—curiously—most high-tech companies, in particular, are failing to pick them up and use them to position themselves in the New America. "US high-tech companies are missing out on a major opportunity," said Martha Geller, a multicultural marketing specialist quoted in the January 1998 issue of *Red Herring* magazine. "The impression," she says, "is that ethnic communities in the US are poor and uneducated and can therefore be covered with general market advertising. Nothing could be further from the truth."

The facts bear out Geller's claim. Arab-Americans, for example, have a median per-household income of almost $40,000, a full 11 percent higher than the national average, while the Hispanic market in the US is valued at more than $350 billion. And more than 55 percent of Asian-Americans (age 25 and older) hold at least a bachelor's degree, compared with 22 percent for the rest of the population. In addition, some 28 percent of the US Asian population use the Internet, while close to one-half own a personal computer, with other ethnic groups close behind.

According to Geller, vice president of YAR Communications in New York, few, if any, of the foreign-born people in the country are targeted "by few, if any, of the large-scale marketing strategies of consumer-oriented technology companies." This lack of focus (a failure to saturate broader consumer segments and utilize specifically targeted advertising), Geller said, "is surprising given the fact that, over the last few years, personal computer and other hardware manufacturers have been steadily expanding their marketing efforts overseas, starting with Europe and more recently turning their attention to Asia and Latin America." He added that software companies, following the trend toward localizing their products, have just begun to customize their international advertising.

Another marketer interviewed for the article says that high-tech firms "were among the first to use the Internet to address markets overseas...and the 'net' affords advertisers the potential to cover ethnic communities in the United States at little incremental cost while looking toward overseas markets."

The potential interplay between domestic ethnic markets and overseas markets, says writer Paul Ross, "has not been lost on multicultural marketers. They note that—thanks to improved technology and declining telephone tariffs—foreign students, recent immigrants, and tourists in the United States now keep in much closer touch with colleagues, friends, and family back home, and these informal conversations can have a substantial impact on the way a US company's products and brands are perceived overseas."

Alluding to AT&T's successful "Acceso Latino" bilingual Internet web site, Martha Geller said, "High-tech companies that want to reach these consumers will follow AT&T's lead, particularly if they recognize the value of getting there first. Our experience has shown that, given the unusually high brand loyalty among ethnic communities, the first PC company...to advertise to these markets will enjoy a significant advantage."

The transformation of America from a primarily industrial economy to an increasingly information-based one has compelled companies to rethink their marketing strategies. The marketing efforts once based on touting a "one-size-fits-all, take-it-or-leave-it" premise have radically shifted to a sharp focus on the needs of the consumer—a consumer that must be understood no matter who he is and no matter where he comes from.

In the future, the most successful international companies will be those who can transform themselves—like Betty Crocker—in ways that make them more receptive to the needs of the consumers. After all, one by one, and group by group, they compose the changing face of America.

THE MORAL: Trains don't wait for stragglers. If you haven't climbed on board before the last whistle, find another train.

CHAPTER 8

Applying the Lessons Learned

IT'S NOT WHAT YOU KNOW, IT'S WHAT YOU DO

INTERNATIONAL MARKETING "is the performance of business activities in more than one nation. But more than that, it is not simply doing business in more than one nation, but doing business in more than one culture," according to international business educator and writer Paul Herbig.

He states that a company, "could perform all of its business in the same country and still be considered to be involved in international marketing." How? "If the company does business with the domestic subsidiaries of a multinational located in another country, it can still be considered involved in international marketing. And since over 70 percent of all companies in the United States either source from or count among their customers, international concerns," in effect they are doing international business.

Herbig calls the US "the last bastion of parochial beliefs," and he notes that "even small companies are realizing they have only three options: go global, get out of the business, or go broke. International marketing, he says, "must exist for the survival of the firm, any firms, all firms."

Mistakes Do Have their Value

Some people say that one of the best ways to learn is from our mistakes, while others say that the best teacher is not making the mistakes in the first place. Both are valid statements: Sometimes blunders—whether experienced or seen and avoided—lead to a change of course onto the right path; other times blunders prove to be expensive stumblings on a company's downhill slope to eventual extinction. Either way, blunders teach lessons—some that seem almost choreographed. They can help smooth the road ahead.

Suffer the Little Children (Beech-Nut Nutrition Corporation)

On June 25, 1982, the top management at the Beech-Nut Nutrition Corporation were at a fork in the road. Their secret was out and they had to make a decision, quickly.

They—namely president and chief executive officer Niels Hoyvald and vice president of operations John Lavery—could admit publicly that the company's apple juice sold to millions of babies around the world as "nutritious and wholesome" was a fraud, or they could try to hide the fact and continue to sell it to unsuspecting customers. Concluding that an admission of such magnitude would ruin a company that had prided itself on purity and quality, they opted for the latter.

For months afterward, container-loads of the juice were shuffled around like the cups in a sideshow "shell game" from its manufacturing plant in Canajoharie, New York, to its warehouse in Secaucus, New Jersey, and thence to distributors across the country. Then, in record numbers, they went overseas to distributors in the Virgin Islands, Puerto Rico, and the Middle East. A complicated game of deception played out so the company could quickly unload the juice (valued at about $7.5 million), minimize its projected losses, and stay one step ahead of the federal and state authorities who wanted to seize the product as evidence.

As reported extensively in the *Philadelphia Inquirer,* an investigation later showed that Beech-Nut had, unknowingly, begun selling phony juice in 1977 when it switched to a new supplier of apple juice concentrate. The concentrate was a component of many of its products. The following year, however, the company learned that the concentrate it was buying from its new New York-based supplier contained absolutely no apple juice at all—it was nothing more than a bland mixture of water, beet sugar, corn syrup, and artificial ingredients.

Beech-Nut executives made visits to the supplier's plant, which raised serious questions about the company's manufacturing capabilities, and the lab tests confirmed that the "concentrate" wasn't concentrate at all. Despite all that, Beech-Nut took no action and continued to buy hundreds of thousands of gallons of the stuff.

COST VERSUS VALUE...AND INTEGRITY

It all came down to cost. Buying the phony concentrate saved Beech-Nut some 20 percent over prevailing prices for the genuine article—savings that amounted to about $1.75 per gallon. Multiplied by hundreds of thousands of gallons, the savings were significant. Thomas Roche, the assistant US Attorney who prosecuted the case, added that "the savings were especially attractive to a company awash in red ink."

Hoyvald joined Beech-Nut after the company had been purchased by Nestlé SA in 1979. Tasked with turning the company into a profit-maker, Hoyvald (who claimed his subordinates had kept him "in the dark" before the June 25, 1979, "revelation") found himself under tremendous pressure. The company had lost $1 million after his first year at the helm; promising to increase sales and produce profits by as much as $700,000, he found himself backed into a corner. He decided to bury the apple juice problem for fear that a change to a legitimate concentrate supplier would add millions of dollars to his costs and negate his promise to turn a profit.

Indicted and convicted in federal court, both Hoyvald and Lavery faced lengthy prison terms and upwards of $8 million in fines. Beech-Nut pleaded guilty to 215 criminal counts of intentionally shipping millions of bottles of the phony juice, and was fined $2 million.

But the company paid in other ways, too. Its reputation trashed, Beech-Nut never really recovered from the scandal. In 1987 alone, the company lost $10.8 million in business, and its reputation was dented even further when it was determined that the phony apple concentrate was also being used in other Beech-Nut products. Despite injunctions from the US Food and Drug Administration, the company continued to sell products using the adulterated apple juice for five months after it was supposed to stop selling it and five years after first receiving word that the concentrate was fake.

LESSON: Don't let the desire to build the bottom line cloud the duty of providing the customer with the best possible product. Beech-Nut, though struggling, had a very good reputation before the apple juice fiasco. Pressure from above caused the company's management to panic and implement a serious lack of judgement. They reacted like persons involved in a high-speed chase with the police. Everyone knows how it's going to end—the driver speeds to get away from the authorities and eventually winds up in handcuffs, sitting in the back of a patrol car. It was only a matter of time before the truth was revealed. Beech-Nuts's Hoyvald and Lavery would have done better had they made a public statement accepting responsibility before taking all the steps necessary to correct the situation. The public will forgive a corporation that makes an honest effort to right a wrong; it will not forgive a company that lies for profit.

What's in a Name? (Bic)

In a November 1990 issue of the *Adweek* magazine *Marketing Week*, the story was told of Bic, the manufacturer that had for generations been synonymous with a broad range of commodity consumer products—from disposable ballpoint pens and razors to cigarette lighters. In mid-1988, the New Milford, Connecticut-based company decided to venture into the fragrance business in an effort to extend its brand name and reputation into an entirely new product line. Early the following year, *Parfum Bic* fragrances—four of them—appeared on the shelves of drugstores, supermarkets, and mass merchandisers across the US, with plans calling for the eventual entry of the new product line in several overseas markets.

The company invested $20 million into the marketing campaign for Parfum Bic fragrances, but in its first year on the shelves, poor sales of the new product were tagged as the primary cause of a drop in company profits of almost 23 percent for the year. Despite hopes for a renewed marketing and sales effort, Parfum Bic fragrances—*Jour, Nuit for Women, Bic,* and *Bic Sport for Men*—were yanked from store shelves in 1989. They left only a slight odor behind to mark their passing.

Pricing wasn't the issue. With a suggested retail price of $5, the fragrances should have flown off the shelves. But the company seemed more infatuated with the product than with paying attention to creating the image that is crucial in selling any fragrance product, concluded the article. Industry analysts at the time said that Bic should have marketed the product more like a fragrance and "less like a cigarette lighter," suggesting that "the Bic name might had a better chance" that way of carrying over into the fragrance category.

Thoughts of creating the right appeal stopped after the company came up with the slogan, "Put Paris in Your Pocket." It was a step in the right direction, but one that proved to be the outer limit of the company's creativity. The fragrance bottles, said one observer, resembled cigarette lighters and carried only the company logo and the fragrance name to identify the contents. In addition, there were no spray testers at the points of purchase, a fatal mistake: perfume and fragrance purchasers unfailingly want to test the smell of a product before they buy it.

Interestingly, the Parfum Bic fragrance fiasco was only one of a string of blunders that made the company a laughingstock. In the mid-1970s, the company fell on its face after investing millions in two failed attempts to develop and market a brand of hosiery called *Fannyhose*. Bic president Marcel Bich led the company into another pothole when it tried to develop Bic sailboards, losing millions more in the process.

Bic survived, but barely. Quoted in an article in *Forbes* shortly before his death in 1994, Bich said, "The more you risk, the more you have the chance to win, or lose." Words to live by "for flamboyant entrepreneurs tempted to stretch the limits of their famous monikers," commented *Forbes*.

LESSON: Don't let past success cloud your objectivity. Even the most flexible and experienced marketers can fail when they assume "one size fits all" in stretching a brand name—they might pull it beyond its limits. The company should have stuck to its core competency, or at least partnered with another company that knew something about the new business. "It's actually a good thing that they didn't make it as far as getting the product overseas," said one observer later. "They became very arrogant in thinking that their name would do all the work for them. Bic would have been eaten alive in overseas markets where the fragrance industry has generations of experience and sophistication. I wouldn't have been surprised if potential customers used to seeing the "Bic" name on other products like throw-away pens and cigarette lighters would have laughed off new fragrances by assuming they'd smell like ink or butane."

Game, Set, and Match (Donnay Sporting Goods SA)

Family-owned Donnay Sporting Goods SA profited handsomely from affiliating itself in promotions with tennis superstar Bjorn Borg—the Swedish champion who had almost become a cult figure, winning tournament after tournament in the late 1970s. The Belgian company saw its global sales skyrocket as tennis players around the world identified its signature wooden racket with Borg's success, wrote *The Wall Street Journal* in its September 13, 1988, issue.

Within a year or two, however, Borg slowly cut back on his tournament schedule. Then, in 1983, he retired from the game altogether. Shackled to Borg's success, the company lost money for four years straight until 1987—when it went out of business.

Observers tell that, for the Donnay company, Borg's move out of the limelight was actually primarily a catalyst for problems that were spawned within the company years before. The real problem started in 1973 when US-based Wilson Sporting Goods decided to drop Donnay as its major supplier of wooden rackets in favor of cheaper rackets supplied by manufacturers in Taiwan. The blow was staggering: Donnay had produced rackets for Wilson for almost 20 years, and by the 1970s it was reportedly shipping 1.3 million of its annual production run of 2 million rackets to Wilson for sale in the US.

In addition, the company failed to adapt its production facility in Couvin, Belgium, to meet the demand for lightweight graphite rackets. The company produced only 3,500 graphite rackets in 1980, choosing instead to concentrate on aluminum rackets—and it continued to make wooden ones until 1986 when the demand virtually dried up.

LESSON: The company simply put most of its eggs in one basket. Donnay decided to disregard the fact that its competitors were cashing in on the booming tennis market in the late 1970s by offering customers the latest in lighter, easier-to-handle graphite models. And they seemed to ignore the evidence that the now-outmoded wooden racket that had become their brand signature piece was swiftly becoming an anachronism. In effect, Bjorn Borg had become the sun around which virtually all of Donnay's marketing, advertising, and product development orbited. The company's other blunders were a recipe for disaster: Donnay had no in-house marketing manager until the year before it went bankrupt. The company's assembly line was ten times longer than any of its more efficient competitors'. The Donnay family insisted on keeping all of the company's production in Belgium, while its competitors were moving theirs to Asia. And, shortly after Borg's retirement, Donnay began distributing its cheaper rackets to mass distributors in the US, effectively blowing the company's image.

Nestlé's Tragic Mistake

Sometimes marketing blunders take a tragic turn, providing lessons in what can happen when an innovation is introduced into cultures, which are not appropriate. In their book, *Marketing: An International Perspective,* authors Philip Cateora and Susan Keavenay chronicle a sad occurrence of just such a corporate strategy.

In the mid-1970s, they wrote, the giant Swiss multinational Nestlé decided to introduce powdered baby formula to developing countries in the Third World. Although no profit-making company could ever be perceived as altruistic, to a degree the company was motivated by the feeling that it actually could relieve a tragic situation plaguing the world's lesser-developed, poverty-stricken countries—thousands of infants in those countries were dying each year because their mothers were themselves malnourished. The company was convinced that the baby formula, when mixed with water, would provide the basic nutrients the infants needed to survive. So arrangements were made with both public and private sector agencies and organizations to distribute the formula through medical clinics, hospitals, missions, and other channels.

The tragedy occurred when mothers, many illiterate and uneducated on the use of the formula, mixed it with unsterilized water, or "stretched" it by diluting it too much to make their supply of the formula last longer. Unfortunately, many of those infants fed with the formula prepared with contaminated water did not survive. To make matters worse, Nestlé learned that mother's milk passed on essential nutrients that weren't contained in the formula. And, because the mothers' milk dried up once the infants were introduced to the formula, there was no recourse.

As a result of the situation, in 1981 the United Nations' World Health Organization (WHO) adopted a set of guidelines for the worldwide marketing of infant formula. The code is mandatory for most nations and is legally binding in more than 25 countries. For Nestlé's part, the company strictly abides by the code whenever it markets infant products and makes all instructions in picture-diagram form for those consumers who can't read.

LESSON: Be aware that good intentions alone do not guarantee helping others. Give all marketing efforts the same care and attention. Nestlé should have given the infant formula program the same attention that it paid to the marketing of a product in more-developed countries. The company should have realized the difficulties that would be encountered in introducing what was, in effect, a sophisticated product into an "unsophisticated" market. Nestlé had allowed its better judgment and proven marketing experience to be clouded by a rush to "do the right thing." In the end, thousands of lives might have been saved had the company created a strategy that accurately fit the precise needs of the people who would be using the product.

A "Technically Superior" Product Fails (Johnson and Tambrands)

Despite the range of "superior products available on the market, only about 3% of women in Hong Kong use feminine tampons—which were introduced on the Hong Kong market in 1946—while in most developed countries usage is roughly equal to that of sanitary napkins." This data comes from a market survey synopsized in an article in the Spring 1996 edition of the *Journal of Health Care Marketing*. In fact, the article stated, most of that small number of users were expatriate residents of Hong Kong rather than the ethnic Chinese that comprised 98 percent of the then-British Crown Colony's population.

The reason for tampons' lack of popularity in Hong Kong puzzled major companies that were looking at Hong Kong—on the eve of its turnover to the People's Republic of China—as a springboard into the potentially huge mainland Chinese market. Two of those companies were Johnson & Johnson and Tambrands, which by the mid-1990s had established production facilities in two Chinese cities. They wanted to firmly establish their position in the feminine-sanitary-products niche.

In the years following World War II and into the 1960s, the feminine-hygiene-products needs of women in Hong Kong were largely served by homemade napkins of cloth or tissue paper, supplemented by unbranded commercially produced variants—either manufactured locally or imported from China. These napkins were sold prewrapped in plain, brown paper or in newspaper to prevent the buyer's embarrassment; as a result, women had no prior knowledge of exactly what they were purchasing. The only method of "comparative" shopping was to buy the products blindly and compare them once the wrappers were off.

Meanwhile, research showed tremendous potential for branded feminine napkins. Government statistics indicated that the female population of Hong

Kong grew by nearly 30 percent between 1961 and 1971, while the median monthly household income rose by a staggering 262 percent, and the expenditure on personal health care items climbed by more than 80 percent. Finally, in the mid-1960s branded feminine napkins began to appear on store shelves in Hong Kong. Suppliers started providing a much wider selection of products: domestic providers concentrated on the production of napkins, while international companies offered both napkins and tampons.

In the tampon segment of the market, Johnson & Johnson and Tambrands battled for market share in Hong Kong. Both US-based corporations had years of domestic and international experience (which included introducing their respective *o.b.* and *Tampax* brands to Hong Kong in the mid-1960s). Research conducted by napkin manufacturers before the companies entered the market concluded that the most significant product values sought by consumers of feminine hygiene products there were, first, safety; next, comfort; and then, convenience.

No such research was carried out by either Johnson & Johnson or Tambrands before they attempted to market their tampons to Hong Kong consumers. Both companies were satisfied that their tampons were technically superior to sanitary napkins in giving potential customers the desired benefits. Tampons, both companies asserted, are more comfortable as they can't be felt during use, unlike a napkin; they are easier to carry and dispose of; and, they are more bio-degradable than sanitary napkins.

Despite these benefits, tampons have never held a significant share of the Hong Kong market—even though both Johnson & Johnson and Tambrands have spent millions on advertising and instructional programs for adolescent girls presented by trained nurses. The market share peaked in 1982 with 3.2 percent, and then dropped to 2 percent at the time of the article in 1996.

LESSON: Both Johnson & Johnson and Tambrands failed to conduct proper research on the cultural differences between napkin and tampon usage. In Hong Kong Chinese culture, respect for family and for education has been found to be a strong influence on consumer behavior, which suggests that a woman is likely to seek the advice of a family member, particularly a mother, about products. Since older Chinese women had no experience with tampons, they could not be expected to recommend them to their daughters. Also, several studies available at the time would have told marketing researchers at both companies that sex and feminine hygiene, in particular, are topics that elicit a strict and austere response in a Chinese family setting. This would have led researchers to conclude that the implications of the penetrative attributes of tampons lauded by both Johnson & Johnson and Tambrands would be, in reality, a powerful disincentive for young Chinese women. Simply put, both companies should have made the effort to understand the particular needs and idiosyncrasies of the Hong Kong market for their products. Such an effort would have clearly delineated the conflict that existed between the product (and its promotional message) and Hong Kong's distinct values and norms.

When the Shine Wears Off (Goddards)

In 1959, Robert McGrath was hired by a US importer to market *Goddards* silver polish, the most famous brand name in the UK for silver polish. The company had been in business for generations, and housekeepers at estates as well as museum curators across the country considered Goddards brand the polish of choice. The company also held a prestigious Royal Warrant because of its approved use at Buckingham Palace. So, Goddards was a high-quality, high-class product with impeccable credentials.

According to McGrath, that year the company was selling about $5,000-worth of polish a month in the US. By the time US-based S.C. Johnson bought the English company and canceled Goddards's contract with McGrath's import firm in 1969, that figure had soared to more than $400,000 per month. Less than three years later, S.C. Johnson offered the line back to the importer—monthly sales had plummeted to $60,000 monthly.

LESSON: It's a story reminiscent of the Quaker Oats/Snapple disaster related in Chapter 6. Bigger and flashier doesn't necessarily mean better. Says McGrath, "During the 1960s, we established relationships with our customers. We ran ads in antique and museum publications, and in the *NEW YORKER* and *SUNSET* magazines. The campaign wasn't big and splashy, but deliberate. Consumers came to trust Goddards' polishes just the way the English did." Sales, he said, "doubled year after year until S.C. Johnson took over and applied its brand of 'marketing savvy'—mass production, pallet-load shipments, and 'big thinking.' Goddard polishes are still on the market but a shadow of their former selves." By the time McGrath took back the line, the damage had already been done. It was too late to "put the shine back on the silver."

Fade to Black

There once was a time when US manufacturers had a "textbook monopoly" over televisions, as told by Herb Kleiman in the September 18, 1995, edition of *Industry Week*. "Every manufacturer was US-based; every TV was made domestically; and American workers had all the jobs, from research and design through manufacturing and marketing." President of a management consultancy in Shaker Heights, Ohio, Kleiman wrote the article just a few weeks after the last domestic US television manufacturer, Zenith Electronics, was acquired by LG Electronics of South Korea.

With the sale of Zenith, Kleiman said, "Our last vestige as a television design-manufacturing creative force vanishes. Soon every TV sold here will be the product of a foreign-owned company." Ironically, he added, "about two-thirds of the nearly 25 million color TVs sold in the US last year were assembled domestically, providing jobs for the American workforce. But the entire front-end of the business, with all the associated knowledge-intensive, highly skilled positions, is outside our shores. Of course, any profits realized are repatriated overseas."

Television manufacturers in America failed to market to the increasingly affluent markets of the developing world. They neglected to adapt and customize their products for overseas sale. And they didn't compensate for high labor and production costs by moving at least some of their production—particularly assembly operations—offshore.

Many of the industry's wounds, Kleiman wrote, "were self-inflicted and have been repeated by companies in other industries. US companies anticipated poorly, underestimated the commitment and prowess of the new competition, lagged in applying advanced technology, and altogether misjudged the dynamics of a sharply altered marketplace."

Unfortunately, Kleiman concluded, "In an era when research budgets are shrinking and caution outranks daring, the low-risk, short-term approach is the overwhelming strategy of choice. We really excel, however, when we create and then dominate new markets. Our history of the past century confirms this contention, with the television experience only one example of many where we did it right—initially."

LESSON: Basically, American television manufacturers were content to sit tight and ignore the global—and domestic—developments that would eventually swamp them. According to Kleiman, everyone on a company's management team "should be involved in the process—research and development, production, marketing, even finance" with the objective of "bringing improved products to market faster, with a high probability of market success." Companies should, he concludes, "draw on their fundamental strengths to out-invent and out-innovate" the competition.

Diebold Fumbles and Recovers

In the summer of 1998, Diebold Inc. found itself in big trouble. The North Canton, Ohio, manufacturer of automated teller machines (ATMs) had just tallied up the figures and found that its second quarter revenues had plunged 7 percent to $281 million, a full loss of $14.4 million for the three-month period.

The loss, analysts said, could be pegged on several issues: the company had an all-consuming preoccupation with the Y2K (Year 2000) problem, banks were continuing a trend of mergers, and, most important, the company failed to create an effective European distribution channel.

According to *American Banker* magazine, International Business Machines Corp. (IBM or "Big Blue," as it's universally known) had been Diebold's major reseller in the international market. The two companies operated a joint venture called Interbold, which lasted for seven years until IBM decided to pull out of the deal in 1997.

Diebold's lack of a stand-by distribution plan came as a surprise, said Richard Sporrer, a financial industry analyst based in Pittsburgh, Pennsylvania. "A lot of analysts thought they had one in place, but that really wasn't the case. I wouldn't say they are starting from scratch, but they have a lot to do. They think they can get it done between now and the end of the year."

Well, almost. In January 1999, after a year of planning, the company took the first steps to recover the ground lost when it split with IBM. "We are now moving forward with our plans for our own international distribution [system], which involves basically the model of direct sales representation for the major accounts and distributors for the middle market," said Diebold chairman and chief executive officer Robert Mahoney.

Diebold's first step was the creation of its own sales subsidiary in Canada. Just two months later, Diebold acquired a 55 percent share of a Bogota, Colombia, financial services company—a former partner of IBM—to handle the distribution, sales, and service of its automated teller machines there. In April, it signed a 5-year agreement with the Standard Bank of South Africa to service the bank's 2,500 automated teller machines throughout the country; it formed a subsidiary, Diebold South Africa S.A., in Johannesburg to develop new business throughout the region. And, that fall, the company acquired total control of Procomp Amazonica Industria Electronica, its former Brazilian software developer and manufacturing partner.

Shortly after, Diebold made the decision to outsource system software developed at a center operated by Diebold HMA Private Ltd., a joint venture partner based in Pondicherry, India. "India is a very important market for us," said a company spokesman. "We expect 100% growth in each of the next two years."

Then, in February 2000 Diebold announced that it would pay $160 million in cash to buy the joint ATM manufacturing operations of Amsterdam-based Getronics NV and Groupe Bull of France. The deal was sweet for Diebold—the acquisition made the company the second-largest provider of automated teller machines in Europe (the company had ranked number four in 1998).

LESSON: Diebold found out very quickly that the international corporate identity of IBM would not automatically transfer over to "Big Blue's" distribution partners. Diebold had assumed that the relationships with vendors that IBM had established over the years would fall into place with them. The company's management hierarchy had failed to realize that Diebold needed to establish its own distribution network and could not hang on to IBM's coattails after IBM decided to end their joint venture. Fortunately, Diebold quickly recovered and was able to recoup on a grand scale.

Aussie Suds Go Flat (Foster's)

Through the 1980s, Foster's Australian Lager beer rode the wave of approval created by the popularity of actor Mel Gibson and a string of films portraying the free-spirited caricature of all things Australian in the movie character "Crocodile Dundee." The beer proved to be very well-liked in the US, particularly in California, which shares an affinity with Australia based on the mutually laid-back "3B" lifestyle—beach, beer, and barbecue.

But the company ran into problems. The beer landed on shelves already sagging under the weight of a huge influx of imported brands from a growing number of countries—including Canada, The Netherlands, Germany, Mexico, Belgium, Great Britain, Ireland, China, Japan, and the Philippines. Not only that, but the company also discovered it had to go head to head with a flood of domestic US beers produced by a host of so-called microbreweries.

Failure to size up the competition accurately was only part of the problem. Foster's failed to establish a brand and added an even greater blunder: the "Down Under" trend had begun to cool, and US sales plummeted from 3.8 million cases in 1988 to 2.8 million the following year. Panic set in. The company decided to switch US distributors in midstream. By the time the sales slide bottomed out, the company found that 40 percent of its business had evaporated.

LESSON: Foster's tried to shift the blame for its own failure at establishing a brand identity to its distributor, All Brands Importers Inc. of Hartford, Connecticut. But when the company split with All Brands, the move created a break in the distribution chain; that further alienated consumers who were already confused by Foster's trying to be the "universal beer" for the Australian every American really wanted to be. "Once you break the pipeline, you have major problems because it's just such a tight market," said Peter LaFrance, associate editor of *Beverage Media*. "If you lose shelf space, and the trust of wholesalers and distributors, it's tough to get it back again, especially for an import that wants a national market."

Polaroid's Instant Failure

According to Philip Cateora and Susan Keaveney in their book, *Marketing: An International Perspective*, one company that neglected to modify its US strategy to fit an overseas market was Polaroid. In the 1970s, the company decided to tap the camera market in France for the first time by introducing its *Swinger* model instant camera there. After two decades of success with the instant camera concept, Polaroid unveiled its Swinger Model 20 in 1965 to a market saturated with small cameras. After a very successful run in the mature US market, the company started selling the camera in France—but the entire effort failed miserably.

Polaroid hadn't understood that, as far as the French market was concerned, the concept of instant photography was a complete mystery. The product was in the introductory stage of its life cycle in France, but Polaroid was using a marketing strategy designed for a product that would be introduced into a mature market like the US, where the company had 20 years of experience and market identity.

The company eventually pulled the Swinger camera from France, restructured its advertising and marketing strategy, and reintroduced the camera into the market. It did so with some success.

In 1994, Polaroid decided to modify its European marketing strategy to concentrate on Germany and Eastern Europe. After concluding that the trend towards faster 35mm film development and instant video playback in Western Europe had significantly eroded its market share there, the company decided to cultivate untapped markets. Polaroid hired a new advertising agency and earmarked about $40 million for an advertising and promotional campaign in the new target markets.

Also in 1994, a year's time of orchestrated lobbying paid off when the Indian government decided to lower its duty on imported "instant" film. The tariff reduction—from 158 percent to 54 percent—came when Indian Prime Minister Narasimha Rao was rethinking the country's long-standing closed door trade policies. The cut in tariffs allowed the company to drop its prices, which made the products more affordable to the average Indian customer.

LESSON: Often international marketers will take a product from the US that is either in the maturity or declining stage of its product life cycle and will try to extend its life by introducing it into a foreign market. To be successful with such a strategy, a company must remember that the product is being inserted into an environment completely different from that in the US; pricing, distribution, advertising, and promotional strategies have to be adequately modified to fit the needs of the new market. On the other hand, Polaroid showed great skill in penetrating the closed Indian market. It was able to convince the Indian government that its presence in the market would benefit consumers, create jobs through its Indian partner, and not harm any domestic Indian business (as Polaroid's only competitor at the time was Fuji of Japan).

A False Sense of Security (Merck & Co.)

The term "pluralistic ignorance" is defined as "a social phenomenon that reflects a situation where people operate within a false social world creating patterns of false beliefs that are either individually inferred or collectively shared," according to Michael Harvey, of the University of Oklahoma, and Milorad Novicevic, of the University of Wisconsin. In the spring 2000 edition of the *Journal of World Business,* they point to the global pharmaceutical giant Merck & Co. as a company where pluralistic ignorance has taken a heavy toll.

In 1998, they said, Merck's sales and profit grew by 19 percent over the preceding year, based on sales of almost $24 billion and a net income of close to $5 billion. An industry analyst they quote warned, however, that Merck's success in markets around the world can be expected to end soon. The analyst said that by the end of 2001 the company's US patents expire on five "big ticket" drugs that currently generate more than $5 billion in annual global sales. The analyst predicted that Merck's global business will drop to 8 percent of its total operations by the end of 2001 and to 6 percent by 2002, slowing its net income growth to 9 percent and 6 percent, respectively.

Merck Chairman Raymond Gilmartin, the writers wrote, "has attempted to sustain the power of the shareholders' pluralistic ignorance spell by asserting that 'Merck has defied conventional wisdom before,' [and] by saying that the company's new line of products—which will be first launched on the domestic market—will more than offset the anticipated drop" in revenues.

Gilmartin's claim initially bore some weight as sales of Merck's *Zucor,* a drug used to treat high blood pressure, generated $3.6 billion by early 1997. But the writers postulate that the development cycle of a drug is dramatically shortened today, which increases the uncertainty of a newly launched drug's success.

In 1997 one of Merck's biggest global rivals, Warner-Lampert, received accelerated approval from the US Food & Drug Administration to start selling *Lipitor* drugs, a counterpart of Merck's Zucor brand. In a strong effort to gain competitive advantage, Warner-Lampert also formed a comarketing alliance with Pfizer Inc.—another US-based pharmaceuticals company—to create a combined sales force of almost 3,000 sales representatives. Merck's sales force at the time numbered only 1,400. As a result, by the end of the second quarter of 1998, the Lipitor brand held a 31.1 share of the market compared with the Zucor brand at only 24.5 percent; the resulting drop in stock value reflected "shareholders' loss of confidence in the continuation of Merck's past global success."

LESSON: Pluralistic ignorance, Harvey and Novicevic write, allows for individuals recognizing the discrepancy between their own private feelings and behavior, but they would not assume or recognize that any others share those feelings. Therefore, they believe that the actions of others accurately reflect those people's thoughts and feelings. In Merck's case, they say, the shareholders recognized the growing importance of global markets for the company, but saw plans from top-level management only indicating that they would maintain a domestic base for future growth. The company's managers also assumed that top management had some prepared plans—which they were not aware of—for effective action. The pluralistic ignorance of both the shareholders and Merck's mid-level management prevented them from asking questions or voicing any concerns.

Sometimes "Cool" Isn't (California Raisin Advisory Board)

In the early 1990s, the California Raisin Advisory Board developed what was considered to be one of the most imaginative promotional advertisements ever to come off the drawing board. The promotion featured "The California Raisins," animated clay-figure raisins, dancing in step like a Motown singing group to the tune of Marvin Gaye's classic pop hit, "I Heard It Through the Grapevine." Decked out in "shades" (sunglasses), the Raisins were the epitome of "cool" as they jived their way to a pair of Clio Awards—the highest award given by the US advertising industry—and into their own exhibit at the National Museum of American History.

The goal of the promotion, of course, was to sell raisins, one of California's largest and most exportable agricultural commodities. The Board was trying to reach undertapped markets, particularly overseas. With Japan as a major potential buyer, the US Department of Agriculture gave the California Raisin Advisory Board a grant of $3 million to get the ball rolling to find buyers in Japan for a goal of 900 tons of raisins annually. Cocky promoters, assured of the campaign's success in Japan, were already crafting plans to introduce the California Raisins to television audiences in other parts of Asia, as well as Latin America and Europe.

But the campaign failed. The promotion cost $3,000 per ton of raisins sold to the Japanese—almost twice what the California producers earned per ton.

Rejected and misunderstood, the California Raisins were forced to pack up their cool image and head back to Sacramento.

LESSON: Don't assume that "cute" or "cool" will sell a product in Japan, or in any other country for that matter. While immensely popular in the US, the California Raisins were not created to seamlessly segue into a foreign commercial environment. Few advertising or promotional campaigns ever do.

An analysis of the California Raisins promotional campaign that appeared in the July 27, 1994, issue of The Oregonian newspaper discusses the reasons why the promotion fell flat: First, the commercials were broadcast "out of the can"—no one even bothered to translate them into Japanese. Second, the dancing raisins—misshapen, dark, and shriveled—frightened children; Japanese parents called television stations in Tokyo to complain. Third, many viewers couldn't figure out what product was being advertised; others confused the raisins with potatoes or chocolate candies.

Welcome to the 21st Century (Royal Dutch/Shell)

Just a few weeks after the confrontational World Trade Organization ministerial summit in Seattle, Washington, *Newsweek International* published a story focusing on the impact of globalization. It highlighted the responsibility of multinational companies to understand their new role in the world marketplace.

For a hundred years Royal Dutch/Shell had prided itself on being one of the first real multinationals. And it acted like one, the story read. "It was monarchical in manner and arrogant as hell, paying scant attention to locals as it marched in and out of the countries where Shell's legion of drillers, refiners and traders planted the company flag."

But in the 1990s, it continued, "the noise of protest outside Shell's boardroom in The Hague, once as faint as distant sirens below, grew into a roar that rattled the company's foundations. In Europe, youths who were angered by Shell's decision to junk an oil platform in the North Sea—forget the environmental damage—began boycotting and burning its service stations. Newspaper editorialists howled in 1995 when Shell only mildly protested as the corrupt government of Nigeria—which got about half its revenues from Shell—hanged writer Ken Saro-Wiwa and other activists who had protested [Shell's] drilling practices."

That's when Cornelius Herkstroter, then the self-described "bookkeeper" chairman of Shell, "began to feel the ground shift under his feet." At a certain moment, the now retired executive said, "you realize that you are beginning to lose touch...that the world is much more open and that communications, opinions and ideas are moving fast. And perhaps you begin to underestimate the forces out there."

LESSON: Today, concluded the Newsweek International piece, multinational corporations like Shell are driving the most phenomenal economic growth in human history. "As they grow even more enormous...they are doing the hard work of globalization. In some ways, multinational may even be the most powerful social glue left in a world where governments and ideologies are growing weaker and ethnic tensions stronger." But there is a flip side to this new prominence, the writers assert. "Increasingly the rest of the globe no longer expects them to act as mere companies. If multinationals have become the world's new power elite, then the public expects them to be good global citizens, and indeed to show leadership and some 'noblesse oblige,' as well." Responding to the criticism, Shell's Herkstroter quickly drafted a code of ethical principles for the company. He opened the company's doors to meetings with activist groups and began publishing an environmental section in its annual report. Now, shareholder activists rate Shell, along with competitor BP-Amoco, as one of the world's most ethical oil companies.

Lessons to Keep Learning

- Any marketing strategy should revolve around the premise that the needs of the customer are paramount. A company should never let a bottom-line mentality drive them to enter into an international market or to lie to turn a profit.

- Past success must not cloud good judgment. "One size" of a product or name brand does not "fit all," particularly in overseas markets. If a company lacks the wherewithal to modify or adapt its product to meet a specific market need, it should join forces with a partner who does, or commit to developing the necessary infrastructure itself.

- Any company wanting to succeed in the global marketplace should stay aware of the developing trends affecting the consumption of their product. Be willing to make hard decisions, even if they go against the grain of years of experience. Have access to experienced marketing professionals who can do the research and guide the process along.

- International marketing should be given the same investment of time and effort as any domestic campaign. The levels of sophistication in diverse markets should also be taken into consideration before a product is introduced into a market that may be incapable of using it properly. Wanting to do good things for people doesn't ensure the result—don't skip steps in the planning and evaluation phases.

- Culture plays an enormous role in the decisions that consumers the world over make every day. The nuances of culture—from the role of gender and family in daily life to religious beliefs and ethics—must be studied and taken into consideration as a core component of any successful international marketing plan. Too many otherwise worthy global business ventures have failed because of something as innocuous as the color of a package or an "unlucky" number used in a promotional campaign.

- Business partnerships are based on mutual benefit. Probably nothing has done more to derail successful international businesses than an emphasis on form over substance and flashy "new management" styles. These have probably ruined the chances of international businesses more than all other factors combined. A good product is a good product and should be treated as the treasure that it is.

- A company that wants to succeed—not just survive—in the global marketplace has to have everyone in the company be part of the team striving to achieve the goal. Labor and management, shop worker and financial officer, all must be sold on the idea of making the company competitive. Without a unified effort, the company can easily become embroiled in activities that will eventually sap its strength and its ability to stay in the race.

■ It's dangerous to assume that a partnership with a much larger multinational company will create a glow that will keep you basking in the sunlight forever. Their business is just that—their business, it's not yours. A company must be ready to take up the strain if a crucial relationship they have suddenly ends.

■ It's never a good idea to break a distribution chain in the middle of dealing with other internal corporate issues. Consumers rightfully expect a product to be readily available. They will transfer their allegiance to the competition if they become alienated by circumstances that could have been better handled. People want to feel that their supplier's management had chosen to take care of business rather than choosing to seek a scapegoat.

■ Products should never be arbitrarily introduced into a foreign market simply to extend their life cycle. Unaltered products rarely succeed in foreign markets. It's important to remember that such a move not only involves the product itself, but also its pricing, distribution, advertising, and marketing.

■ Every company should foster an environment encouraging the free expression of ideas. It is dangerous to assume that because nobody is complaining, everything must be all right. An employee brings the sum total of their experience to their job, which is worth much more than many companies will admit. Also remember that the most effective communication in a corporate environment moves both up and down.

■ Remember that what's chic in one place may cause furrowed eyebrows elsewhere. Concepts of what is avant garde, "cool," and "cutting edge" are relative. Industry sectors that sometimes cater to extremes in tastes, such as the apparel and entertainment industries, can foster a dangerously condescending attitude towards other cultures and people. These marketers assume that what is acceptable at home, for example, swimsuits conceived outlandishly for design rather than function, will be and should be acceptable to other cultures. This "hipper than thou" attitude displayed so frequently in some industries has done much to skew an appropriate understanding of a more common—and less "sophisticated"—global culture.

■ Any company—large or small—with global aspirations must see itself as a responsible partner in the global community. While not possessing the vast and almost limitless capabilities of a powerful giant company, small and medium-sized companies are the actual drivers of the world economy. It's incumbent on them to develop a sense of accountability that combines an understandable desire to succeed in an increasingly competitive global economy with a realization that the world is inhabited by many diverse peoples who have the right to make decisions about what they will or will not consume, and the price they're willing to pay for that right. A company will gain more respect for understanding, adapting to, and promoting acceptance of cultural diversity than it will for insensitively filling the marketplace with negative and even offensive portrayals of the extremes of human nature. The attempted humor simply falls flat.

CHAPTER 9

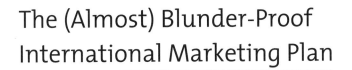

The (Almost) Blunder-Proof International Marketing Plan

NOW THAT YOU'VE MADE IT THIS FAR, an obvious question jumps off the page: "Is there a foolproof way to avoid the kinds of mistakes made by the companies chronicled in this book?" The answer is no, as there is not now, nor will there ever be, a foolproof way to do anything. Without putting too fine a philosophical point on it, anything devised by human beings is inherently flawed; that is an immutable truth.

It's almost laughable to consider that one would need to convince mature and experienced businesspeople of the advantage—not to say the criticality—of taking a long, hard look at a potential overseas market before making the decision whether to do business there. But, alas, the examples in this book have shown otherwise. Suffice it to say, though, that if one approaches an international business deal—whether the first or fiftieth—after having studiously followed a clearheaded course of action, the possibility of committing the kinds of mistakes and blunders—big and small, innocent and almost deliberate—mentioned in this book will be proportionally reduced.

Study hard, do your homework, ask questions—and take the answers to heart. Then, while everything may not go according to plan, at least you will have developed the kind of mindset to take it all in stride, follow with whatever corrective measures are necessary, and not lose sight of your ultimate goal.

Quite literally, hundreds of schematic marketing plans have laid out, to a greater or lesser degree, the elements of a successful international marketing strategy. And while all of them differ in many ways, they orbit around the same core formed by a few immutable truths. That is, they may differ in detail, but almost all are identical in approach.

This chapter builds on what a company anywhere and at any time can do to apply with practicality the lessons outlined in the preceding chapters.

"Country Books" and Research Sources

The first step in constructing an international marketing plan free from the blunders that have stopped so many companies dead in their tracks is to make a detailed country or regional analysis.

The basic information you need to create such an analysis includes three elements: (1) an evaluation of the target market's potential; (2) the identification of any problems or issues that might possibly eliminate the potential market from consideration; and (3) an evaluation to see whether any adaptation of your product or service is necessary to make it marketable.

THE COUNTRY NOTEBOOK

According to Philip Cateora in his book *International Marketing,* many companies compile a "country notebook" for each country in which they do business. Each notebook should contain up-to-date information that a marketer should be aware of when making decisions about a specific country market. The information should be gleaned from as many sources as possible. Publications of all kinds—both international and those published within the target country or region—should be read on a regular basis. The Internet also provides an outstanding source of qualified information, from both public- and private-sector sources, that in many cases is updated daily.

What to do with all this information? "Study it," Cateora says.

Whenever a marketing decision is made, he says, the country notebook should be the first source consulted. Keep an eye out for any conceivable issue that could impact the market's business environment—from political and economic issues to information on both domestic and international competitors. Organizing country notebooks and cultivating useful sources of information is only the first step, however.

MARKETING STRATEGY

Many international traders, particularly those new to the experience, make the common mistake of failing to seek qualified counseling to help them develop a marketing strategy that clearly defines their goals and objectives. They need a strategy that enables them to reach their goals despite whatever problems may arise during the process.

The sources for useful information are almost limitless. Public-sector assistance is available from a variety of government agencies at national, regional, and local levels, while private-sector groups such as bilateral chambers of commerce, world trade centers, industry-specific trade associations, and other trade promotion entities can also provide very useful information on trade trends and developments. Also, many schools cooperate with government agencies to operate trade promotion and business development centers that offer both counseling and classes on a wide variety of topics for business executives and others interested in international trade.

The Distribution "Partnership"

Another element that must be carefully considered is the selection of overseas distributors and the crafting of a seamless distribution plan to get your product to market.

It usually takes much more time to establish a presence in a target market overseas than in a domestic one. This is where a long-range, long-term perspective proves invaluable: the initial costs in time, money, and manpower necessary to establish a foothold in an international market have often frightened away many neophyte global traders from what could have been a very worthwhile experience. This initial skittishness can be minimized by carefully monitoring your company's efforts at every predetermined benchmark; stop, analyze, and make sure that every possibility has been taken into account.

The heart of this is determining the type of representation your company wants in the target market. Would it be best to hire someone on-site to act as a company representative—perhaps a native with invaluable language and cultural skills? Or would it be better to deal through an agent who represents a number of other similar products? Perhaps it would be best to assign a manager with international experience as an expatriate? Or would it be best to create a joint venture with an in-market partner to produce and distribute your product within the market itself?

While each has its own advantages and disadvantages, the decision on the type of distribution channel that is best for your company will have a tremendous impact on the way you structure your international effort. Some things to keep in mind are:

- Your existing manufacturing operation's capability to keep up with the increased demand that an overseas market will create;

- Top management's commitment to support an overseas operation as an equal to your firm's domestic business;

- Management's ability to adapt to the unique needs that an international operation requires; and

- Your company's willingness to perform the due diligence that's a crucial part of any global business transaction.

Determining the right type of relationship with the right overseas partner is crucial because, while your company may have an identity at home, more than likely it is an entirely unknown entity in your chosen target market. Thus, in all likelihood, customers in the foreign market will buy your product almost solely on the strength and reputation of your distributor. A personal evaluation of the person or persons handling your account is essential, as is a critical analysis of their facilities, management styles, and experience.

INTERNAL CAPABILITIES AND THE EMC

This leads to a very important point. Some companies, for a variety of reasons, don't have the internal capacity to handle the management of an international operation. They take a cursory first glance at their existing facilities and management structure, shake their heads, and walk away convinced that they could never be competitive in an overseas market.

Very often, though, nothing could be further from the truth. Any company, no matter how small or seemingly inconsequential, should, in a sense, step out of itself and see what its potential is from the outside. By this I mean that the management of many smaller companies are sometimes so caught up with their day-to-day struggle to survive that they don't see things in the long term from the perspective of someone in a far-off land who just might be very interested in buying their product. Such companies may not have what it takes to operate their own internal international department, but can still be a global competitor by working with an export management company or other entity that can provide, as a proxy, exactly the services performed by in-house staff.

Many export management companies, or EMCs, act as the global marketing, promotion, and sales arm of a company that can't, or doesn't have the desire to, perform that service itself. In the US alone, about 1,200 EMCs management companies are currently in operation providing services to more than 10,000 companies; these companies, in turn, account for between five percent and ten percent of all US-sourced exports of manufactured goods.

There are a number of advantages for a small company utilizing an EMC: the investment to enter an international market is significantly minimized; the number of company personnel needed to monitor or oversee the international operation is reduced; and one of the greatest strengths of an EMC is its established network of sales offices, as well as a wealth of international marketing and distribution experience. The one downside is that a company, by necessity, hands over the direct control of its global marketing and sales to another company. This can be successfully offset, though, by working with an export management company as a partner, rather than as a surrogate.

EXPORT AGENTS

Another distribution alternative that bears some consideration is working with an export agent. Export agents are, in essence, consultants who provide limited services compared to an EMC, but they tend to specialize in specific industry sectors, countries, or geographic regions. While they understand the requirements of getting goods through the customs process, they usually stop short at providing the kind of marketing expertise that an export management company provides. In effect, agents focus more on the handling and the sale of the goods, therefore becoming an export manager for documentation and shipping responsibilities. A disadvantage in using an export agent is that they are usually country-specific in their expertise; you will require a number of agents if your company's sales expand into multiple markets.

An important element that can't be overemphasized is the necessity of treating your international distributor or agent on an equal basis with their domestic counterparts. Too often, a company will create advertising and marketing campaigns, special credit-term programs, warranty offers, and sales incentive programs in their home country without taking the time to adapt the same incentives for use by their distributors in their overseas sales areas.

Licensing or joint venture agreements with overseas partners should also be considered. While it's true that many products that are competitive in your home country can be competitive elsewhere, a joint venture with an overseas partner can provide many advantages unavailable through other means. This is particularly true if a product needs to be technologically enhanced or modified, a costly process that often is beyond the capability of most small manufacturers.

Logistics: The "X" Factor

Anyone who's spent months piecing together a complicated international business transaction will tell you that few things are more disconcerting than finding out that it has been quashed because a company let its guard down and failed to develop a relationship with its logistics provider.

Similar to the critical role of due diligence in determining who should represent your company overseas, it's equally important to develop partnerships with the company, or companies, that will have the ultimate responsibility for getting your shipment where it needs to be, when it needs to be there. The logistics side of distribution was virtually ignored for many years by high-level managers. They usually left the decisions on how products would move in the hands of a traffic manager, who usually learned his business only through on-the-job training. The movement of cargo would happen at a more leisurely pace as weeks went by, and sometimes months would pass before a shipment arrived at its final destination.

But all that changed. Containerization, intermodalism, computerization, and technology have revolutionized the speed of goods moving through an arterial system of sea lanes, air routes, rail lines, and highways—linking virtually every business and population center on the globe. The traffic managers of days gone by now often have a degree and a title to go with it, such as "vice president of logistics." Their responsibilities impact every domestic and international transaction of their organization.

Logistics—the science of getting product A to point B in a timely, efficient, and cost-effective manner—has come into its own. It's now seen as a component equal in value to the strategies implemented for product development, marketing, advertising, sales, and customer relations.

There are a number of professional logistics associations around; they can help a company new to international business in finding the right logistics partner to craft a strategy that fits the company's specific needs. In the US, the Illinois-based Council of Logistics Management offers programs and classes. Other useful resources include the National Customs Brokers and Freight Forwarders Association in New York, the National Industrial Transporting League, and the Supply Chain Council. Similar groups include The Council of Logistics Management in Asia, the European Logistics Federation in Europe, and the Mexican Institute of Transport in Mexico.

International traders with infrequent shipments or shipments that are smaller than those usually handled by larger logistics providers should look into a shippers' association for help. Shippers' associations are comprised of small shippers who band together to collectively negotiate volume discount rates with cargo carriers. Those rates are usually only provided to larger shippers who can guarantee large significant volumes on a regular basis.

"Target" Marketing

An old expression goes, "If you aim at nothing, that's what you're going to hit—nothing." In international business, in particular, a targeted approach is infinitely more effective; otherwise, you can find yourself chasing down orders from all over the world in a willy-nilly fashion that wastes time, strains your capabilities, and spreads your resources to the breaking point. The smartest approach is to establish a base for orderly, profitable growth. For a company that's a new player in the international arena, more often than not it's best to concentrate efforts in one or perhaps two geographic regions until enough business is generated to support expansion into other areas in springboard fashion.

Unfortunately, many companies see international trade only as an alternative to consider when their domestic business slows or comes close to drying up. Even worse, an equal number of firms relegate their international operations to the back burner, or even worse yet, they put the brakes on their global business altogether after their domestic economies reverberate. It is absolutely essential that top management of your company see its international commitment in an equal light with your existing domestic business. A failure to do so can only lead to lost overseas market potential, alienated overseas business partners, and disaffected customers who have long memories and whose loyalty will be difficult, if not impossible, to reclaim.

Adaptability

Another common error in doing international business comes from fostering the delusion that a market technique that has proven its value elsewhere, or a product that has brand identity and a reputation either domestically or in another international market, can automatically be inserted into a new overseas environment. Remember: What works in one market more than likely *won't* work in another. Every factor, from local advertising and packaging regulations to safety and environmental issues, must be taken into consideration. If the necessary adaptations or modifications aren't identified by management and carried out on the shop floor, the distributor is put into the position of having to take care of what needs to be done at his end—usually at a greater cost in both time and money than if the issues had been taken care of at home.

The Language of Communications

As we've seen in Chapter 2, language is a lot more than just words. It comprises the sum total of how people communicate with one another based on their collective experience. Don't fall into the trap of thinking that all (or even a majority) of the potential end users of your product in a specific target market speak your language. In all likelihood, most of the people you want to have buy your product *don't* speak your language. In fact, they probably don't think the way you do or act like you do. Nor do they necessarily have the same ethics, morals, or social values that you have.

As a wag once observed, "God must love foreigners; he made so many of them." If your message isn't clear to you (or your distributor), it will not be clear to your potential customers—no matter how good your product is or how much you invested to develop it.

Hold on the Paperweights

"Companies of almost any national origin and size make common, basic errors when they try to grow their international business," says John Anderson, an international business consultant and former vice president-international of the Rubbermaid Inc. Office Products Group. "These mistakes are time-consuming and expensive, and they usually stem from a combination of inexperience, ignorance, and/or arrogance."

Quoted in the January 10, 2000, edition of *Industry Week* magazine, Anderson said, "Don't proclaim your firm to be a "global company"—gleefully handing out globe-shaped paperweights—unless you fully understand the resources, commitment, and actions required to back up that proclamation."

Attacking faraway markets "wisely and prudently," the Anderson interview concluded, "can generate growth and profits for years to come. However, half-hearted or ill-conceived globalization efforts produce nothing more than a deep hole into which you'll pour money, time, and effort with little or no return."

Remember the Basics

- Use common sense and clearly appraise your company's overseas potential.
- Create an information database around "country books."
- Craft an overseas distribution plan that best suits your company.
- Give logistics equal weight to the other elements of your marketing plan.
- Think in terms of "targeting" specific overseas markets.
- Be adjustable and flexible in terms of product development and adaptation.
- Remember that language involves total communications—verbal and nonverbal.

CHAPTER 10

Glossary

AGENT An individual or legal entity authorized to act on behalf of another individual or legal entity (the principal). An agent's authorized acts will bind the principal. A sales representative, for example, is an agent of the seller.

ASSOCIATION OF SOUTH EAST ASIAN NATIONS The economic and trade bloc founded in 1967 and comprised of Indonesia, Malaysia, the Philippines, Singapore, Thailand, and Brunei. Acronym: ASEAN.

BOTTOM LINE That which a company calls "profit" after all has been said and done. In itself it is not a bad thing, but many in the corporate world consider the bottom line a sanctified litmus test of a company's value. Problems arise when it's seen as the sole indication of a company's value. The true value of any company should be viewed by its viability to compete and serve its customers in the long term— not month to month or fiscal year to fiscal year. In other words, build a good company and well-served customers will continue to buy your product.

BRAND A name, term, design, symbol, or any other feature that identifies a seller's goods or services as distinct from any offered by the competition.

BRAND EQUITY The value a company derives from the fact that their product name is recognized and well-thought-of in the marketplace.

BRAND EXTENSION The introduction of a new product or service by associating it in promotion with an already existing and well-established brand name.

BRAND LOYALTY The degree to which a buying unit, such as a household, concentrates its purchases over time on a particular brand within a particular product category.

BRAND REPETITION The constant repetition of a brand name to consumers using different advertising media.

BREAKING INTO A MARKET The process of introducing a product into a new market.

BROKER An individual or company that negotiates contracts with a third party on behalf of a principal. Typically a wholesale intermediary who facilitates sales.

CHANNEL The pathway and the intermediaries necessary for moving products from the producer to the seller. This may include distributors, agents, wholesalers, agents and retailers.

CO-BRANDING A strategy of building brand equity that combines two or more brand-name products or producers into a single new product, with the goal of benefiting from each brand's reputation, (e.g., IBM computer with Intel Inside label).

COMMUNICATION The sharing of meaning. Five elements are necessary for communication to occur: source, message, receiver, and the processes of coding and encoding.

COMPARATIVE ADVANTAGE (economics) An economic theory which holds that a company or nation should sell and export those goods or services that it produces more efficiently than other companies or nations and buy or import those goods or services that it produces less efficiently that other companies or nations.

COMPARATIVE ADVERTISING Advertising in which the marketer compares its brand to rival brands that are actually identified by brand name.

COMPETITION The rivalry among marketers who seek to satisfy the same markets.

CONSUMER PRODUCTS Goods purchased by individuals or households for their personal use, as opposed to products purchased by businesses.

CONTAINERIZATION A materials-handling system that uses standardized shipping containers of varied length to ship goods from a shipper to a consignee without the actual goods being physically handled during the shipment. Sometimes the contents of a container come from multiple sources.

CORPORATE PHILOSOPHY The core essence, ethics, values and fundamental beliefs of a business entity.

CULTURE The sum total of beliefs, knowledge, values, customs, and artifacts that we use to adapt to our environment and that we hand down to succeeding generations.

CULTURAL ANALYSIS The process whereby a marketeer studies the target culture in order to gain insights into the wants, needs and buying habits of the local population prior to market entry. This analysis enables the company to formulate product design and promotional efforts to please (rather than offend) local tastes.

DEMOGRAPHIC SEGMENTATION The division of a mass market on the basis of statistical data such as age, gender, and buying power.

DIRECT MARKETING A system of marketing that uses a variety of communication techniques to contact potential customers in order to elicit a measurable and almost immediate response. It includes DIRECT MAIL, DATABASE MARKETING, DOOR-TO-DOOR, and COUPONS.

DISTRIBUTOR A company that undertakes to purchase products from the manufacturer for resale in a given market.

DIVERSIFICATION A strategy of developing new products and selling them in new markets.

DOWNSIZE To redesign in a small size. Specifically to redesign a business entity in a smaller size requiring fewer workers.

DUMBING DOWN A product of the Information Age, this term refers to the negative impact resulting from too much information—including untrue informa-tion—influencing both corporate and personal decision-making processes. Based on the axiom that he who controls the flow of information controls thought, the receiver of the information bears the burden of filtering in the data that is credible and, therefore, not destructive.

ECONOMIES OF SCALE The decline in average cost per unit that results from spreading fixed costs over a large number of units.

EUROPEAN UNION The trade, economic, and political bloc comprised of 18 countries: Austria, Belgium, the Czech Republic, Denmark, Finland, France, Germany, Greece, Hungary, Ireland, Italy, Luxembourg, the Netherlands, Poland, Portugal, Spain, Sweden, and the United Kingdom. As of the summer of 2000, there were 11 other countries that had applied for membership: Albania, Bulgaria, Cyprus, Estonia, Hungary, Latvia, Lithuania, Malta, Romania, Slovakia, and Turkey.

EXPORT MANAGEMENT COMPANY A business entity that serves as the export department for a number of other companies in exchange for a commission, fee or retainer.

FRANCHISING The granting by a company (franchisor) of a license to another company (franchisee) to sell the franchisor's goods or services in return for a fee. The franchise agreement binds the franchisee to specific standards of operation, in return for which they gain the value of the franchisor's brand recognition.

GLOBALIZATION A worldwide marketing strategy by which a firm uses the same or very similar marketing mixes in all its markets.

GRAY MARKET Unauthorized intermediaries that circumvent legitimate marketing channels by buying in low-price markets and reselling in high-price markets at prices that are lower than those charged by authorized channel members.

INDUSTRIAL MARKETING The sale of goods and services to companies that will use the products to make other goods and services available for sale to end-users.

INTERMODAL The use of more than one mode of transportation to complete a cargo move. For example, cargo might be loaded onto a truck at a factory for shipment to a railhead where the cargo is placed onto a train for forwarding to an ocean terminal. There the cargo is loaded aboard a ship bound for a port, where the entire process is reversed using either the same or other modes of transport in any combination.

INTERNAL MARKETING The marketing of goods and services of one department to another department inside of a company's operation. Or, the process that occurs when a company attracts, hires, trains and retains employees. All other marketing is considered external.

KEIRETSU The Japanese term for "industrial group." These groups are almost self-reliant because they can count on the support of any other member of the keiretsu for financial or material support. Such groups include the Mitsui Group—comprised of Mitsui & Company (trading), Mitsui OSK Lines (ocean shipping), Mitsui Bank (finance), and more; Sumitomo; Mitsubishi; and several others. All members of the keiretsu rely upon each other for the core of their existence. It is an almost a perfect example of the Japanese concept of mutual reliance and community.

Keiretsu are the lineal descendants of the pre-World War II "zaibatsu"; these were rendered illegal after the war because they were thought to be a driving economic force behind Japan's prewar militarism and expansion into China and Southeast Asia.

LICENSING AGREEMENT A contract whereby the holder of a trademark, patent, or copyright transfers a limited right to another person or company to use a process, sell or manufacture a product, or provide specific services covered by the license.

MARKET A set or other group of individuals or organizations that desire a product and are willing and able to buy it.

MARKET AUDIT The systematic and formal review of all areas of a marketing plan after its implementation to examine the current environment, strategies, tactics and results.

MARKET DRIVEN 1) A company that produces goods, services or modifications based upon what consumers demand. 2) An economic system in which supply, demand and price are the determinants of which products will enter the marketplace. See PRODUCT DRIVEN below.

MARKETEER A person or company that promotes the sale of goods and services.

MARKETING The process of planning and executing the conception, pricing, promotion, and distribution of ideas, goods, and services to create exchanges that satisfy both individual and industrial objectives.

MARKETING MIX The combination of the marketing elements of product, price, place and promotion to generate the sale of goods or services.

MARKETING PLAN A detailed, heavily researched and organized plan of a company's goals and objectives for the development, production, promotion, sale and service of its product line. It defines specific strategies and timelines for which the appropriate personnel will be assigned responsibility.

MARKET POTENTIAL The maximum possible number of sales of a specific product in a specific market (or market segment) over a particular time period for all sellers in the industry, given that all sellers would be performing their maximum marketing effort under an assumed set of environmental conditions.

MARKET RESEARCH The process of identifying and defining a marketing problem or opportunity, specifying and collecting the data required to address those issues, analyzing the results, and communicating the information to decision makers.

MARKET SHARE (a.k.a. brand share)   The amount of sales a company has as a portion of the entire market it has targeted.

MEDIA   All forms of communications that can carry advertising and promotional messages. Includes print, radio, television, direct mail, billboards, the Internet, skywriting and more.

MEDIA MIX   Any combination of advertising and promotional outlets used during an advertising campaign. A company varies its mix based on quantifiable results and product positioning.

MERCHANDISING   The activities of a marketeer's sales force, distribution chain, and retailers that promote the sale of goods to consumers.

MERCOSUR   The regional trade alliance between Argentina, Brazil, Paraguay, and Uruguay. Also known as the Southern Common Market.

MULTINATIONAL COMPANY   A firm that is based in one parent or home country and produces goods or services in one or more foreign or "host" countries. Acronym: MNC.

NICHE MARKETING   Marketing strategy in which a company focuses its entire effort on a small, specialized segment of a larger market. Niche marketing is usually practiced by small companies after significant research into the long-term profitability of the niche.

NORTH AMERICAN FREE TRADE AGREEMENT   The free trade pact between the US, Canada, and Mexico that took effect in 1994. Over a 15-year period, the agreement is expected to eliminate barriers to trade, promote fair competition, increase investment opportunities, provide protection for intellectual property rights, and establish a framework for the resolution of trade disputes between the three countries. Acronym: NAFTA.

ONE SIZE FITS ALL   The concept (in this context it is a fallacy) that one answer or solution fits every conceivable situation or problem. While some general rules apply to almost every endeavor, flexibility and a clearheaded approach to problem solving are crucial for crafting the correct solution to any given, unique problem.

ON-THE-GROUND   Research or information acquired in the actual market that's the subject of the research. This is the best form of research for cultural studies.

ORIGINAL EQUIPMENT MANUFACTURER   A firm that buys industrial products from a supplier and incorporates them into the product it produces and markets. Acronym: OEM.

PACKAGING   The exterior container of a product or service as seen by the purchaser. The package may serve to advertise, describe, promote, deter the theft of, or set portion controls for the product. Packaging is used to create brand awareness.

PENETRATION   The degree to which a product and its promotion have attained market share in any targeted market segment. Usually describes a company's first effort in any particular marketplace.

PERCEIVED VALUE   The benefits (tangible and intangible) beyond the monetary value that a consumer expects to receive from the purchase of goods or services.

PERSONAL SELLING   Person-to-person communication between a buyer and a seller that may include face-to-face meetings, telephone conversations, faxes, email or other direct correspondence.

POSITIONING   The way that customers perceive a company's product in relation to that of its competition. It may be based on quality, size, price, brand recognition, packaging or a host of other "subjective" features that affect consumer decisions.

PRICE COMPETITION   Competition between producers or sellers of like products which are of roughly the same quality, based on price alone. At this point, competition and consumer preference is based strictly on the price of the product.

PRICED OUT OF THE MARKET (to be)   The failure of a product in a given market based upon its price being either too high or too low for that market.

PRICE DRIVEN   A method of positioning a product in the marketplace based primarily on its price as compared to that of the competition.

PRODUCT AFFINITY   The favorable attitudes that a customer exhibits toward a product or a company, as a result of positive experiences with the product, advertising, or public relations efforts.

PRODUCT AWARENESS   The degree of perception that a customer has regarding a product, as established by advertising and promotional efforts.

PRODUCT CONFIDENCE   The belief that customers have in a product and its value. Confidence is most often engendered during the promotion of a product rather than after its first usage, since customers rarely buy what they believe is useless.

PRODUCT DISCONNECT   Lack of recognition (on the part of the marketers) that the positive benefits of a product are canceled out for many consumers by the product's negative side effects or disadvantages.

PRODUCT LIFE CYCLE   The series of stages through which a product passes, including development, introduction, growth, maturity and decline.

PRODUCT LINE   A group of products closely related because they satisfy a class of needs, are used together, are sold to the same customer group, are distributed through the same outlets, or fall within a given price range.

PRODUCT MATURITY   The state at which demand for a product consistently absorbs allocated supply, with all pricing objectives being met by the marketeer. A product may remain mature for some time before decline begins to occur.

PROMOTION   Any of the various techniques used to create a positive image of a seller's product in the minds of potential buyers. Includes advertising, personal selling, public relations and discounts.

PROTECTIONISM   The shielding of one or more of a country's industry sectors from import competition by the erection of either high tariffs, or nontariff barriers such as cumbersome restrictions and overly complicated regulatory controls.

QUALITY   The totality of features and characteristics of a product or service that bear on its ability to satisfy stated or implied needs.

RETURN ON INVESTMENT   The ratio of after-tax net profit to the investment used to earn that profit. Acronym: ROI.

ROLL-OUT   Marketing term used to describe a product introduction. Applies to new products as well as the introduction of old products to new markets.

SALES FORECAST   What one company expects to sell under conditions specified for the uncontrollable and controllable factors that affect the forecast.

TARIFF   In international marketing, a government tax on goods or services entering a country.

TRADEMARK   The sign, emblem, word, or other symbol that a company uses in commerce to distinguish its goods or services from those of another company. It may or may not be the company's trade name. Usually, a company asserts exclusive rights to use the trademark or service mark. Also known as a logo.

VALDEZ PRINCIPLES   Guidelines that encourage firms to focus attention on environmental concerns and corporate responsibility. Coined after the oil spill caused by the 1989 grounding of the tanker *Exxon Valdez* that spilled 11 million gallons of oil into Alaska's Prince William Sound.

VALUE-ADDED   In retail strategy decisions, a dimension of the retail positioning matrix that refers to the service level and method of operation of the retailer. A factor that adds value to the core product, for example, in terms of the consumer's psychological or monetary benefit from the purchase.

CHAPTER 11

Resources

Books

Allen, Frederick. *Secret Formula*
   HarperCollins, New York, New York. 1994.

Anholt, Simon. *Another One Bites the Grass*
   John Wiley & Sons, New York, New York. 2000.

Axtell, Roger E. *Do's and Taboos Around the World*
   John Wiley & Sons, New York, New York. 1990.

Axtell, Roger E. *Do's and Taboos of International Trade*
   John Wiley & Sons, New York, New York. 1994.

Brislin, Richard W. *Cross-Cultural Encounters: Face to Face Interaction*
   Pergamon Press, New York, New York. 1981.

Bryan, Lowell, Jane Fraser, Jeremy Oppenheim, and Wilhelm Rall. *Race for the World*
   Harvard Business School Press, Boston, Massachusetts. 1999.

Copeland, Lennie, and Lewis Griggs. *Going International*
   Random House, New York, New York. 1985.

Fields, George. *From Bonsai to Levis*
   MacMillian Publishing Company, New York, New York. 1983.

Foley, James F. *The Global Entrepreneur*
   Dearborn Financial Publishers, Chicago, Illinois. 1999.

Haden-Guest, Anthony. *The Paradise Program*
   William Morrow & Co., New York, New York. 1973.

Halberstam, David. *The Reckoning*
   William Morrow & Company, New York, New York. 1986.

Hay, Peter. *The Book of Business Anecdotes*
   Wings Books, New York, New York. 1993.

Herbig, Paul A. *Handbook of Cross-Cultural Marketing*
   International Business Press, Binghampton, New York. 1998.

James, David L. *Doing Business in Asia*
   Betterway Books, Cincinnati, Ohio. 1993.

Jeannet, Jean-Pierre and H. David Hennessey. *Global Marketing Strategies,* 3rd edition
   Houghton Mifflin Company, Boston, Massachusetts. 1995.

Kazenstein, Gary. *Funny Business: An Outsider's Year in Japan*
   Soho Press, New York, New York. 1989.

Kotler, Philip and Gary Armstrong. *Principles of Marketing*
   Prentice Hall, Englewood Cliffs, New Jersey. 1994.

Love, John F. *McDonald's: Behind the Arches*
Bantam Books, New York, New York. 1986.

Mackiewicz, Andrea. *Guide to Building a Global Image*
McGraw-Hill Inc., New York, New York. 1993.

Malloy, Mary A. and Michael K. Malloy. *The Buck Starts Here*
Thomson Executive Press, Cincinnati, Ohio. 1996.

Mattera, Philip. *Inside U.S. Business*
Business One Irwin, Homewood, Illinois. 1991.

Morgan, James C. and Jeffrey J. Morgan. *Cracking the Japanese Market*
The Free Press, Detroit, Michigan. 1991.

Moskowitz, Milton. *The Global Marketplace*
MacMillan Publishing Company, New York, New York. 1987.

Ogilvy, David. *All Consumers Are Not Created Equal*
John Wiley & Sons, New York, New York. 1995.

Paley, Norton. *The Strategic Marketing Planner*
The American Management Association, New York, New York. 1991.

Porter, Glenn and Harold C. Livesay. *Merchants & Manufacturers*
Ivan R. Dee Inc., Chicago, Illinois. 1971.

Reischauer, Edwin O. *Japan: The Story of a Nation*
Alfred A. Knopf Inc., New York, New York. 1970.

Reischauer, Edwin O. *The Japanese*
Harvard University Press, Boston, Massachusetts. 1977.

Ricks, David A. *Blunders in International Business*
Blackwell Publishers, Cambridge, Massachusetts. 1993.

Rosenweig, Jeffrey A. *Winning the Global Game*
The Free Press, New York, New York. 1998.

Rossman, Marlene L. *Multicultural Marketing*
American Marketing Association, New York, New York. 1994.

Schoell, William F. and Joseph P. Guiltinan. *Marketing: Contemporary Concepts and Practices*
Allyn & Bacon Publishers, Needham Heights, Massachusetts. 1990.

Seelye, H. Ned and Alan Seelye-James. *Culture Clash: Managing in a Multi-Cultural World*
NTC Business Books, Lincolnwood, Illinois. 1995.

Sobel, Robert. *When Giants Stumble*
Prentice Hall Press, Paramus, New Jersey. 1999.

Stanat, Ruth and Chris West. *Global Jumpstart*
Perseus Books, Reading, Massachusetts. 1999.

Walden, Gene and Edmund O. Lawler. *Marketing Masters: Secrets of America's Best Companies*
HarperBusiness, New York, New York. 1993.

Winkworth, Stephen. *Great Commercial Disasters*
MacMillan London Ltd., London, UK. 1980.

Wong, Angi Ma. *Target the US Asian Market*
Pacific Heritage Books, Palos Verdes, California. 1998.

1465